Handbook for Enhancing Undergraduate Education in Psychology

Edited by Thomas V. McGovern

American Psychological Association
Washington, DC

Published by the
American Psychological Association
750 First Street, NE
Washington, DC 20002

Copies may be ordered from
APA Order Department
P.O. Box 2710
Hyattsville, MD 20784

Typeset in Goudy by Techna Type, Inc., York, PA

Printer: Wickersham Printing Company, Inc., Lancaster, PA
Cover designer: Michael David Brown, Inc., Rockville, MD
Technical/production editor: Valerie Montenegro

Library of Congress Cataloging-in-Publication Data

Handbook for enhancing undergraduate education in psychology / edited
   by Thomas V. McGovern.
        p.   cm.
   "Based on the American Psychological Association (APA) National
Conference on Enhancing the Quality of Undergraduate Education in
Psychology, held at St. Mary's College of Maryland in June 1991"—Pref.
   Includes bibliographical references and index.
   ISBN 1-55798-196-5 (pbk.; acid-free paper)
   1. Psychology—Study and teaching (Higher)—United States—
Congresses.   2. Psychologists—Training of—United States—
Congresses.   I. McGovern, Thomas V.
BF80.7.U6H36   1993
150'.71'173—dc20   93-7081
                                                                 CIP

Printed in the United States of America
First edition

To Bill McKeachie
Player on the Cornell (1951), Michigan (1960), and St. Mary's (1991) teams;
coach to faculty and students of higher education; and
scholar, teacher, and citizen of psychology.

CONTENTS

PREFACE

Faculty are often prompted to examine their undergraduate programs because "something is broken and not working right." Each of the chapters in this book, read separately, offers the means to diagnose problems and to develop alternative remedies.

Faculty who are committed to undergraduate education in general and to psychology in particular seek scholarly expositions about their craft. Reading this book will be an excellent faculty development activity for an individual or for a group of faculty. Faculty are energized when they are given the opportunity to talk about their teaching. Teaching is one topic in academic life in which values, beliefs, and personal commitments come to the foreground with little more than a provocative stimulus.

This book is just such a stimulus. It is based on the American Psychological Association (APA) National Conference on Enhancing the Quality of Undergraduate Education in Psychology, held at St. Mary's College of Maryland in June 1991. In contrast to other national conferences on other topics sponsored by the APA, the St. Mary's gathering was organized with a single purpose in mind. Its goal was to synthesize the scholarship and practice of the teaching and learning of psychology in order to produce a practical handbook for faculty who work with undergraduates in our discipline.

The conference was the result of 3 years of planning, discussion, and writing by more than 100 psychologists. At the conference, 60 psychologists were organized into small groups to discuss critical questions for undergraduate educators in our discipline. By the end of the conference, the participants had composed first drafts of chapters 1 through 7 in this book and generated a set of recommendations to the APA. As a result of the conference discussions, the Steering Committee subsequently developed the overarching Principles for Quality Undergraduate Psychology Programs.

This book is designed to enable faculty to enhance their efforts in a broad spectrum of institutional settings. It can become a catalyst for undergraduate program initiatives at the departmental, institutional, regional, and national levels.

THOMAS V. MCGOVERN

ACKNOWLEDGMENTS

There are three groups of people whom I want to acknowledge. Their combined efforts made possible both this conference itself and its eventual role as a catalyst for enhancing undergraduate education in psychology.

The first group is the conference participants, especially the chairs of the conference task forces. More than 200 individuals submitted applications to participate in this conference, and of those, the Steering Committee selected 50. The participants' capacity to listen to one another, to influence one another, and to set aside solely individual perspectives to generate a group product was nonpareil. The chairs of the seven task forces facilitated this outcome with persistent diplomacy and produced this book with style.

The second group to acknowledge are the administrators, faculty, and staff at St. Mary's. President Edward T. Lewis, Provost Melvin Endy, Jr., Executive Vice President John Underwood, Vice President for Advancement Brian Clarke, and Human Development Division Head Michael Berger provided resources and support without which the conference would not have been implemented. Anne Loker, director of public events, and William Caplins, director of information processing, also provided resources and support. In addition, I acknowledge the faculty, especially our site manager Roy Hopkins, and the undergraduate students of the Human Development Division, who became true colleagues during our stay at St. Mary's.

The third group of individuals I want to acknowledge are the many psychologists in the APA governance groups and on the APA staff who nurtured this conference when it was being planned and implemented. The following members of the Education and Training Board and the Interim Board of Educational Affairs were its principal advocates: Norman Abeles, Irwin Altman, Cynthia Belar, Ludy Benjamin, Joanne Callan, Henry Ellis,

Seymour Feshbach, Lucia Gilbert, Bernadette Gray-Little, Joseph Grosslight, Diane Halpern, David Holmes, Dorothy Evans Holmes, Nadine Lambert, Paul Lloyd, Joseph Matarazzo, Ruth Matarazzo, Janet Matthews, Kathleen McCluskey-Fawcett, Asher Pacht, Nathan Perry, Tommy Stigall, George Stricker, Richard Suinn, Samuel Turner, and Harry Yamaguchi.

APA President Charles Spielberger's focus on education and his presentation during the conference were important, as were remarks by Edward T. Lewis; APA Chief Executive Officer Raymond Fowler; Wayne Camara of the APA Science Directorate; Phil Guzman of the Public Interest Directorate; and Paul Nelson of the Education Directorate. Also, Bill McKeachie was recognized for his 40 years of contributions to undergraduate education and his participation in all the conferences.

While meeting in Washington, DC, concurrently with the conference, President-Elect Jack Wiggins and members of the APA Board of Directors conveyed their messages of support. Dick Suinn's membership on the Board of Directors and the conference Steering Committee empowered our efforts in more ways than we will probably ever know.

I want to acknowledge the Steering Committee who, for 3 years, worked as a truly effective group in motivating, editing, and enabling one another to make the outcomes of this conference so rich.

The conference was planned during the transition from the APA Education and Training Board to the Board of Educational Affairs and during the formation of the Education Directorate. Cynthia Baum, Joanne Callan, Ira Cohen, Paul Nelson, and Martha Braswell were ever attuned to the project during these difficult transition years. Raymond Fowler's support as chief executive officer of the APA was invaluable.

Finally, I want to acknowledge my administrative assistant at Arizona State University West, Priscilla Van Dam, who expanded her considerable literary skills by learning APA style in order to edit with me the multiple drafts of this book. I also want to thank Judy Nemes, development editor, and Valerie Montenegro, technical/production editor, both of APA Books, as well as copyeditor Stephen Pazdan, who brought the final text to life; without their help, these ideas might not have had the felicity of expression that now characterizes these pages.

THOMAS V. McGOVERN, Chair of the Steering Committee
Arizona State University West

I

ESTABLISHING THE FRAMEWORK

INTRODUCTION

THOMAS V. McGOVERN

Over the past 20 years, undergraduate education in psychology has been affected by major changes in the field that have affected curricular practice, teaching methods, and the substantive content of coursework. Furthermore, the broader landscape of higher education has changed as dramatically as that of the discipline. These changes have been the objects of numerous "blue ribbon panel" reports and the topics for *Chronicle of Higher Education* feature stories on a regular basis. A sample of the most frequently debated issue might include:

- the assessment of student learning
- the renewal of advising and student development programs
- the changing demographics of student enrollments
- ethnic minority student recruitment and retention
- changes in faculty roles and rewards
- a redefinition of the nature and balance between teaching and scholarship in faculty lives
- the effectiveness of general education curricula and overspecialization in major fields
- the role of active learning, critical thinking, and innovative pedagogy to achieve complex, liberal learning objectives.

The American Psychological Association (APA) has a long history of involvement in education issues and has traditionally used national conferences as a vehicle for bringing together knowledgeable faculty to discuss the changing needs of the field. For example, conferences have been held on graduate education and training for the professional practice of psychology. A future conference is planned on postdoctoral education and training. Past conferences on undergraduate education were held in 1951 and 1960, and participants in both produced a book that was used by psychology faculty at their own institutions. The last major national project on psychology education sponsored by the APA was the Kulik (1973) report *Undergraduate Education in Psychology*, a national research study that grew out of the tumultuous decade of the sixties and was published 20 years ago. It has been clear for some time that today's faculty need a comprehensive resource with which to update their understanding of undergraduate program issues.

A CONFERENCE FOR THE NINETIES

The APA National Conference on Enhancing the Quality of Undergraduate Education in Psychology was held at St. Mary's College of Maryland June 18–23, 1991, with that need and with past conference formats and products in mind. Its goal was to synthesize the scholarship and practice of the teaching and learning of psychology in order to produce a practical handbook for faculty who work with undergraduates in our discipline. The conference Steering Committee was fully aware of the need to address changes in the discipline of psychology and to do so in the larger context of changes taking place in higher education. Seven critical areas were identified: assessment, advising, ethnic minority recruitment and retention, faculty development, faculty networks, curriculum, and active learning. The faculty assembled at St. Mary's researched and discussed these seven areas in depth; the fruits of their work are reflected in the core chapters of this handbook. The central themes and coverage of these seven areas are summarized later in this chapter. Moreover, the Steering Committee abstracted from the conference discussions and the consequent chapters a set of Principles for Quality Undergraduate Psychology Programs. This important conceptual statement about psychology students, faculty, and curriculum immediately follows this introduction.

What is most important to understand is that the conference participants, who addressed the critical issues for contemporary undergraduate education, came from research and comprehensive universities, liberal arts colleges, community colleges, and high schools. Never before had such different institutional perspectives been brought to bear on undergraduate psychology problems. We hoped that by drawing on such a variety of perspectives this handbook would be applicable to an exceptionally broad audience, that is, anyone who teaches students preparing for or in the midst of their undergraduate psychology education.

THE HISTORICAL ROOTS OF THE ST. MARY'S CONFERENCE

Cornell Conference

Forty years before this conference, six psychologists from Cornell University, the University of Maryland, the University of Michigan, Vanderbilt University, and Yale University met at Cornell as a study group on the topic of undergraduate psychology. For 8 weeks in the summer of 1951, they met to accomplish "an audit to determine the objectives, examine the content, and appraise the results of the instruction we have been giving" (Buxton et al., 1952, p. v). The product of their work, *Improving Undergraduate Instruction in Psychology* (Buxton et al., 1952), described their analysis of the goals of the curriculum. The authors recommended a model curriculum to accomplish the liberal arts goals they identified as most important.

Michigan Conference

Another study group of six psychologists from the University of Michigan, Oberlin College, Northwestern University, University of Oregon, and Bethany College met at the University of Michigan in the summer of 1960. Before they met, the group collected survey data from 411 departments, assessing the extent to which recommendations from the 1951 Cornell meeting had been implemented. More than 50% of the responding departments had revised their curricula since the publication of the Buxton et al. (1952) report. Of the departments that had revised their curricula, 26% reported using the report's recommended curriculum model "as much as possible" or "quite extensively," and 31% "made no attempt to use it" (p. 16).

The Michigan group's work resulted in the publication of *Undergraduate Curricula in Psychology* (McKeachie & Milholland, 1961). They were motivated by a belief that teaching had lost its prestige in university settings and that research consumed inordinate amounts of faculties' time and creativity. They recognized that a new generation of students populated undergraduate classrooms and that the curriculum in psychology was under pressure to respond to their needs. McKeachie and Milholland described three model curricula that would enable different types of institutions with increasingly different types of students to provide a liberal arts education in psychology.

Kulik Report

Another 10 years elapsed before the APA sponsored a third study of the undergraduate psychology curriculum. Forty-eight individuals from different institutions were involved in this study. From 1969 to 1972, the project faculty collected and analyzed survey data from 463 baccalaureate programs and 99 two-year institutions. They conducted 17 site-visit case studies as well. In *Undergraduate Education in Psychology*, Kulik (1973) described the project results, characterizing undergraduate psychology curricula as reflecting the different institutions in which they were developed. Institutional innovations were based on faculty's creative responses to the changes in their student populations. The quest for a single model curriculum was put to rest in this report: "The diverse goals of students in psychology courses suggest that pluralism may be a valuable concept in the design of programs in psychology" (Kulik, 1973, p. 203). Moreover, even the singular definition of psychology as a liberal arts discipline was questioned: "Is it conceivable that for some students, occupationally oriented programs may provide a better road?" (Kulik, 1973, pp. 202–203).

More Recent Initiatives

In 1980, the APA Committee on Undergraduate Education (CUE) developed a preliminary proposal for a national conference that was subsequently approved by the Education and Training Board and the Board of Directors. The three prior projects had been supported by external funding, in 1951 from the Carnegie Corporation and the Grant Foundation and in 1960 and 1969 from the National Science Foundation. Thus, the CUE submitted a grant proposal to the Fund to Improve Postsecondary Education (FIPSE), requesting support for a 3-year project that included commissioned papers written in the 1st year, a national conference convened in the 2nd year, and dissemination workshops held at state and regional conventions in the 3rd year. The proposal was not funded by FIPSE and the conference was not held.

The APA (1983) sponsored a telephone survey of undergraduate department chairs conducted by CUE members. This survey was an effort to respond to criticisms by FIPSE that the APA should provide more direct support for the study of its undergraduate curriculum. The chairs who responded to the survey identified two pressing concerns: (a) balancing competing demands on the curriculum and (b) responding to increasing vocational needs expressed by students.

In 1984, two staff members of the APA Educational Affairs Office completed a national survey of the undergraduate psychology curriculum that was based on the preliminary work of the telephone survey. In *The Undergraduate Psychology Curriculum: 1984*, Scheirer and Rogers (1985) summarized the curricular practices of a random sample of 165 four-year and 122 two-year institutions and compared their findings with those reported by Kulik (1973).

Finally, from 1988 to 1991, the APA collaborated with the Association of American Colleges (AAC) on a national review of arts and sciences majors funded by the Ford Foundation and FIPSE. The APA was 1 of 12 learned societies to convene a task force, addressing a common set of questions about purposes and practices of liberal arts education in general and of the psychological field in particular. A study group of 5 psychologists worked on the project with more than 60 faculty from 11 other disciplines. Preliminary drafts of the psychology report were reviewed by more than 200 psychologists with special efforts made to solicit comments from ethnic minority faculty. The final report, "Liberal Education, Study in Depth, and the Arts and Sciences Major— Psychology" (McGovern, Furumoto, Halpern, Kimble, & McKeachie, 1991), was published in the *American Psychologist* and sent to every undergraduate psychology department chairperson in the country. The psychology report was published also in two AAC texts on the entire project, *The Challenge of Connecting Learning* (Project on Liberal Learning, Study-in-Depth, and the Arts and Sciences Major, 1991a) and *Reports from the Fields* (Project on Liberal Learning, Study-in-Depth, and the Arts and Sciences Major, 1991b).

The substance of these psychology reports from the 1950s through the current decade will be analyzed in chapter 6 on curriculum. In addition, the interested reader should review selected chapters in *Teaching Psychology in America: A History* (Puente, Matthews, & Brewer, 1992) for an in-depth review of these reports, especially for the historical contexts in which they were framed.

It is important to understand that the intellectual roots of the 1991 APA National Conference held at St. Mary's were informed by these prior reports and meetings. The organizing principles and group dynamic were influenced by organizational factors in the APA.

Beginning in 1980, there was growing concern about the undergraduate curriculum in psychology. An August 1983 resolution of the APA's Council of Representatives requested that the CUE review undergraduate curricula and recommend whether the APA should establish guidelines for a model curriculum. The CUE recommended and the Council of Representatives approved a resolution in August 1985 that (a) undergraduate psychology should be a liberal arts discipline and not a preprofessional or vocational training, (b) the APA should *not* prescribe curricular requirements for undergraduate education as it does for accredited doctoral programs, and (c) the APA should periodically monitor the status of undergraduate education to possibly reevaluate the need for curricular guidelines.

In 1986, an *American Psychologist* article by Howard et al. entitled "The Changing Face of American Psychology" addressed several concerns about the undergraduate psychology curriculum. Recruitment, education, advising for career development, and retention of women and ethnic minority students at the undergraduate level directly affected the quality of graduate education and the future of the discipline and the profession. The recruitment of individuals to scientific areas of the discipline was related also to enhanced opportunities for research training at the undergraduate level.

In "Resolutions Approved by the National Conference on Graduate Education in Psychology" (Bickman, 1987), issues were identified for undergraduate educators, including structure and content of the major, recruitment and retention, student and faculty diversity, program quality control, and the preparation of future teachers of psychology. Both of these highly visible reports were used to support the CUE's efforts for increasing the APA's attention to undergraduate concerns.

THE DEVELOPMENT OF THE ST. MARY'S CONFERENCE

In 1987, the CUE resurrected the idea of a national conference; its members felt that any discussion of the undergraduate curriculum should engage a broad spectrum of participants to generate and disseminate their recommendations. The CUE approved a preliminary proposal. Five problem areas were identified as the original objectives for this conference: (a) the changing profile of undergraduates and the implications for the discipline; (b) undergraduate curriculum models; (c) advising and career preparation for students; (d) research and program evaluation; and (e) faculty development and delivery systems for information on teaching and program development. A revised proposal was developed by the CUE members in 1988, approved by the Education and Training Board and, in principle, by the Board of Directors at its June 1988 meeting. It is important to note that the proposal spotlighted the need to increase psychologists' awareness of the APA as a significant resource for undergraduate program development. At a time when many academic and scientific psychologists saw the APA being consumed by clinical practitioner agendas, support of an undergraduate conference represented support for multiple levels of education.

Because of the APA's severe fiscal crisis during this period, funding was delayed for 1 year. At its June 1989 meeting, the Board of Directors approved the Education and Training Board recommendation to name Thomas McGovern as chair of the Steering Committee for the conference and to fund planning for the project over a 2-year period. At its August

1989 meeting, the Council of Representatives, on the recommendation of the Board of Directors and the Education and Training Board, voted to support the conference and allocated additional funds, matching the sum already committed by the Board of Directors. A proposal for additional funding was submitted to FIPSE in November 1989. Like the 1981 proposal to FIPSE, however, it was not approved. Despite uniformly positive ratings by the reviewers, FIPSE regarded such a project as the responsibility of the APA, commenting that more resources were available in the APA than in FIPSE's federally funded program.

Steering Committee Activities

In December 1989, the Board of Directors approved a Steering Committee that was nominated by the Interim Board of Educational Affairs. The committee included continuing members of the CUE and six additional faculty. (Their names are listed in appendix A.)

The Steering Committee met for the first time on March 23, 1990 and established preliminary plans for solicitation of site proposals, recruitment of participants, and a group dynamic for the conference. A vision for the conference was established at this very first meeting with the Steering Committee's clarification of the conference outcomes and the seven critical questions to be addressed as well as the defining characteristics of the participants.

Several members of the Steering Committee had attended the National Conference on Graduate Education held at the University of Utah in 1987. Their experience as well as that of Wilbert McKeachie who attended the 1951 and 1960 undergraduate conferences provided an important perspective on what could be expected from the participants. The Steering Committee decided that the outcome of this conference should *not* be a long list of recommendations for improving undergraduate education, the exact language of which would be debated first at the conference and then for several years by APA governance groups. We decided instead to produce a scholarly and practical resource book for undergraduate psychology faculty teaching in multiple types of institutions across the country. Recommendations to the APA about resource development for undergraduate concerns would be generated by the participants, but as a secondary goal.

To shape the development of this handbook, the Steering Committee focused its attention on refining the original questions proposed for the conference. Seven critical questions became the study topics for the participants and are the primary chapter topics for this book.

In planning the conference, the selection of a site and participants was accomplished before the format of the meeting was determined. Details about the selection of the participants are contained in appendix B; details about the selection of St. Mary's as the conference site and how this environment contributed to the overall outcomes are contained in appendix C.

GROUP DYNAMIC FOR THE CONFERENCE

The group dynamic for the conference followed from the decision by the Steering Committee to produce a scholarly and practical book. First, we kept in mind the research literature on forming task-oriented groups as well as our commitment to including many different perspectives in the discussion. Group size was limited to 6 to 10 members and included individuals from different types of institutions. Ethnic minority perspectives were distributed across all seven areas. Second, we kept in mind prior conference experiences about structuring the activities before, during, and after the meeting.

Activities Before the Conference

In November 1990, we sent participants a letter informing them of their selection, their assignment to one of the seven groups with their topic, and specific expectations for their work. Participants were informed they would (a) spend most of the 5-day conference discussing the background readings, considering the issues, and composing a chapter; and (b) in addition to preliminary reading and writing and full participation during the week of the conference, disseminate the results of the conference at the local or regional level by networking, lecturing, influencing policy, and publishing. The seven critical questions, an acceptance form, a biographical data sheet, and instructions for writing a three-page paper that provided participants' perspectives on their assigned topic were sent with the letter. In the instructions for the three-page paper, the Steering Committee asked participants to treat the history of the issues, problems and obstacles, possible solutions, agendas for the 1990s, and translation of their experiences to other campuses. The paper was to be organized around three questions: (a) Where is the field of undergraduate psychology, (b) how did it get there, and (c) what shall we do to move forward? The Steering Committee reviewed these papers before its final planning meeting for the conference.

At its final planning meeting in March 1991, the Steering Committee completed the plan for the preconference preparation and established the format for the 5-day conference. We sent all participants a book of preliminary readings to shape their expectations about work at the conference and to introduce them to the ideas of one another. The chairs of the seven groups also distributed a list of readings that they wanted their members to review before the conference. Finally, we sent the chairs a description of the proposed conference book including a uniform outline for their chapters and our expected deadlines for submitting the texts during and after the meeting.

Activities During the Conference

The Steering Committee gave the participants a daunting task. In 4½ working days, we expected small groups of 6 to 10 psychologists, who had not previously met or worked with each other, to produce the first drafts of 50-page chapters on seven complex topics.

To accomplish this feat, four things were done during the conference. First, the Steering Committee shifted its role from that of providing an active direction of the conference to that of being a resource provider for each of the seven groups, providing a perspective about overall conference goals and expectations for other groups' work. Second, the chairs of the groups along with Tom McGovern, Cynthia Baum, and Roy Hopkins assumed primary leadership for the daily conference activities as well as for the seven working groups. Third, we scheduled large blocks of time for small group discussions and for writing text. Fourth, every effort was made to schedule time during the days and evenings when participants could fashion collegial ties and reinforce what brought them to St. Mary's.

Meals were both social and business forums. Breakfast was a time to set the day's agenda and to give the whole group progress reports on the previous day's accomplishments. Jigsaw groups after breakfast were used on the last 2 days of the conference to exchange ideas across working groups and to build dissemination networks. Lunch was a time for planned and impromptu meetings of chairs, Steering Committee members, and new and old colleagues. Dinner was a time to toast different individuals who were making the conference a success.

We devoted the morning of the last day to participants' networking by geographical region to establish preliminary dissemination plans. It was also a time to say good-bye and to savor the work that had been done in such a short time.

In sum, 16-hour work days became medleys of group and individual writing; persuasive arguments; conflicts and compromises; and learning about others and their high school, community college, and university programs. These days were a celebration of the commitments to teaching and learning that brought the participants to St. Mary's. Our group dynamic was successful in accomplishing its objectives. All seven groups completed a first-draft chapter before they left St. Mary's.

Activities After the Conference

Participants left the conference with a copy of their group's chapter and work assignments for completing the next draft. Thomas McGovern and Cynthia Baum met with the chairs at the APA Annual Meeting in San Francisco in August 1991 to clarify expectations and timetables for completing this book. The chairs solicited input from their members and composed second and third drafts of the chapters. The Steering Committee met in January 1992 to set priorities for conference recommendations to the APA (see appendix D) and to refine the text for the Principles for Quality Undergraduate Psychology Programs.

The participants began their dissemination of the conference activities almost immediately after leaving St. Mary's. At the APA Annual Meeting in San Francisco, the chairs of the seven groups gave summary presentations of their work; an overview of the conference results and dissemination efforts was presented also to the Council of Graduate Departments of Psychology (COGDOP) meeting in San Francisco. Participants from the New England Psychological Association gave a presentation on the conference at their fall meeting. Participants offered symposia at the Mid-America Conference for Teachers of Psychology, the Southeastern Conference on the Teaching of Psychology, and the National Institute on the Teaching of Psychology. Additional presentations were given at regional psychological association meetings held in the spring of 1992. A series of roundtable discussions were offered on faculty development, active learning, and ethnic minority student recruitment and retention at the APA Annual Convention in Washington, DC, in August 1992.

At its spring 1992 meetings, the Board of Education Affairs began its reviews of the Principles for Quality Undergraduate Psychology Programs and Recommendations for Undergraduate Education Activities. The former are being evaluated by multiple governance groups within the APA in anticipation of eventual approval as a policy statement. The latter has already been the catalyst for change, prompting new activities initiated by the Education Directorate.

SEVEN CRITICAL QUESTIONS FOR UNDERGRADUATE EDUCATION IN PSYCHOLOGY

To organize the conference discussions, the Steering Committee determined seven questions on the basis of its evaluation of prior conference topics, current literature on undergraduate education in psychology, and emerging issues in higher education that will shape discipline-based programs. The following paragraphs list those questions and summarize the corresponding chapter or section in this handbook that addresses each question.

Sections I and III serve as the intellectual bookends for the entire text. In section I, the Steering Committee for the conference articulates the Principles for Quality Undergraduate Psychology Programs. The principles are our syntheses of the scholarly and practical discussions and the recommendations in the rest of the book. The principles should serve as the primary catalyst for discussion among scholars, teachers, and administrators of undergraduate psychology.

In section III, "Transforming Undergraduate Psychology for the Next Century," I place the outcomes from the St. Mary's conference in their historical context by comparing the authors' conclusions with those from previous reports by psychology faculty in the 1950s, 1960s, 1970s, and 1980s. Finally, I discuss issues shaping higher education at the national level that will affect psychology programs into the next century.

Section II, consisting of chapters 1 through 7, addresses the following questions:

How can instruction in psychology more effectively address and assess student learning in key educational outcomes such as critical thinking, written and oral expression, scientific and quantitative reasoning, sensitivity to people and cultures, and ethical judgment? How can curricular or program effectiveness be evaluated?

In chapter 1, Halpern and her colleagues address "Targeting Outcomes: Covering Your Assessment Concerns and Needs." This chapter was placed before the others because assessment initiatives from state, university, and departmental groups will be a primary stimulus for comprehensive program renewal and evaluation efforts in the coming decade.

Given the large numbers of students considering psychology and their diverse goals, what are the advising problems for students and faculty, and what strategies are available to resolve these problems?

In chapter 2, Ware and his colleagues address "Developing and Improving Advising: Challenges to Prepare Students for Life." For faculty to respond to the changing demographics of higher education, the authors offer specific suggestions to shape the components of advising for all students and for program implementation and evaluation.

What strategies are available or might be developed for recruiting and retaining ethnic minority students as psychology majors?

In chapter 3, Puente and his colleagues focus our attention on ethnic minority students and faculty in particular. "Toward a Psychology of Variance: Increasing the Presence and Understanding of Ethnic Minorities in Psychology" establishes a rationale and offers specific recommendations to enhance recruitment of and retention efforts for ethnic minority individuals.

With regard to faculty development of full-time and part-time instructors and graduate teaching assistants, what improvements are needed in teacher preparation, continuing education, and systematic instructional evaluation? How can faculty better address the diversity of perspectives and values among their colleagues?

In chapter 4, Fretz and his colleagues use a developmental perspective to understand academic faculty lives. "The Compleat Scholar: Faculty Development for Those Who Teach Psychology" identifies barriers to faculty development and effective strategies applicable to a broad spectrum of institutions and individuals.

How can instructors from various levels of psychology education—high schools, 2-year colleges, and 4-year colleges and universities—develop better networks for sharing ideas, solving common problems, providing mutual support, and developing a greater sense of community?

In chapter 5, Weiten and his colleagues analyze an issue that has become increasingly important for psychology instructors. In "From Isolation to Community: Increasing Communication and Collegiality Among Psychology Teachers," they describe innovative linkages among faculty at all levels of educational institutions, providing case studies for further assistance.

How are departments meeting the challenge of the curriculum? What models have been (or could be) developed for the major? How can departments balance the needs of the major with interdisciplinary pursuits and service courses?

In chapter 6, Brewer and his colleagues tackle the topic of curriculum. Although the chapter title, "Curriculum," is the shortest, there is a long history of debate on the form and substance of the psychology curriculum. Brewer and associates review these debates and analyze curricular goals and structure. The community college curriculum, interdisciplinary courses, and service courses are analyzed as well.

How can active learning be enhanced in all psychology courses, regardless of level, size, setting, or resources?

In chapter 7, Mathie and her colleagues bring the reader full circle from assessing student learning to providing effective teaching strategies to accomplish that learning. "Promoting Active Learning in Psychology Courses" offers faculty a rationale, specific teaching practices, and recommendations to enhance active learning across the curriculum.

Summary

Each of the chapters in this handbook can stand alone. The authors offer faculty a scholarly overview of the critical issues and provide specific strategies to modify undergraduate programs. When read together, the chapters form a comprehensive framework for renewal and change in undergraduate psychology. The Principles for Quality Undergraduate Psychology Programs that immediately follow this introduction are the starting point for any discussion of students, faculty, and the curriculum.

REFERENCES

American Psychological Association. (1983). *Results: Phase I survey of undergraduate department chairs*. Washington, DC: Author.

Bickman, L. (Ed.). (1987). Resolutions approved by the National Conference on Graduate Education in Psychology. *American Psychologist, 42,* 1070–1084.

Buxton, C. E., Cofer, C. N., Gustad, J. W., MacLeod, R. B., McKeachie, W. J., & Wolfle, D. (1952). *Improving undergraduate instruction in psychology*. New York: Macmillan.

Howard, A., Pion, G. M., Gottfredson, G. D., Flatteau, P. E., Oskamp, S., Pfafflin, S. M., Bray, D. W., & Burstein, A. G. (1986). The changing face of American psychology: A report from the Committee on Employment and Human Resources. *American Psychologist, 41,* 1311–1327.

Kulik, J. (1973). *Undergraduate education in psychology*. Washington, DC: American Psychological Association.

McGovern, T. V., Furumoto, L., Halpern, D. F., Kimble, G. A., & McKeachie, W. J. (1991). Liberal education, study in depth, and the arts and sciences major—Psychology. *American Psychologist, 46,* 598–605.

McKeachie, W. J., & Milholland, J. E. (1961). *Undergraduate curricula in psychology*. Fair Lawn, NJ: Scott, Foresman.

Project on Liberal Learning, Study-in-Depth, and the Arts and Sciences Major. (1991a). *Liberal learning and the arts and sciences major: Vol. 1. The challenge of connecting learning*. Washington, DC: Association of American Colleges.

Project on Liberal Learning, Study-in-Depth, and the Arts and Sciences Major. (1991b). *Liberal learning and the arts and sciences major: Vol. 2. Reports from the fields*. Washington, DC: Association of American Colleges.

Puente, A. E., Matthews, J., & Brewer, C. (Eds.). (1992). *Teaching psychology in America: A history*. Washington, DC: American Psychological Association.

Scheirer, C. J., & Rogers, A. M. (1985). *The undergraduate psychology curriculum: 1984*. Washington, DC: American Psychological Association.

PRINCIPLES FOR QUALITY UNDERGRADUATE PSYCHOLOGY PROGRAMS

CYNTHIA BAUM, LUDY T. BENJAMIN, JR., DOUGLAS BERNSTEIN,
ANDREW B. CRIDER, JANE HALONEN, J. ROY HOPKINS,
THOMAS V. McGOVERN (CHAIR), WILBERT J. McKEACHIE,
BARBARA NODINE, PAMELA T. REID, RICHARD SUINN, and
CAROLE WADE

The American Psychological Association (APA) recognizes the importance of undergraduate education in advancing psychology as a science and as a means of promoting human welfare. There are inevitable and desirable differences among undergraduate programs, based on institutional missions, faculty, student populations, and available resources. There are also common principles that characterize quality undergraduate programs.

These principles are intended to guide faculty and administrators in their ongoing efforts to renew undergraduate psychology. The principles emphasize (a) students who enroll in psychology programs and individual courses; (b) faculty whose teaching, scholarship, and collegial affiliations enhance their students' learning; and (c) curriculum that shapes students' study.

These principles are based on recommendations from the APA National Conference on Enhancing the Quality of Undergraduate Education in Psychology, held at St. Mary's College of Maryland, June 1991.

STUDENTS

Quality undergraduate psychology programs should:

1. Set clear and high expectations for students, promote active learning, and give students systematic assessment and feedback on their progress.
2. Recognize that students learn about psychology in multiple settings—classrooms, laboratories, field experience, cocurricular programs (e.g., psychology clubs and science fairs)—and through formal and informal contacts with faculty and student peers.
3. Be enriched by the diverse characteristics of students, drawing on and responding to their differences in age, gender, race, ethnicity, national origin, religion, sexual orientation, disability, and socioeconomic status.
4. Foster effective student advising that goes beyond providing information about institutional procedures and policies by motivating students
   a. to explore and develop their values, interests, abilities, and career and life goals
   b. to become increasingly independent in their decision making
   c. to play an active role in shaping advising policies and procedures.
5. Support effective student advising by providing faculty
   a. unequivocal administrative support for the activity
   b. continuing education opportunities in innovative advising methods
   c. tangible rewards for excellence.

FACULTY

In quality undergraduate programs,

1. Faculty foster students' learning through teaching, scholarship, and service. These three activities are complementary, and quality programs recognize excellent performance in all three.
2. Faculty are enriched by differences among individuals, by

different cultural and ethnic minority perspectives, by different specialization areas and theoretical orientations, and by different contributions to excellence made at different stages of one's academic career.

3. Faculty are enriched by learning from colleagues at different institutions and levels, including secondary schools, community colleges, liberal arts colleges, and universities.

4. Faculty development is considered a lifelong process and is nurtured by
   a. periodic opportunities to enrich one's teaching and scholarship
   b. opportunities for senior faculty to "mentor" new faculty
   c. periodic evaluation and feedback to all faculty on their teaching and intellectual development.

CURRICULUM

In quality undergraduate programs,

1. The curriculum enables students
   a. to think scientifically about behavior and mental processes
   b. to appreciate and respect others
   c. to pursue a variety of postbaccalaureate alternatives including employment and graduate or professional school.

2. The curriculum is based on clear and rigorous goals. These include
   a. synthesizing the natural science and social science aspects of the discipline by requiring students to take courses in both knowledge bases
   b. evaluating research methods (quantitative, qualitative, archival), research designs (experimental, correlational, case study), statistics, and psychometric principles
   c. appreciating the ethical practice of scientific inquiry
   d. thinking scientifically, distinguishing observations from conclusions and distinguishing theories and findings based on evidence from those without such support
   e. speaking and writing effectively in the discourse of the discipline
   f. respecting the diversity of human behavior and experience and appreciating the rich opportunities for science and social relationships that such differences provide

g. understanding how the study of psychology enables individuals to contribute to making their community a better place.

3. Faculty determine the best structure of a curriculum to achieve the goals they identify. A common structure for the baccalaureate curriculum includes
    a. a required introductory course
    b. methodology courses
    c. advanced content courses
    d. an integrating capstone experience.

4. Faculty determine the essential elements of a curriculum to achieve the goals they identify. Common elements of the curriculum include
    a. multiple opportunities for students to be active and collaborative learners
    b. research projects to help students learn the science of psychology
    c. fieldwork, practica, and community service experiences to help students learn the applications of psychology
    d. an emphasis on learning across the curriculum about ethical issues and values
    e. multiple courses emphasizing the diversity of human behavior.

5. Faculty establish mechanisms to assess the curriculum. Essential elements of an assessment program include
    a. clearly stated and achievable outcomes for the curriculum and other program-related experiences
    b. multiple measures of students' learning
    c. planned opportunities for systematic feedback to students on their progress
    d. specific plans to use assessment data to improve individual course instruction and the overall curriculum
    e. opportunities to communicate assessment results to the multiple constituencies of undergraduate psychology.

II

EXAMINING CRITICAL AREAS

1

TARGETING OUTCOMES: COVERING YOUR ASSESSMENT CONCERNS AND NEEDS

DIANE F. HALPERN, in collaboration with DREW C. APPLEBY,
SUSAN E. BEERS, CATHARINE L. COWAN, JOHN J. FUREDY,
JANE S. HALONEN, CARRELL P. HORTON, BLAINE F. PEDEN, and
DAVID J. PITTENGER

The term *assessment* conveys multiple meanings in the debate about student outcomes in higher education. In this chapter, assessment refers to a wide range of activities that involve gathering and examining data for the purpose of improving teaching and learning. Recent trends in higher education and in the nation have elevated the role that assessment plays in the undergraduate experience (Boyer, 1987; Halpern, 1987; McMillan, 1990). For psychology departments, assessment initiatives will be the stimuli in the coming decade for faculty review of its students, its curricula, its advising programs, and its teaching strategies.

WHY ASSESSMENT? WHY NOW?

A number of factors have come together to create a climate for assessment. The first and perhaps most persuasive reason for embarking on a nationwide effort to assess educational outcomes in higher education is the concern over a crisis in human capital. Students from North America routinely rank below those from other parts of the world in academic areas such as scientific knowledge, mathematical problem solving, and general literacy (Lapointe, Mead, & Phillips, 1989). Economists and politicians argue that the poor performance of North American students is a threat to our ability to remain a world leader in science and technology. Individuals and agencies with this same concern believe that the information gained from outcomes assessment can provide the necessary direction to keep America's work force strong and competitive in the 21st century.

A second reason for assessing what and how much students are learning in higher education comes from national groups such as the Association of American Colleges and provocative reports such as *Integrity in the College Curriculum* (Project on Redefining the Meaning and Purpose of Baccalaureate Degrees, 1985). A coherent and well-planned program of outcomes assessment requires clearly articulated educational goals. When faculty and administrators discuss what they want their students to know or to be able to do, these goals must be explicit, and educational practices designed as a means to achieve these goals are examined for their effectiveness. Thus, the process of planning and implementing an outcomes assessment program will enhance educational quality and produce better educated students and graduates.

A third reason is that taxpayers, state legislators, and employers are demanding assurance that scarce educational dollars are being well spent. The director of the Center for the Study of the States recently commented that "Education is going to have a lot more competition for dollars" (quoted in Brownstein, 1991, p. A5). When an outcomes assessment program is used to justify the cost of education, institutions of higher education must become accountable for the quality of educated individuals they produce.

In response to mounting pressures to conduct student outcomes assessment, departmental faculty at colleges and universities are seeking information about implementing or improving such a program. This chapter provides a framework for the assessment of student learning and program effectiveness, adaptable for use by any higher education discipline, although primarily for undergraduate institutions that offer psychology courses as a part of general education or baccalaureate degree programs.

The recommendations for outcomes assessment presented in this chapter are based on two common assumptions: (a) there are multiple assessment goals, and any programmatic examination of higher education needs to begin with a clear statement of these goals; and (b) outcomes assessment should be student-centered. Students' academic, attitudinal, and behavioral outcomes are the primary sources of assessment data. A student-centered outcomes assessment program provides information about the effectiveness of the curriculum, advising, faculty development, ethnic diversity goals, and external linkages with the other segments of education (e.g., high schools, community colleges, and graduate and professional schools). All of these topics are covered in depth in subsequent chapters in this handbook.

Assessment should be a supportive process that takes place in an environment conceptualized as a series of concentric circles (see Figure 1). Students occupy the innermost circle, and faculty, academic departments, colleges or universities, and society form the ever-expanding layers. A properly conducted, multifaceted assessment program serves the needs of every group in the circles. In a well-designed outcomes assessment program, students will be informed of their teachers' academic expectations and will receive regular feedback on their academic performance for use in academic and career planning. Faculty will communicate their expectations to students in a clear manner and in turn will receive feedback on the effectiveness of their teaching for use in their own development. (See chapter 4 for a discussion of faculty development goals and practices.) At the departmental level, faculty and chairs will develop statements of mission and purpose to plan empirical data collection for use in curricular change. Academic programs will be examined to allow administrators or trustees to determine the extent to which institutional missions are being accomplished. Society as a whole can determine the efficacy of higher education and the extent to which it is populated by a literate, numerate, and ethical citizenry. Thus, when assessment is done well, it provides valuable information to all of the participants and stakeholders in higher education.

Despite the potential of outcomes assessment for improving student growth, fostering faculty development, and accomplishing educational objectives, it has not been embraced enthusiastically by everyone. Faculty,

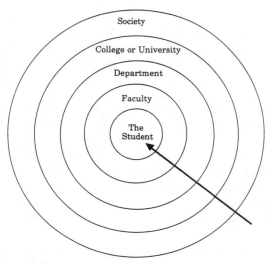

Figure 1: A student-centered model of outcomes assessment.

in particular, may be reluctant to engage in assessment for several reasons. Assessment generates unfamiliar language and is fueled by uncertain purposes. Assessment poses a threat to the status quo, and many of those involved in higher education perceive change unfavorably (Hutchings, 1990a). Many faculty view assessment activities as an "add-on" to their fundamental teaching and scholarship responsibilities. Assessment is yet another task imposed on an already overworked and underpaid faculty. Attitudes toward assessment are even more negative when external agents mandate assessment as a means of accountability. In this instance, assessment can be perceived as punishment, especially when the mandate carries a potential reduction in funding as a consequence of a poor evaluation. Such pressures encourage departments to build superficial assessment programs or to collect data that will make them "look good" and avoid possible negative consequences. Therefore, for many reasons we believe that assessment should be developed internally by a department rather than imposed externally. Assessments should not provide a platform for administrators or politicians to use the results to make foolish comparisons between departments, between institutions, or worse, between faculty.

Similar to the position of curricular pluralism espoused by Brewer and his colleagues in chapter 6, we believe that there is no single assessment method appropriate for all departments and institutions. The search for a perfect assessment plan is like the quest for the Holy Grail. We encourage departments to quest instead for fair assessment, to establish an ongoing process in which the dynamics among faculty and between faculty and students change for the better.

Our assessment model and its underlying assumptions resonate with Boyer's (1987) sentiments:

> The outcomes of collegiate education should be measured by the student's performance in the classroom as he or she becomes proficient in the use of language, acquires a basic solid education, and becomes competent in a specific field. Further, the impact of the undergraduate experience is to be assessed by the performance of the graduate in the work place and further education. But in the end, students must be inspired by a larger vision, using the knowledge they have acquired to discover patterns, form values, and advance the common good. (pp. 283–284)

We hope that those who embark on a program of student outcomes assessment follow Boyer's advice and become inspired by the larger vision. To avoid our own myopic tendencies, the remainder of this chapter is organized around the following broad questions:

1. What is unique about psychology's contribution to student outcomes assessment?

2. What outcomes should psychology foster and can these be organized developmentally?
3. What forms of assessment show the greatest promise for assessing psychological abilities and knowledge?
4. What elements contribute to an effective outcomes assessment plan?
5. How can faculty develop more meaningful and effective assessment?
6. How can an assessment program be created on an individual campus?

The answers to these questions can guide those who want to begin or to improve an outcomes assessment program.

PSYCHOLOGY'S UNIQUE CONTRIBUTION TO ASSESSMENT

Administrators and other faculty expect psychologists to take the lead in assessing student outcomes because of their expertise in areas such as learning, adult development, psychometrics, program evaluation, and cognition. Both quantitative and qualitative approaches to assessing educational outcomes are natural domains for the psychologist-educator.

Although there are many similarities among programs for different academic majors, every field of study has unique characteristics that require a more specialized perspective on the outcomes that are measured. Psychology students learn principles in their study of human thoughts, feelings, and behavior. The experimental method is at the core of psychology, influencing what we want our students to know and how we go about assessing their knowledge. Another assumption of psychology is that people can change with intervention. This assumption is at the heart of all schools of psychotherapy and all theories of learning and cognition. Psychologists, therefore, expect to use an experimental approach to answer others' questions about how and how much students have changed during their college years. Those who identify with the humanist tradition in psychology may care about the quality of education we are providing to students; experimental colleagues may want to see just the data.

PSYCHOLOGY OUTCOMES AND THEIR DEVELOPMENTAL ORGANIZATION

How do we want our students to change as a result of their education? We identified three ways in which successful psychology students change as a result of their undergraduate education. First, they accumulate a body

Knowledge base

    Content areas
        Specific areas (vary depending on objectives and specifics of curriculum)
        Knowledge of psychology's role in liberal arts
    Methods
        Research design
        Statistics
        Psychometrics
    Theory
        Schools of thought
    History
        Origins of psychological thought
        Great person vs. zeitgeist approaches
        Historiography of psychology

Intellectual skills

    Thinking skills
        Thinks logically, creatively, and critically
        Synthesizes multiple sources of information
        Evaluates at a sophisticated level
        Generalizes results from research findings
        Defends ideas in an objective, clear, and nondogmatic manner
    Communication skills
        Writes effectively
        Speaks clearly and persuasively
        Creates understandable graphs and tables
        Writes in accord with APA style
    Information gathering and synthesis skills
        Makes careful, systematic observations
        Conducts traditional and electronic library searches
        Detects, comprehends, and retains key points from written and verbal
            sources
    Quantitative, scientific, and technological skills
        Uses scientific methodology
        Uses statistical methodology
        Interprets results

Personal characteristics

    Thinking
        Creative
        Open-minded
        Organized
        Tolerant of ambiguity
        Nondefensive
        Flexible
    Interpersonal and intrapersonal skills
        Deals sensitively and effectively with a wide variety of people
        Collaborates effectively
        Adapts to organizational rules and procedures
        Interacts with research participants in an ethical manner

(Continued on next page)

(Exhibit 1—*Continued from previous page*)

Motivation
    Motivated and hard working
    Positive about learning
    Enthusiastic
    Displays initiative
    Begins and completes tasks with a minimum of supervision
Ethics
    Displays and supports high ethical standards
Sensitivity to people and cultures
    Appreciative of individual differences
    Enthusiastic about cultural diversity

of knowledge. Second, they master intellectual skills that enable them to use their knowledge wisely. These skills include the abilities to think critically, to express themselves clearly in writing and speaking, to reason empirically, and to demonstrate ethical judgment and sensitivity to other people and cultures. Third, psychology students acquire or strengthen personal characteristics such as maturity, rigor, tolerance, flexibility, high ethical standards, and a positive attitude toward lifelong learning.

Like nature and nurture, these three broad goals of higher education are intertwined. For example, suppose a student has the ability to use a variety of statistical procedures. Without a psychological knowledge base or the motivation to apply these skills, successful use of this knowledge will not be possible. Similarly, students who have a desire to use psychological principles to benefit society but do not have the knowledge or skill to do so will be unable to accomplish their goal.

The outcomes that departments target for the knowledge base, intellectual skills, and personal characteristics will vary depending on faculty strengths, university missions, student goals, and other variables. In Exhibit 1 we offer an example of specific outcomes that a department might generate. Again, every department's list of outcomes should be uniquely determined by its faculty.

Depending on departmental philosophy and goals, some outcomes can be organized into a developmental hierarchy such as those proposed by Bloom (1956) and Perry (1970). Such an organization can lend itself to the sequencing of the curriculum. Walker, Newcomb, and Hopkins (1987) described such a curriculum organized by developmental goals. Another such developmental hierarchy might evolve as a result of a department deciding that its freshmen should have basic reading, writing, and library skills; its sophomores should be able to synthesize information from multiple original and secondary sources; its juniors should be able to evaluate conflicting claims and apply information to novel situations; and its seniors should be able to tie all of these skills together and defend the results.

Formal programmatic assessment can be administered at any time in a student's academic career—when leaving the institution (graduation or otherwise); at entrance and again at exit (known as a "gains" measure); and at frequent intervals such as at entry, after the completion of the sophomore year or a portion of the general education program, and again at graduation. The timing of assessment administrations will depend on purpose. For example, exit-only measures may be sufficient for external agencies interested in certifying the abilities of students at graduation. Faculty and others concerned with student development will emphasize assessment conducted periodically during a student's academic career, so that changes can be monitored longitudinally. The assessment of a developmental hierarchy should cover a 4-year period, and the skills and knowledge assessed should increase in complexity commensurate with developmental expectations.

FORMS OF ASSESSMENT FOR MEASURING PSYCHOLOGICAL ABILITIES AND KNOWLEDGE

This section describes an array of assessment methods. First, we will examine conventional techniques that are being used already and will consider how they can be improved and incorporated into the larger scheme of outcomes assessment. Second, we will consider procedures that may be novel for some departments. These procedures build on available material and provide additional information about unique departmental goals. Third, we will consider how individual assessment techniques contribute to the convergent validity of an overall assessment program.

Conventional Techniques

Archival Forms of Assessment Data

Numerous campus offices already may be collecting data that are useful for an assessment program, although the results are probably scattered over several places on campus. For example, most admissions offices collect information on student demographics, performance on standardized tests, and writing samples. The records office collects information about the types of classes students are taking and generates transcripts. It may be instructive to examine transcripts for the patterns of courses that psychology majors take for their general education requirements and elective course options. Libraries maintain records of books withdrawn, bibliographic searches completed, and resources used. Student affairs offices maintain information about student activity in clubs, volunteer work, and campus leadership activities. Finally, the alumni office should have information on postbaccalaureate job placements, on the level and nature of additional education, and on indices of satisfaction with the college.

Class Assessment Activities

A well-planned assessment program builds on assessment that takes place regularly in individual classrooms. All college courses assess student performance. In the typical class, students take exams, write papers, make presentations, contribute to class discussions, respond to extemporaneous questions, and interact with fellow students. These classroom activities may be modified to include an assessment program and to provide information at the departmental level (Cross & Angelo, 1988).

Exams. The single ubiquitous form of assessment is the in-class exam. Exams are used to determine if students have achieved a specific level of knowledge in a subject matter. Instructors use multiple-choice exams because they are easy to administer and score and because the tests appear to be an objective measure of student knowledge. Like every other form of assessment, multiple-choice exams have both advantages and disadvantages (Aiken, 1987; Cantor, 1987). They offer obvious benefits when class sizes are large. Many psychology lecture classes, especially introductory courses, have hundreds of students. Large classes make the option of lengthy essay questions graded by a single professor a daunting task. Multiple-choice exams can be used to assess higher level cognitive skills (Appleby, 1990), although they are often used only to measure basic knowledge.

The speed and ease of scoring multiple-choice exams, however, is offset by their inability to tap the effective communication of students' knowledge. If departments are committed to developing students' writing skills, then multiple-choice tests are inappropriate unless used in conjunction with written assignments. The alternative to multiple-choice exams is a significant writing component within each exam. The grading of the essay can then reflect several components. First, the essay can be assessed for accuracy of information. If the question is worded well, the student should have sufficient information to provide a well-informed response. Second, the essay can be evaluated for quality of writing. Scoring criteria are available that make grading of the essay meaningful for the student (Braun, 1986, 1988). It is possible for the instructor to provide two grades to the student; one grade reflects the accuracy of the material presented in the essay and another grade reflects the quality of the writing.

Papers. There has been a greal deal of recent interest in student writing in psychology (Nodine, 1990). Papers foster students' assimilation of information from a variety of sources and stimulate them to reflect on larger issues in psychology. Papers can be incorporated into a student portfolio to allow for a longitudinal assessment of intellectual development.

Classroom presentation and activities. The development of oral communication is often part of the mission of an institution or department. Students may be required to make oral presentations in their classes or be evaluated on less formal indicators of their oral expression such as their contributions to class discussion. Such activities foster oral skills by giving students instruction, practice, and feedback in speaking, as well as in course content. Classroom speaking can provide the opportunity for assessment of thinking skills and personal characteristics, such as sensitivity to others and willingness to tolerate disparate ideas. Other techniques to foster the development of oral communication skills include having students act as leaders in a class discussion and observing how students perform when asked a specific question during class.

Standardized Testing

Standardized testing refers to some form of cohort testing designed to measure the achievement of a group. Typically, departments perform such tests during the fourth year of an academic program. The timing of the testing depends on how test results will be used and on the design of the curriculum. Departments without a linearly organized curriculum, which requires students to have achieved specific goals by specific times, may find that such testing should be done at the end of the senior year. Other departments with a more sequenced curriculum will find that the test may be given earlier in the student's education.

There are several standardized test options available for undergraduate psychology. The Educational Testing Service (ETS) offers objective instruments to assess content knowledge. The Advanced Psychology Test is one measure designed and normed for use as a screening device for admission to graduate schools. The Major Field Achievement Tests were designed by the ETS to measure content knowledge in areas such as psychology. The primary difference between these two tests is that the Advanced Psychology Test is normed for a higher level of achievement.

Although these tests are relatively inexpensive and easy to administer and score, they may not meet the specific needs of a department, such as any special emphasis on specific content areas (e.g., health psychology or industrial psychology). Likewise, a department that places little or no emphasis on a particular topic (e.g., physiological psychology) may find that too much of a standardized test focuses on underemphasized topics.

There are several alternatives to these commercially created tests. For example, groups of colleges can develop a pool of test items indexed by topic and type of question (e.g., multiple choice, short answer essay). The advantage of a question pool is that faculty from any participating institution can sample questions and tailor an instrument to very specific assessment needs. Because every question is tested with large numbers of students, the psychometric properties of questions can be determined (e.g., indices of discriminability).

Some departments use a senior-level test as a final determination of whether students should be allowed to graduate. It is our recommendation that a senior-level test not be used for this purpose; such a test is only a partial reflection of the integrity of the whole department's curriculum, not a measure of individual performance.

Capstone Courses and Other Integration Experiences

A senior capstone course can be incorporated into an assessment program. The general goal of any capstone course is to enable students to synthesize the skills that have been developed through an entire program of study. There are several alternative types of experience available. A common one is the *research project*, which requires students to design and conduct an original experiment. Students prepare a final report that is formally presented. An alternative capstone experience is the *applied externship*, in which students are placed in work settings (e.g., mental health facilities, tutoring centers, or industry settings) in which there is an active applied psychology component. A well-planned externship will include direct supervision from the psychology faculty as well as from the staff at the host setting. The academic component includes meeting with faculty to discuss issues such as ethics and various principles demonstrated in the work setting. Students can benefit also from journal assignments in which they reflect on their work experiences. As with the research report, the student may be required to prepare a final report that includes an oral presentation.

Nontraditional Qualitative Measures

There is a large number of student-centered, performance-based methods that can be used to provide information about student and programmatic outcomes. We list several here that are relatively easy to administer.

Portfolio analysis

This qualitative measure was developed as a means of assessing writing, but it has been adapted to the assessment of a variety of educational goals (Hutchings, 1990b). Portfolios are simply files of students' work that are reviewed periodically. The work selected represents various educational objectives. Portfolios may be developed for individual courses, majors, or colleges (Beers, 1985). For example, a portfolio compiled to chart students' development in reading, writing, and library skills could require freshman-year papers summarizing information from single sources, sophomore papers reporting links among articles and books, junior-level term papers in which literature is reviewed and critiqued, and a senior thesis. Portfolios can include videotapes and audiotapes that measure student achievement of other communication skills.

Recently, Schulman (1991) advocated the creation of portfolios as an alternative means of assessing the quality of teachers at all levels of education. Thus, portfolios can be applicable in a wide variety of situations, but have as a disadvantage the psychometric problems of unknown reliability and validity.

Interviews

This qualitative measure can be conducted periodically throughout students' academic careers or as part of their senior-year experience (Doll & Jacobs, 1989). Interviews may cover students' experiences in the major or in college as a whole. They can be designed to assess specific skills. In *situational assessments,* the interview consists of presenting students with specific hypothetical situations for which they present their analysis or indicate appropriate actions. Situational assessments may be particularly useful for examining students' ethical judgment or for examining the dimensions of their sensitivity to people and cultures. *Focus groups,* which are structured interviews conducted with students in a group format, are also worthy of consideration.

External Examiners

This strategy has been a meaningful part of assessment in a variety of institutions. When complex educational objectives such as the disposition to challenge assumptions and beliefs are to be assessed, external evaluators are necessary. Although the faculty supervisor of a student's project may be able to evaluate the student's thinking up to the production of the final product, that product can be evaluated more impartially by an external reader. Senior theses or comprehensive exams easily lend themselves to external examination. The Association of American Colleges' External Examiner Project (Association of American Colleges, 1989) recently expanded this concept by creating teams of scholars from schools of similar sizes and missions to create a meaningful external oral examination for member schools. Although external evaluators are costly in terms of time and effort, the students and assessors report that they are invigorated by the process (Halonen, 1990).

External evaluation can be used in other ways as part of an assessment program. Institutions with similar goals and missions can exchange faculty who serve as external examiners to each other. The job of these examiners is to make general assessments of standards. By exchanging faculty, the process is reciprocal (i.e., the assessors are themselves assessed), and this symmetry helps to mitigate negative emotional impacts (and keep the assessors reasonably honest).

Performance-Based Assessment

This measure is uniquely appropriate for psychology given the discipline's history of behavioral research. Direct behavioral assessment was also suggested by the National Institute of Education's (1984) report on involvement in learning as a means of assessing achievements in general education. Performance-based assessment asks students to "do the discipline" in discussions, projects, speeches, and other active learning situations (Loaker, 1990). For example, in a seminar course, students may be assigned related articles to read that provide them the opportunity to assert, challenge, and defend various points of view. This type of exercise provides faculty the opportunity to assess the critical thinking skills of evaluation and analysis and personal characteristics such as nondefensiveness, open-mindedness, and tolerance of ambiguity. Performance-based assessment provides faculty, students, and external constituencies with particularly clear indicators of students' skills. Effective performance-based assessment requires (a) the specification of goals and criteria for assessment and (b) multiple opportunities for student learning.

Conflict of Ideas Approach

Another active learning method focuses on argumentation as a vehicle for skill acquisition. This approach is modeled on the life of Socrates, whose teaching sharpened the differences among competing positions through inquiry (Furedy & Furedy, 1982, 1986). This approach, which can lead to conflict between people as well as ideas, is poorly suited to political interactions (as demonstrated, though not for the last time, by the fate of Socrates at the hands of the Athenian democracy). It is well suited for the examination of complex issues because the emphasis on the conflict of ideas is a hallmark of higher education. One force, however, that mitigates against the successful use of the conflict of ideas approach is the grading power that professors have over students. Many students believe that disagreement with the professor will result in lower grades.

Assessment that uses the conflict of ideas approach centers around the degree to which students recognize alternative possibilities and can engage in intellectual conflicts. The best measures for this approach are a sample of written work (e.g., thesis, literature review term paper) or oral responses to a thoughtful question. Moreover, because the critical skill involves disagreeing with the professor, the evaluation may require an external examiner. The term *external* here does not necessarily mean external to the department, but only that the evaluator must not have been involved with the work itself. One measure of how well the student has developed the propensity to question the ideas of others is the degree to which the student's work has challenged the ideas of the instructor, or, more generally, the extent to which a student essay has challenged the grader's views.

Assessment of Critical Thinking

Critical thinking is a widely used term that includes skills in applying, analyzing, synthesizing, and evaluating information and the disposition to apply these skills (National Center for Excellence in Critical Thinking Instruction, 1991). Critical thinking is almost always listed as one of the desirable outcomes of undergraduate education (Halpern, 1988). A review of the literature on the assessment of critical thinking skills shows that there are many assessment options. For example, written and oral work can be evaluated on the extent to which conclusions are supported by evidence or other reasons. Some researchers have used student self-reports to measure students' ability to think critically, although such reports are questionable because of the multiple biases inherent in self-report data. Several researchers have measured gains in cognitive growth and development using developmental frameworks such as those proposed by Piaget (Inhelder & Piaget, 1958), Kohlberg (1976), and Perry (1970).

One of the most theoretically advanced means of exploring changes in critical thinking is to examine changes in the underlying structure of cognitive skills and knowledge. Several researchers have shown that when students become better thinkers about a topic, their internal representations of topic-related knowledge will become more similar to the internal representations of experts in the field (Schoenfeld & Hermann, 1982). In other words, students come to think more like experts. Other researchers have used a cognitive skills approach that begins with a specification of the skills that are needed for effective thinking. There are many lists of cognitive skills (e.g., Halpern, 1989), most of which include constructs such as understanding the distinction between correlation and cause, weighing evidence in support of a conclusion, recognizing regression to the mean, making appropriate generalizations, and using "if ... then" reasoning appropriately. A multiple-choice test has been devised that purports to assess students' ability to use these skills (Facione, 1991).

The real goal of any program to improve students' ability to think effectively is transfer of training, that is, the spontaneous use of these skills in novel, out-of-class situations. Nisbett (Lehman & Nisbett, 1990) and his colleagues completed a series of studies in which they examined the spontaneous transfer of thinking skills to real-world problems that occur outside the classroom. In one study, they phoned students at home several months after they completed their course work. Students were told that the caller was taking a poll and they were asked to comment on several contemporary topics. Results demonstrated that students had learned the critical thinking skills required to answer the questions that were posed over the phone. All of these methods have shown that it is possible to promote and assess critical thinking and that improved thinking ability can be an outcome of higher education.

This list of assessment techniques highlights two basic and inescapable facts: educational goals are complex, and all measurement is imperfect. Assessment will be most useful when multiple methods are used to examine clearly specified objectives. A comprehensive assessment plan should not overburden the resources of a department or overtax faculty and students, but should, within reason, provide for both qualitative and quantitative types of evaluation.

ELEMENTS OF EFFECTIVE PSYCHOLOGICAL ASSESSMENT PLANS

Assessment of educational outcomes can take many forms, but regardless of the specific decisions about who, what, and how to assess, good programs share some common attributes. The following guidelines are applicable to all outcomes assessment programs.

Student-Centered

The purpose of student outcomes assessment is to improve teaching and learning. Therefore, one feature of a good outcomes assessment program is that it be student-centered. Information about individual students should be used to help them select courses, plan careers, and develop life views. This information should be provided in ways that enable students to monitor their own cognitive and attitudinal gains (or losses) while they are enrolled in college. Faculty should receive information that they can use to improve individual classes and the way they teach, and institutions can use the data to direct curricular change and development. Outcomes assessment serves as a quality assurance indicator so that taxpayers and prospective employers can be assured that their tax dollars are being well spent and that future employees are being well educated.

Multiple Measures

There is no single indicator of educational effectiveness. No single measure or score captures the multifaceted nature of an effective college education or the cognitive growth of an adult. All good programs will use multiple measures that are qualitatively different.

Faculty Ownership

Successful assessment programs are owned by faculty. It is the faculty who are responsible for the curriculum and the process of higher education and who must direct any assessment of the educational effectiveness of their courses and their teaching. Decisions about the way data are generated and used rest with appropriate faculty committees.

Recognition for Quality Assessment

The expertise and hard work involved in the quality assessment of educational objectives must be recognized and rewarded in a manner that is comparable with that of other professional activities. Faculty appointed as directors of assessment programs should receive the same consideration in the retention, promotion, tenure, and merit evaluation processes as faculty engaged in traditional research and committee assignments. Similarly, departments that engage in a thoughtful analysis of their programs and that follow sound educational practices should reap some of the customary rewards such as increases in budget or support staff.

Linkages

Outcomes assessment programs create natural links with other segments of higher education (i.e., 2- and 4-year colleges, high schools, doctoral programs). Institutions can form regional collectives to track student progress and to monitor success-related variables such as course-taking patterns, contiguous enrollment, preparation for transfer, and other relationships. (See chapter 5 for specific examples of effective linkages.)

Judicious Use of Data

No outcomes assessment program can succeed unless care is taken to ensure that data are not misused. Student outcomes assessment is not a sole indicator of faculty performance. It is not appropriate for use in the faculty promotion, retention, tenure, or merit evaluation processes unless an individual faculty member wishes to include it as ancillary data. If faculty believe that such data will be misused, the program will not succeed.

THE DEVELOPMENT OF MORE MEANINGFUL AND EFFECTIVE ASSESSMENT

As departments design assessment initiatives, psychology faculty discover that there are limits to the resources available to assist them in planning and executing their assessment program. The purpose of this section is to review the kinds of needs that exist in developing effective assessment.

Department chairs find it helpful to arrange for a faculty retreat to signal a different kind of faculty collaboration in the design of assessment work. An off-campus gathering facilitates "breaking set" and transcends the traditional ways of thinking about the ways we work. At such a gathering, faculty can be encouraged to self-assess the following: How satisfying is the undergraduate experience in the curriculum? How do we know we are doing what we say we are doing? What must be tweaked and what must be trashed?

This chapter and others in this handbook will serve as a stimulus for faculty discussion. Every chapter highlights dimensions of undergraduate faculty activity. As McGovern suggested in the Preface, the whole book can be assigned to faculty members over a course of time, or individual faculty or faculty teams may be asked to apply the principles in certain chapters to existing practices at their institution.

As assessment plans develop, faculty should be encouraged to work in pairs. Creative assignments may be more reliably completed when one faculty member has a sense of accountability to another. The assessment plan needs to include clear deadlines for implementation and revision.

These activities cannot take place without appropriate time and funding. Faculty are unlikely to take this activity seriously if they are unrewarded for their efforts. In addition, attendance at assessment-oriented workshops and conferences could receive higher priority in travel funding for department members, so that such members can learn more about the options and issues in assessment.

Administrators need to collaborate at some central level to develop institutional approaches to assessment. This collaboration can be accomplished by creating interdepartmental task forces. The more explicit the charge, the more likely the success of the task force. Time will need to be allotted for faculty gatherings to communicate directions or tentative plans to those not assigned to the task force. Release time from teaching will facilitate more rapid progress in developing the assessment strategy.

The original model posed in this chapter can clarify the level of assessment activity required. Faculty who are learning about classroom assessment techniques can focus primarily in this area. Other faculty may wish to pursue departmental level objectives. Others may be more interested in the interdisciplinary collaboration involved in institutional assessment design. All activities will need to be modified as future assessment requirements from accrediting agencies become more focused and more stringent. In addition, knowledge of a variety of processes provides flexibility in designing and revising effective assessment programs.

Assessment consultation is available through several sources. The Education Directorate of the APA maintains a list of consultants to assist departments. Requests for assessment specialists should be clearly identified. Other organizations that can help in institutional activities include the Association of American Colleges and the American Association of Higher Education, both located in Washington, DC.

A less tangible but equally important need in developing meaningful and effective assessment programs is trust in the way the data will be used. There are several apparent paradoxes in student outcomes assessment. If they are not addressed, the entire enterprise will fail because a successful program cannot be initiated without the support of faculty.

The Comparison Paradox

There is a contradiction between the desire to provide valid and reliable assessment and the wish to avoid invidious comparisons between individuals and between institutions. Such comparisons inevitably have winners and losers in a zero-sum game. One solution to this paradox is to reject all such comparisons and to collect only within-individual or within-institution developmental data. Advocates of this solution cite examples of the gross misuse of single quantitative indices to compare institutions with widely differing goals.

The comparison paradox needs to be considered in light of the legitimate reasons for making comparative decisions. For example, a parent or student choosing between institutions of higher education with similar goals is entitled to comparative information to make that choice. But, for assessment to be fair (perfect assessment is not possible) and appropriate, multiple measures (both quantitative and qualitative) must be used, and comparisons can only be made among institutions that are similar with respect to their missions, students, and geography. It is only through the provision of fair comparisons that the assessment paradox is adequately resolved.

The Funding Paradox

The constituencies that provide funds for higher education desire evidence that those funds are not wasted. Student outcomes are tied to further funding so that the institutions with the best outcomes receive the most funding. However, this practice can adulterate the assessment process, in which, to avoid losing funding, assessment is either superficial or is slanted to ensure favorable outcomes. This, in turn, makes it unlikely that the institution will confront and improve its practices, because reporting negative outcomes may eliminate the program. So the prima facie reasonable practice of tying funding to outcomes can actually result in poorer teaching and learning. One way to resolve this paradox is to reject funding that is based on outcomes data.

Performance-based funding also denies funds to those programs that are most in need of improvement and provides funds instead to programs that are already doing the best job. This unfortunate state of affairs can be resolved by rewarding sound educational practices such as those that are advocated in this and other chapters in this book. Good outcomes result from good practices.

The Faculty Development Paradox

We have stated in numerous places that a good outcomes assessment program will provide feedback to faculty about how well they are teaching along with appropriate feedback for the other audiences in the higher education arena. Although the information that faculty receive will be a partial index of how well they are teaching, we maintain that this information is inappropriate for retention and promotion decisions, unless an individual faculty member decides to include it along with the usual documentation of teaching and professional activities. In fact, the data must be collected and disseminated in such a way that individual faculty members cannot be identified. This level of confidentiality is imperative to ensure that assessment programs examine crucial data and ask the "hard" questions about effectiveness.

There are better ways than outcomes assessment to determine whether faculty are performing well. Faculty assessment will require a different set of procedures if it is to be fair and valid. The teaching portfolio described earlier is one such approach, as are peer visitations, collections of syllabi and exams, student evaluations, and statements of teaching goals and philosophies.

THE CREATION OF ASSESSMENT PROGRAMS

What follows is a step-by-step guide to establishing or improving a student outcomes assessment program. In recognition of the significant differences among programs, there is no single program that can be reproduced on every campus. This list is intended as a guide to be modified in accord with individual campus needs and priorities.

Small-Group Support

Begin with a small group of faculty and administrators who believe that outcomes assessment is beneficial. Assessment programs work best in a climate of support. An important first step is to convince a cadre of faculty and administrators that assessment yields tangible gains for students, faculty, and institutions. Faculty may need to present some of the reasons for assessment that are presented in the opening section of this chapter to obtain the commitment of key colleagues and administrators. Support from a majority of the faculty or acknowledgment from every level of administration is not necessary; a small group of faculty and administrators who are willing to support initial efforts is sufficient. It is unrealistic to expect that more than a handful of faculty will be willing to get involved in initial planning.

Flexibility

The planning stages of any undertaking are fraught with delays and setbacks. Outcomes assessment is not a quick fix. Expect frustrations and do not be disappointed. If a particular form of assessment is mandated by the state or by the institution, there will be fewer local decisions. If the institution is in the United States, contact a campus liaison to the local accreditation association. Each association now requires some form of outcomes assessment, so it makes good sense to incorporate accreditation requirements into an overall plan.

Early Planning

Put time and effort into the early planning stages. A good plan will involve a great deal of consultation. By consulting widely with department chairs, curriculum committees, offices of institutional research, deans, chairs from other departments, student government, and other groups and individuals, the process will go more smoothly and quickly later on. A plan always benefits from the diversity of the input. Wide consultation will increase support for the activity. If possible, solicit public and written forms of support from committee chairs and administrators.

Visibility of Program and Its Coordination

Create a visible center or location where assessment information will be compiled, and identify the people who are responsible for making the plan work. Clear ownership is an important part of getting the job done well. All segments of the academic community will need to know where assessment is being coordinated. A visible location for assessment activities conveys the message that assessment is being taken seriously.

Faculty Discussions

Get faculty talking about desired outcomes for their students. What should students know when they complete their academic program? What skills and dispositions are expected? This may be the most valuable part of the entire assessment program. Faculty willingness to tackle such difficult questions and to begin to formulate answers is a critical component in an assessment plan. After faculty plan an assessment program, many report that these discussions are the first time that they ever articulated goals for their students. Discussions of this sort build a sense of community for faculty, clarify programmatic goals, and require interdisciplinary colleagues to consider their students' needs and their institutional mission. Goals will vary depending on the needs and expectations of students, type of institution, faculty background and expertise, available resources, and a host of other variables. Despite differences in the specific nature of the desired outcomes for students, the very process of articulating what students should get out of the curriculum and the college experience is a valuable end in itself. It is a way of bringing coherence into pluralistic curricula that are becoming increasingly fragmented.

Operationalization of Outcomes

Operationalize desired outcomes. How will it be determined whether a department is achieving its educational objectives? There are suggestions in earlier sections of this chapter for determining, for example, if students are graduating with content area knowledge or with high levels of critical thinking abilities or with skills in written and oral communication. Some measures are easy to obtain, such as a simple count of the number of courses that require written or oral assignments. Supporting data can also be found in student databases such as standardized test scores, placement and proficiency exams, survey data, and persistence rates. Other data require new assessment techniques such as comprehensive exams, capstone experiences, or reviews of student portfolios. Decisions about which types of measurement and how many indicators of progress are included in the assessment will depend on individual campus variables.

Plan and Time Line

Make a concrete plan with a realistic time line. Good planning with extensive communication among all interested parties is vital to the success of an outcomes assessment program. The identity of the interested parties will vary from campus to campus, but probably will include faculty, curriculum and assessment committees, general education committees, academic deans, student affairs professionals, student government groups, institutional research staff, and academic vice-presidents.

Use of Information

Make sure that the information collected is usable and used by students, faculty, and the institution. Students need to know their strengths and weaknesses so that they can plan for their future. Faculty need to know

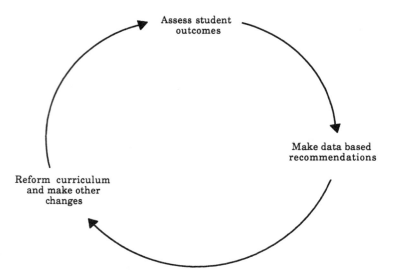

Figure 2: Outcomes assessment is an iterative process that functions like a continuous feedback loop. The results of an assessment are used to change programs, which are then reassessed.

if they have an effective curriculum and whether they are teaching in a manner that facilitates learning. Institutions need to know how well they are educating their students. Information should be provided in a way that it can be used to revise curricula and suggest ways of improving teaching and learning.

Data-Based Recommendations

Make data-based suggestions for improving teaching and learning. Outcomes assessment is an iterative process in which the results of one cycle are used to modify the educational process, which is then assessed for its effectiveness in the next assessment wave. The assessment cycle is depicted in Figure 2. It is important to have structures for change in place.

Student outcomes assessment is not only a tool for improving the teaching and learning process, it is the only way of determining what works in higher education. As Hutchings and Reuben (1988) so eloquently described, "Assessment may mean headaches, squabbles, and threats to faculty autonomy; it can also give faculty something most of them have never heard very clearly: a signal that teaching matters" (p. 55).

REFERENCES

Aiken, L. R. (1987). Testing with multiple-choice items. *Journal of Research and Development in Education, 20,* 44–58.

Appleby, D. C. (1990). A cognitive taxonomy of multiple-choice questions. In V. P. Makosky, C. C. Sileo, L. G. Whittemore, C. P. Landry, & M. L. Skutley (Eds.), *Activities handbook for teaching of psychology* (Vol. 3, pp. 79–81). Washington, DC: American Psychological Association.

Association of American Colleges. (1989). *Using external examiners to assess student learning in arts and sciences majors.* Washington, DC: Author.

Beers, S. E. (1985). Use of a portfolio writing assignment in a course on developmental psychology. *Teaching of Psychology, 12,* 94–96.

Bloom, B. S. (Ed.). (1956). *Taxonomy of educational objectives: The classification of educational goals. Handbook 1: Cognitive domain.* New York: Longman.

Boyer, E. L. (1987). *College: The undergraduate experience in America.* New York: Harper & Row.

Braun, H. I. (1986). *Calibration of essay readers* (Final Report, Program Statistics Research Tech. Rep. No. 86-68). Princeton, NJ: Educational Testing Service.

Braun, H. I. (1988). Understanding scoring reliability: Experiments in calibrating essay readers. *Journal of Educational Statistics, 13,* 1–18.

Brownstein, R. (1991, July 18). More conflicts likely in era of empty pockets. *Los Angeles Times,* p. A5.

Cantor, J. A. (1987). Developing multiple-choice test items. *Training and Development Journal, 20,* 85–88.

Cross, P. K., & Angelo, T. A. (1988). *Classroom assessment techniques: A handbook for faculty.* Ann Arbor, MI: National Center for Research to Improve Postsecondary Teaching and Learning.

Doll, P. A., & Jacobs, K. W. (1989). The exit interview for graduating seniors. *Teaching of Psychology, 15,* 213–214.

Facione, P. (1991, August). *Testing college-level critical thinking skills.* Paper presented at the 11th Annual International Conference on Critical Thinking and Educational Reform, Sonoma, CA.

Furedy, J. J., & Furedy, C. F. (1982). Socratic versus sophistic strains in the teaching of undergraduate psychology: Implicit conflicts made explicit. *Teaching of Psychology, 9,* 14–20.

Furedy, J. J., & Furedy, C. F. (1986). On strengthening the Socratic strain in higher education. *Australian Journal of Education, 30,* 241–255.

Halonen, J. S. (1990, August). *Assessment, outcomes, and decisions in the psychology classroom.* Paper presented at the 98th Annual Convention of the American Psychological Association, Boston, MA.

Halpern, D. F. (Ed.). (1987). *Student outcomes assessment: What institutions stand to gain.* San Francisco: Jossey-Bass.

Halpern, D. F. (1988). Assessing student outcomes for psychology majors. *Teaching of Psychology, 15,* 181–186.

Halpern, D. F. (1989). *Thought and knowledge: An introduction to critical thinking* (2nd ed.). Hillsdale, NJ: Erlbaum.

Hutchings, P. (1990a, June). *Assessment and the way we work.* Paper presented at the Fifth Annual Meeting of the American Association of Higher Education Conference on Assessment, Washington, DC.

Hutchings, P. (1990b). Learning over time: Portfolio assessment. *American Association of Higher Education Bulletin, 42*(8).

Hutchings, P., & Reuben, E. (1988, July/August). Faculty voices on assessment. *Change,* pp. 48–55.

Inhelder, B., & Piaget, J. (1958). *The growth of logical thinking from childhood through adolescence.* New York: Basic Books.

Kohlberg, L. (1976). Moral stages and moralization: The cognitive-developmental approach. In T. Lickona (Ed.), *Moral development and behavior* (pp. 31–53). New York: Holt, Rinehart & Winston.

Lapointe, A., Mead, N., & Phillips, G. (1989). *A world of differences.* Princeton, NJ: Educational Testing Service.

Lehman, D., & Nisbett, R. (1990). A longitudinal study of the effects of undergraduate training on reasoning. *Developmental Psychology, 26,* 952–960.

Loaker, G. (1990). Faculty as a force to improve instruction through assessment. In J. H. McMillan (Ed.), *New directions in teaching and learning: Assessing student learning* (pp. 19–32). San Francisco: Jossey-Bass.

McMillan, J. H. (Ed.). (1990). *New directions in teaching and learning: Assessing student learning.* San Francisco: Jossey-Bass.

National Center for Excellence in Critical Thinking Instruction. (1991). *Defining critical thinking* (Draft Report). Santa Rosa, CA: Sonoma State University.

National Institute of Education. (1984). *Involvement in learning: Realizing the potential of American higher education.* Washington, DC: Author.

Nodine, B. F. (Ed.). (1990). Special issue: Psychologists teach writing. *Teaching of Psychology, 17.*

Perry, W. G., Jr. (1970). *Forms of intellectual and ethical development in the college years: A scheme.* New York: Holt, Rinehart & Winston.

Project on Redefining the Meaning and Purpose of Baccalaureate Degrees. (1985). *Integrity in the college curriculum: A report to the academic community.* Washington, DC: Association of American Colleges.

Schoenfeld, A. H., & Hermann, D. J. (1982). Problem perception and knowledge structure in expert and novice mathematical problem solvers. *Journal of Experimental Psychology: Learning, Memory, and Cognition, 8,* 484–494.

Schulman, L. S. (1991, June). *Dangerous liaison: Connecting the assessment of faculty and the assessment of students.* Paper presented at the Sixth Annual Conference of the American Association of Higher Education, San Francisco, CA.

Walker, W. E., Newcomb, A. F., & Hopkins, W. P. (1987). A model for curriculum evaluation and revision in undergraduate psychology programs. *Teaching of Psychology, 14,* 198–202.

2

DEVELOPING AND IMPROVING ADVISING: CHALLENGES TO PREPARE STUDENTS FOR LIFE

MARK E. WARE, in collaboration with NANCY A. BUSCH-ROSSNAGEL, ANDREW B. CRIDER, LISA GRAY-SHELLBERG, KARYN HALE, MARGARET A. LLOYD, EDUARDO RIVERA-MEDINA, and JOSEPH A. SGRO

As a starting point in our examination of advising issues, we adopted an advising perspective reported by Ender, Winston, and Miller (1984). Their view of advising emphasized (a) building personal relationships between students and advisers; (b) achieving academic, career, and personal goals; and (c) using institutional and community resources. To that view, we added the themes of (d) responding to student diversity and (e) performing evaluations that reflect the students' diverse profile and that reflect the advisers' commitment to empirical scrutiny.

Although theory, research, and practical applications permeate the advising literature, most academic psychologists appear relatively uninterested in advising-related activities and outcomes. As an illustration, consider Zanna and Darley's (1987) *The Compleat Academic.* The book contains an excellent chapter on classroom teaching, but the bulk of the book focuses on faculty members as researchers. Except for a few sentences on advising graduate students, the authors pay no attention to advising per se.

Several surveys noted that faculty advising was the campus service that students used the most, but students gave the service a low rating of satisfaction (Ender et al., 1984). A comment by DeCoster and Mable (1981) is telling: "Students frequently described the idea of approaching one of their instructors as scary, threatening or demeaning. . . . At the same time, the very mention of academic advisers would invariably be met with a roar of laughter" (pp. 43–44). A faculty member at one institution commented that faculty advising at most large institutions was "at best an embarrassment, at worst a disgrace" (Riesman, 1981, p. 258).

By contrast, a popular view is that, prior to the 1960s, college faculties emphasized both the development of individual intellectual ability and a sense of community fostered by frequent contacts between students and faculty outside of the classroom. Early in this century, William Rainey Harper (1905), president of the University of Chicago, recommended that educators assess students to discover their strengths and weaknesses and on the basis of that assessment arrange a program of study. Harper's vision for individualizing college education consisted of personal, social, and academic advising involving a close personal relationship between faculty and students (Engle, 1954).

How then did we arrive at such a negative view of advising, and more important, what can we do to improve it? In part, the decline in the perceived quality of advising is a consequence of the failure to maintain individualized attention to students during a period of dramatic growth in college enrollments from the mid-1950s through the 1970s. The number of recipients of bachelor's degrees in psychology also grew dramatically from about 5,000 in 1955 to a peak of more than 50,000 in 1976 (Howard et al., 1986). The number declined to a low of about 40,000 in 1985 but increased to more than 48,000 in 1988–89 ("Almanac," 1991).

This growth in the number of college enrollments was accompanied by a change in demographic characteristics from primarily young adult, male, and White students to a more heterogeneous group (Chickering & Havighurst, 1981; Merriam & Caffarella, 1991; Schlossberg, Lynch, & Chickering, 1989). The greater number of middle-aged and older adults in the college ranks can be attributed to such factors as shifting needs in the workplace, increased longevity, and greater numbers of high school graduates. In addition, profound legal and social changes affected the gender and ethnic composition of the student population.

Returns from a national survey of psychology departments (Lunneborg & Baker, 1986) indicated that 16% of the departments reported that 25% of their majors were older than 25 years, and 20% of departments said that from 11% to 25% of their majors were older than 25 years. Other data (*Almanac*, 1991; Howard et al., 1986) also revealed that psychology leads arts and sciences disciplines in attracting women (70%) and members of minority groups (16%). Today's students, in general, and psychology students, in particular, are quite different from those of only two generations ago.

By the 1980s, several commentators (e.g., Ender et al., 1984; Kramer & Gardner, 1983) described comprehensive conceptualizations of advising to meet the needs of an increasingly diverse student population. In addition, the emergence of the National Academic Advising Association (NA-CADA) in the late 1970s (Beatty, 1991) brought with it a renewed advocacy for advising at the collegiate level. NACADA encouraged and supported the American College Testing (ACT) program that initiated national surveys of academic advising (Crockett & Levitz, 1984). The findings from those surveys have suggested strengths and weaknesses in advising programs.

The clamorous advising activists of the past decade have contributed to an invigorated interest in the role of advising and the advising process. In the remainder of this chapter, we will (a) identify the components of advising, (b) examine implementation strategies, and (c) summarize our recommendations for advising undergraduate psychology majors.

COMPONENTS OF ADVISING

What can advisers and advising programs do to assist students in developing educational plans that reflect their academic, personal, and career needs? We address this question by analyzing (a) advising relationships, (b) content areas, (c) resources and training, (d) student diversity, and (e) evaluation.

Advising Relationships

Fundamentally, advising is an interaction between two participants, the student and the adviser. The student has a need, sometimes informed but frequently not well formulated, that the adviser must help to identify and act on. At best, this interaction is a partnership characterized by (a) respect for students' talents and interests and (b) shared responsibility that leads to an informed choice using (c) decision-making skills. We examine those characteristics in the following paragraphs.

Having respect for students' knowledge, skills, values, interests, and the like contributes to a humane relationship between students and advisers. By respecting students, faculty can simultaneously acknowledge students' cognitive and motivational capabilities while recognizing their varied life and academic experiences. Moreover, respect for students' values and interests that might differ from those of their advisers' can contribute to a trusting, supportive relationship. Such a trusting relationship promotes an ongoing process of helping students to assess and develop their academic, career, and personal skills.

This partnership also implies that each party has defined responsibilities. Faculty have a responsibility to be available; to let students know how to best make contact; to provide accurate and specific information; to listen to students and help them address their needs; to model essential skills in educational planning and achievement; and to be sensitive and responsive to age, gender, ethnicity, and other differences that affect advising relationships. With all of these responsibilities, advisers are not expected to be infallible sources of information and direction. Moreover, students have responsibilities that include locating their advisers, arranging meetings with them, undertaking preliminary planning for advising tasks, bringing necessary paperwork or forms, and accepting responsibility for their decisions.

Although students enter the advising relationship with the requisite ingredients for decision making and problem solving, the complexity of some tasks requires assistance in identifying and executing a formal process of decision making. The role of decision making is so central to advising that Kramer and Gardner (1984) asserted that "advising can be described as decision-making and an advising interaction as an opportunity to teach students decision-making skills" (p. 424). The prerequisite conditions for teaching decision-making skills consist of the previously mentioned characteristics of respect for students and shared responsibility.

A first step in decision making consists of identifying one's goals. In the next section, we discuss the content areas that frequently arise in the advising relationship.

Content Areas

We found NACADA's advising goals useful and convenient as a comprehensive representation of advising functions (Table 1). The goals, taken from the 1982 ACT national survey (Crockett & Levitz, 1984), are rank ordered in terms of advisers' ratings of degree of satisfaction in achieving each goal. Thus, advisers were relatively satisfied with the first item, "Providing accurate information about institutional policies, procedures, resources, and programs" and relatively dissatisfied with achieving the last item, "Assisting students in developing decision-making skills." The rank ordering indicates that academic institutions, in their own estimation, provide informational and curricular advising (academic programs) more effectively than they provide advising geared toward students' values, interests, and abilities as related to broader life goals (career opportunities and postgraduate educational alternatives). The three content areas (academic programs, career opportunities, and educational alternatives) are compatible with the goals identified in the advising perspective we adopted at the beginning of this chapter.

TABLE 1
Mean Ratings of National Academic Advising Association Goals for Advising Programs

Goals	Mean rating[a]
Providing accurate information about institutional policies, procedures, resources, and programs	3.99
Assisting students in developing an educational plan consistent with life goals and objectives (alternative course of action, alternative career consideration, and selection of courses)	3.35
Assisting students in evaluation or reevaluation of progress toward established goals and educational plans	3.33
Making referrals to other institutional or community support services	3.30
Providing information about students to the institution, colleges, and academic departments	3.25
Assisting students in their consideration of life goals by relating interests, skills, abilities, and values to careers, the world of work, and the nature and purpose of higher education	3.01
Assisting students in self-understanding and self-acceptance (value clarification; an understanding of abilities, interests, and limitations)	2.73
Assisting students in developing decision-making skills	2.55

Note: From "Current Advising Practices in Colleges and Universities" by D. S. Crockett and R. S. Levitz, 1984. In R. B. Winston, Jr., T. K. Miller, S. C. Ender, T. J. Grites, & Associates (Eds.), *Developmental Academic Advising* (p. 51). San Francisco: Jossey-Bass. Copyright 1984 by Jossey-Bass. Adapted by permission.
[a]Ratings are based on a scale from 1 to 5, where 1 = *does not apply, no services have been implemented to address this goal;* 2 = *achievement not very satisfactory;* 3 = *achievement somewhat satisfactory;* 4 = *achievement satisfactory;* and 5 = *achievement very satisfactory.*

Information from the NACADA-ACT survey is consistent with a common dichotomy (informational and developmental advising) made between types of advising (Kramer & Gardner, 1983). Informational advising consists of communicating information "about the requirements, policies, and procedures of the institution, and very likely . . . about courses, resources, and various student services or helping agencies on campus" (p. 38). Developmental advising consists of helping students to come to grips with feelings of uncertainty about "self, goals, and abilities or . . . the nature, rationale, and consequences of academic requirements" (pp. 24–25).

Although it is convenient to think of advising in dichotomous terms, there is evidence to the contrary. Trombley (1984) conducted a factor analysis of students' perceptions of the importance of 13 advising tasks. The author labeled the two resulting factors as *information* and *counseling* roles, with the former including clerical and the latter more professional kinds of responsibilities. However, Trombley also pointed out that the factors shared several tasks, indicating that some advising practices require a combination of informational and developmental approaches. We caution against making a sharp distinction between informational and developmental advising.

Although some faculty may prefer an informational emphasis and others a developmental one, experience indicates that faculty will need at least a modicum of expertise in both areas. Advisers will most likely find a personal comfort zone or limit in performing informational and developmental advising. We believe that students' best interests are served when advisers are skilled in making referrals to other faculty or student personnel professionals after they determine that they have reached the limits of their own advising abilities.

Resources and Training

Faculty advising takes place in a context of departmental and campuswide resources. Faculty advisers should be familiar with those referral resources and comfortable in using them as appropriate. The most immediate resources are one's departmental colleagues, one or more of whom may be called on to help fulfill students' informational and developmental requirements. Other departmental resources may include departmental advising specialists, peer advisers, handbooks and brochures, workshops, and courses. We will consider these resources more fully later in the chapter.

Making referrals to knowledgeable campus professionals is an essential advising task that can significantly increase advising effectiveness. Campus supports include offices of student affairs, psychological counseling, career development and placement, and learning assistance. We emphasize the multicomponent, ongoing nature of advising in which faculty advisers play a leading role but are not responsible for the entire process.

The use of available resources assumes that faculty are familiar with those resources and that faculty have had training in advising. However, one study (Crockett & Levitz, 1984) reported that, although two thirds of academic institutions expected faculty to serve as advisers, about 75% reported offering little or no training. When training was provided, it consisted largely of information about regulations, policies, and procedures or about campus referral sources. Information about careers, employment, or decision-making skills was not common in training programs. On the basis of such evidence, we conclude that a need exists to train faculty to be effective advisers. Our conclusion is consistent with Fretz's observation in chapter 4 that advising students is a pertinent target area for faculty development.

Student Diversity

Even when a relatively homogeneous faculty advises a relatively homogeneous student population, one cannot automatically assume that the advising interaction will flow smoothly. Variations in values, style, interest, and personality always have to be bridged to achieve a viable working relationship. With today's more heterogeneous student body and faculty, there is an even greater need to be sensitive to individual and group differences that contribute to establishing effective advising relationships.

In discussing the relationship between faculty and students, we noted the importance of respect and openness. When advisees or advisers bring preconceived role expectations or sociocultural stereotypes to the relationship, problems can develop. However, roles and sociocultural variables are also an integral part of the advising relationship that can bring meaning and coherence to the students' education.

What are some of the salient variables that contribute to student diversity? As we pointed out earlier, the change in demographic characteristics of the student population reflects greater numbers of mature or adult learners and women. There is a growing descriptive, and sometimes empirical, literature on the special needs and environments for adult students and the opportunities such environments provide for enhanced learning (Daloz, 1986, 1988; Knowles & Associates, 1984; Merriam & Caffarella, 1991; Merriam & Cunningham, 1989; Mezirow & Associates, 1990; Schlossberg et al., 1989).

One example of a specific need of adult learners includes adjusting after reentry into the academic environment. Adult students often must confront issues of balancing family and career demands. Some women who reenter the academic scene have to consider the prospect of taking low-paying jobs in clerical or social services areas. Traditional advising strategies can handle some, but not all, of the special needs of such students.

In chapter 3, Puente points out that attracting and retaining minority students requires additional and different strategies, such as increasing the representation of minority faculty and developing programs in minority communities. We will identify unique applications of strategies for advising adult, female, and minority students in the implementation section of this chapter.

Advisers should also remember that faculty bring their own academic culture to bear on the advising relationship. However else faculty may differ, they are representatives of an academic culture that has a particular set of values, expectations, and behaviors. Part of the advising task is to introduce students to that culture, to facilitate an appreciation of its value, and to teach students how to function effectively within it. In sum, cultural variables are inevitable components of advising and can be valued and incorporated effectively into the process.

Evaluation

Adapting slightly Halpern's observations in the previous chapter, we viewed assessment programs as a means to measure and improve advising. Our primary goal in evaluating advising programs was to determine the conditions under which different advising strategies may be most effective for different groups of students. Failure to incorporate an evaluative component risks implementing and maintaining ineffective or even detrimental programs. We also recognized that some individuals would want to use the results of evaluation techniques for deciding which individuals to recognize or reward. Local campus conditions will emphasize this latter goal to a greater or lesser extent.

IMPLEMENTATION OF ADVISING PROGRAMS

Effective implementation of advising programs presupposes leadership and commitment. The success of advising programs requires advocacy from people in leadership positions. As Crockett (1978) noted, "Unless those in responsible positions . . . [provide support] both fiscally and psychologically, advising will be taken lightly or more likely neglected" (p. 1.22). A departmental chairperson is the most likely candidate to provide such leadership. Chairs need not implement programs themselves, but if they do not, then chairs must designate a responsible and committed person or group of people. A less desirable but effective alternative is one in which a dedicated faculty member serves as an advocate for initiating the advising program.

Advising programs can be implemented by accomplishing the five themes we identified earlier: (a) developing advising relationships, (b) identifying content areas, (c) using resources and training advisers, (d) responding to student diversity, and (e) evaluating advising strategies. We will address these themes in the following pages.

Developing Advising Relationships

In examining the advising relationship, we will describe the dynamics or conditions for enhancing respect and shared responsibility. We will also describe salient features of decision making.

Dynamics of the Process

As described earlier, effective advising requires faculty's respect for advisees. Strategies for increasing respect include (a) developing rapport (e.g., by talking about extracurricular activities and interests), (b) becoming acquainted with relevant information about advisees' backgrounds (e.g., previous academic performance and family history), (c) inquiring about students' previous and current career dreams or plans, and (d) displaying effective listening skills. Crockett (1986, Section 3) described specific exercises and strategies for promoting respect.

Delineating faculty and students' advising tasks helps to clarify the role of shared responsibility. For example, faculty should post and maintain office hours, and students should contact and keep in touch with advisers. Faculty should possess accurate and specific information, and students should prepare specific questions. Faculty should identify alternative courses and careers, and students should make decisions regarding courses and careers (see Crockett, 1986, p. 169).

By maintaining student advising folders, faculty can reduce stress and confusion in advising their students. Up-to-date academic and personal information about students reduces the effort required to remember specific facts. Suggested information for the content of students' advising folders includes the students' nickname, date of birth, previous schooling, standardized test scores, grades, career aspirations, relevant family background, previous volunteer and work experience, and the like. For examples of folders that several institutions have used, refer to "The Advising Folder" in Crockett (1978).

Some larger institutions have adopted systems in which information compiled by advisers can be stored in computer portfolios that are accessible to both students and faculty who possess appropriate access codes. The importance of establishing effective relationships is even more critical when much of the information that students need can be obtained from interactions at a computer terminal. The principle of personalizing the advising contact is applicable in both traditional and more technologically sophisticated environments.

Decision-Making Styles

In evaluating educational and career plans, students make many decisions. As stated previously, advising is largely a decision-making process. Shipton and Steltenpohl (1981) described an educational advising and career counseling decision-making model that includes defining the task, gathering information, establishing a values hierarchy, making a choice, and taking action. To assist their students, advisers should (a) recognize that there are different decision-making styles and (b) distinguish between the process and the outcome of decision making.

Our advising experience has revealed two common decision-making styles. (See Chartrand & Camp, 1991, for a review of the empirical literature on career decision making.) What we call the *rational* style is goal directed and plan-oriented. Individuals using this style often take charge and see themselves as in control of their lives. In a somewhat contrasting approach that we call the *adaptive* style, individuals take advantage of opportunities as they arise. When displaying this style, students view decisions in a larger context of interacting forces. They approach their lives as a series of steps, the importance and sequencing of which may be obvious only in retrospect. Neither style is right or wrong; they are merely different.

Furthermore, our experience has revealed that the advising process contains both linear and iterative elements. An example of the linear element is the systematic planning of tasks that must be accomplished for timely graduation or the pursuit of graduate school immediately following college. The iterative element acknowledges that many tasks associated with advising are done and redone as students change majors, gain maturity, or reenter college in later years.

Combining these two elements is consistent with contemporary views of human development that emphasize the plasticity of developmental tasks (Lerner & Busch-Rossnagel, 1981; Vaillant, 1977) in general and career development in particular (Super, 1990). Not only do we work on identity during adolescence, but we continue to rework it throughout adulthood as Shipton and Steltenpohl (1981) noted:

> Locating oneself on the human development continuum, gaining an understanding of tasks already accomplished and those yet to be achieved, realizing that one's interests and preferences change over time, understanding the crises and strains of transition periods, and visualizing what is yet to come give students of *all ages* [italics added] a broader perspective on future possibilities as well as deeper insight into present needs. (p. 695)

Because tasks can be confronted more than once, career decision making need not be a once-in-a-lifetime event. Moreover, the data indicate that traditional college-age students "will change jobs seven times and careers three times" (Shipton & Steltenpohl, 1981, p. 690) during their lifetimes.

Understanding and using both the linear and iterative elements may be particularly useful with nontraditional students who have not completed college "on time" and with those who perceive themselves as failures because they have not completed or resolved issues on a timetable consistent with their own or others' expectations. Appreciating the iterative element may be a solace for advisers whose advisees do not complete career decision making as students. Recognition of the importance and centrality of careers may come to some individuals only after additional maturity, a divorce, a layoff, or other significant life events.

One of the advantages of approaching advising from a decision-making perspective is that students can acquire transferable skills. These decision-making skills can be applied to different and future situations. There are many books that advisers can use to teach students decision-making skills (e.g., Bartsch & Sandmeyer, 1979; Dunphy, 1976; Gordon, 1984; Scholz, Prince, & Miller, 1985).

Identifying Content Areas

In this section we focus on three aspects of advising: (a) students' academic programs, (b) career opportunities for graduates with a bachelor's degree in psychology, and (c) postbaccalaureate educational alternatives. Moreover, we recognize that effective advising encompasses students' developmental needs and personal crises. Many faculty may feel more comfortable dealing with such problems by referring students to appropriate student personnel professionals (Matthews & Ware, 1988). After elaborating on these three content areas of advising, we will identify implementation strategies for all three in the Using Resources and Training Advisers section.

Content areas for advising (i.e., academic programs, career opportunities, and postbaccalaureate educational alternatives) are likely consistent across institutions. However, the strategies for dealing with those areas may vary among institutions, departments, and advisers.

Academic Programs

Students' entrance into the advising program often results from problems, conflicts, or issues associated with their academic programs. Under those circumstances, advisers provide information about college policies and regulations; requirements for the college, the major, and the minor; and information about academic support services on campus. Kramer and Gardner (1983) stated that a bare minimum of informational advising consisted of "knowledge about the requirements, policies, and procedures of the institution, and very likely . . . about courses, resources, and various student services or helping agencies on campus" (p. 38). They asserted that rarely would students or others criticize advisers who were competent informational advisers and that competence was a laudable goal, particularly for advisers with limited time.

Faculty also find themselves communicating strategies for academic success, such as note-taking skills, study skills, test-taking skills, time management skills, and the like. Advisers with limited time or knowledge in one or more of those areas can usually refer students to professionals trained to teach those skills that transfer across disciplines.

Career Opportunities

There are several reasons for including career opportunities among content areas for advising. Chickering and Havighurst (1981) pointed out that "Choosing and preparing for a career is the organizing center for the lives of most men and women" (p. 32). Helping students to prepare for the world of work requires considerable effort by many individuals, including advisers.

Our experience indicates that a large percentage of advisees ask, "What can I do with a bachelor's degree in psychology?" In addition, psychology majors display an eagerness for information about the salaries that psychology alumni earn. Using the initiatives of a university-wide assessment program, which includes alumni survey data across the institution or data based on more specific measures for psychology majors, departments can report employment data about recent alumni as well as the results of numerous psychology alumni surveys (McGovern & Carr, 1989). This type of information can be supplemented by identifying the types of skills that bachelor-level positions require.

Career advising, however, consists of more than transmitting occupational information. Shipton and Steltenpohl (1981) pointed out that the ideal approach to decision making consists of gathering information about oneself as well as about the external world. Historically, the emphasis has been on providing students with information about the world of work but failing to encourage them to examine their personal attributes and to acquire decision-making skills (Ware, 1991). We believe that besides seeking employment, students equipped with a bachelor's degree in psychology need to increase their knowledge about themselves and develop their decision-making skills.

Postbaccalaureate Educational Alternatives

We advocate supporting and encouraging students whose aspirations, skills, and behaviors are congruent with pursuing postbaccalaureate education as a means for realizing their career goals. Advising students about postbaccalaureate education includes identifying alternative fields (e.g., psychology, education, social work, medicine and other health professions, law, etc.). Advisers can assist students by informing them about the prerequisites or foundation courses required for various programs. Advisers may encourage students to seek a match between personal characteristics (e.g., values, interests, skills, etc.) and characteristics of the graduate program. Additional advising tasks include establishing a realistic time line, preparing applications (including a goals statement), taking the Graduate Record Examination (or other standardized test), and selecting faculty to write letters of recommendation.

Using Resources and Training Advisers

Our views about advising goals for undergraduate psychology majors have set the stage for elaborating on resources for implementation. These resources include delivery systems, materials for advisers and students, and programs for training advisers.

Delivery Systems

Delivery systems are the techniques that advisers use to communicate with advisees and include one-on-one contacts, self-help approaches, small group meetings or conversation hours, peers, and courses. The following paragraphs contain brief descriptions of each system.

The traditional method of advising consists of one-on-one contacts between advisers and students. Although this method may be unsurpassed at individualizing the advising process, it is also the most time-consuming and inefficient method for delivering generic information. Requiring advisees to read printed materials before their appointments can increase the effective use of one-on-one interactions. Another limitation of one-on-one interactions is that they fail to provide students with opportunities to learn through observation of the struggles and success of peers. By combining individual contacts with other methods, we can increase students' breadth of perspective and range of problem-solving skills.

In their national survey of advising practices, Lunneborg and Baker (1986) identified four variations of one-on-one advising structures (or models). The main difference between the structures was primarily in who was responsible for advising premajors (i.e., undecided students) and majors. In the all faculty model, almost all psychology faculty advised undergraduates in their premajor and major stages. In the part faculty model, a centralized advising program took responsibility for advising premajors, but all psychology faculty advised their majors. In the no faculty model, a centralized advising program took responsibility for advising premajors, but a faculty member supervised a departmental advising office for majors. In the central model, a centralized advising program took responsibility for advising all students. The authors excluded the central model from data analysis because only 6 of 842 respondents reported using that model.

Results indicated an overall preference for the all faculty model except for public graduate institutions, where the part faculty model was judged as effective as the all faculty model.

Because the models using faculty as advisers were the most prevalent, and because our intended audience consists primarily of psychology faculty, we will emphasize faculty-centered models. However, we also note evidence for an increasing number of professional advisers at the collegiate level in general (Crockett & Levitz, 1984). The focus on faculty in this section should not undermine the notion that advising is a mutual process; we view students as having a significant responsibility for developing their educational and career plans.

We likewise recognize that most colleges have nonfaculty professionals who are responsible for many tasks associated with or central to the advising process. One can find those professionals in counseling or psychological services centers, career planning and placement offices, academic support services, and other offices falling under the auspices of the student affairs administration. We contend that advising can be facilitated and made more efficient if faculty take advantage of the expertise of all available professionals.

One of the most underused delivery approaches is that of self-help. Because we view the advising process as one with mutual responsibility, we encourage the development of strategies for students to advise themselves. Blocher and Rapoza (1981) noted that

> A major innovation in the delivery of vocational development services is the use of automated data-processing facilities to retrieve information. These can be accessed directly by students in response to their immediate needs or in conjunction with conventional vocational counseling activities. (p. 224)

Appleby (1989), for example, developed a novel and effective technique using a microcomputer to assist psychology majors in becoming more responsible for updating their own advising files. We remind readers about our earlier caveat regarding the importance of establishing and maintaining effective personal relationships, particularly when students spend progressively more time interacting with computers.

An alternative to meeting with students individually is to meet with groups of students who have similar needs or interests. Examples include meetings to familiarize students with the requirements for the major, to introduce psychologists or psychology alumni representing different careers, and to discuss strategies for getting into graduate school.

The use of peers is another neglected strategy. In chapter 7, Mathie and her colleagues also discuss the use of peers as an effective means of active learning, drawing on a program developed at the University of Rochester. Titley and Titley (1982) suggested using peer advisers during registration, but peers can be used beyond registration tasks. At the University of Puerto Rico–Rio Piedras Campus, a faculty member with the assistance of graduate students organized and supervised groups of peer counselors. In any given semester, two groups of peer counselors participated in the program. While one group of about 10 students received training, another group provided services under the supervision of the professor and graduate students. Peer counselors provided information about and preparation for graduate school, assisted in the preparation and search for jobs, and facilitated the referral of students with personal crises. Assessment of similar programs has revealed many more advantages than disadvantages (Grites, 1984).

Academic courses are another forum for advising groups of students. Examples include courses that orient freshmen to college life and that aid upper-level psychology majors in career planning and decision making (Ware, 1988). Other relevant educational opportunities include work experience (e.g., field placement experiences) and programs in career guidance and college placement services (Ware & Millard, 1987). In chapter 6, Brewer and his colleagues identify (a) learning about career opportunities as one of the specific goals for a psychology curriculum and (b) discussing students' career interests as one of the components for internships.

Materials

There are a variety of materials that departments can develop or acquire to assist advisees. Two members of our group had developed handouts and brochures for students seeking information about academic, career, and postbaccalaureate educational areas. Further examination revealed pamphlets containing information about careers (APA, 1986; Ware, 1987) and postbaccalaureate education (APA, 1986; Ware, 1990). There are also books containing information about academic issues (Woods, with Wilkinson, 1987), career pursuits (Woods, with Wilkinson, 1987; Woods, 1988), and postbaccalaureate education in psychology (APA, 1991b; Fretz & Stang, 1980; Keith-Spiegel, 1990; Woods, 1988). Videotape productions cover careers (APA, 1990, 1991a; Ware & Sroufe, 1984a) and postbaccalaureate education (Ware & Sroufe, 1984b). Finally, Appleby (1989) reported using existing computer software to develop a strategy for keeping students actively involved in maintaining their own academic records.

Programs for Training Advisers

The training of advisers is a third component in effective advising. At the outset, we assumed that most effective advisers are not born, they are made. Thus, faculty must acquire the information and skills to be effective informational and developmental advisers. In institutions where expectations for informational advising exist, responsibility for training faculty rests with the academic or departmental administration. For those responsible for training faculty in advising tasks, we suggest Grites's (1986) chapter, which describes guidelines and provides suggestions for faculty training programs. We also recommend Crockett (1978, pp. 5.97–5.108); he describes symptoms suggesting the need for referral, as well as skills required for effective referral. Finally, chapter 4 in this book by Fretz and his colleagues identifies many structures, methods, and techniques for faculty development that generalize to the training of advisers.

Although we might expect all faculty advisers to be knowledgeable about academic and graduate school information, many faculty will not be informed about entry-level careers available to psychology majors or about the academic requirements for admission to graduate programs other than psychology (e.g., law, medicine, or social work). McGovern and Carr (1989) highlighted the extensive literature about career and postbaccalaureate educational opportunities for psychology alumni. When faculty do not possess requisite information, they should refer students to others who do.

An inextricable component for developing advising skills is the concomitant recognition and reward for good advising performance. Crockett (1978) stated that "Good advising, like good teaching, publication, and research needs to be recognized" (p. 1.24). There are many ways for recognizing and rewarding advising, including (a) giving release time for certain advising activities (e.g., serving as advising resource person), (b) scheduling in-service training at attractive off-campus sites, (c) considering advising when making annual salary evaluations, (d) giving advising weight in promotion and tenure review, and (e) recognizing advising excellence in public forums and by awards.

Faculty perceptions about rewards for advising (Larsen & Brown, 1986) indicated that from 48% to 72% of faculty, excluding departmental chairs, strongly disagreed with statements about the adequacy of rewards for advising, the consideration of advising when giving merit raises, and the role of advising in promotion and tenure evaluation. In short, large percentages of faculty do not believe that relevant rewards exist for advising. We will return to the reward issue in the evaluation section of this chapter.

Suggestions for increasing incentives for faculty to improve advising incur a variety of costs. Concomitant with spending greater amounts of time and money on advising is a necessary decrease in the amount of time devoted to teaching and scholarship. In the final analysis, faculty and administrators must answer the question of whether the benefits of improved advising, including increased student development, reduced attrition, and increased alumni and taxpayer support, are consistent with the institution's mission.

Responding to Student Diversity

Earlier in this chapter, we pointed out that the college student population in the latter part of the 20th century has become increasingly heterogeneous. The approaches to advising that we have discussed can be applied, in general, to all students. However, some of the special needs of adults, women, and ethnic minority group members require additional attention because many advisers are not experienced at working with members from these groups. The descriptions that follow are not comprehensive, but they illustrate some of the situations advisers may face.

Adult Students

Adult students confront somewhat novel problems in adjusting to a traditional academic setting. They express fears about competing and fitting in with 18–22-year-old students. They question their ability to understand and retain large quantities of information. Although they may be effective problem solvers for many life demands, adult learners may exhibit fewer skills for coping with an academic environment.

Identifying and discussing reentry concerns can facilitate the reduction of such fears. Encouraging adult learners to find and to discuss their concerns with other adult learners can reveal the common and situational versus personal nature of many fears.

Adults who struggle through demanding courses in study groups with 18–22-year-old students can discover that the two age groups have more in common than they could have imagined. When genuine problems related to study skills or content areas (e.g., mathematics) arise, faculty can clarify that such problems are not unique to adults and can use conventional advising strategies or refer those adults to appropriate professionals.

Many adult learners shy away from advising about job search skills or graduate school. They think that adults should know about getting jobs and that graduate school is only for young people. Exploring and clarifying these and other occupational and educational misconceptions constitute challenges for advisers. Readers can find additional information about adult learners in Lunneborg's (1988) article.

Women

One problem experienced by many adult women (and increasing numbers of men) who major in psychology is balancing the dual commitments to family and career (Betz & Fitzgerald, 1987). Development and use of time management skills can be a boon to otherwise overextended women. Adult women can benefit from learning decision-making or planning strategies for careers or graduate school. Such strategies can help women focus their energy and resources in dramatically more effective ways.

Encouraging women to take courses outside of the social services areas (e.g., management, marketing, political science, environmental sciences, etc.) increases the prospects for employment and for discovering previously unexplored matches between personal and occupational characteristics. Developing leadership and assertiveness skills can contribute to increased self-esteem and opportunities for employment in areas not previously considered possible. Woods (with Wilkinson, 1987, chapter 17) expands on issues affecting adult women.

Events in the 1980s and 1990s have modified any simplified view of traditional role expectations for women and men. Increased career opportunities for women, coupled with day-care facilities, parental leave policies, and prospects for pursuing both family and career, make advising and particularly career advising for women a challenging endeavor.

Members of Ethnic Minority Groups

There are similarities among members of different minority groups that result from their experience of living in a majority culture. Smith (1985) catalogued the many sources of stress for members of ethnic minority groups and their potential responses. The comments that follow concentrate on the similarities among African Americans (Jones, 1988), Hispanics (Cervantes, 1988), Native Americans (McShane, 1988), and Asian Americans (Suinn, 1988).

Ethnic minority members experience various degrees of value conflict. Value conflicts can exist when students have identified to at least a moderate extent with models in the minority culture, whereas value confusion occurs when students have no unified value system because of a lack of or inadequate models in the minority culture. Advisers can assist students who experience value conflict by encouraging them to discover and explore values within and between the two cultures and by discussing value-laden issues with family, friends, academic peers, and other adults. Remaining open to and respectful of cultural differences and discovering the overlapping values between cultures can reduce, although probably not eliminate, value conflicts.

Many ethnic minority students also experience difficulty in their orientation toward change. Because they find themselves between two cultures, students find themselves confronted, at least implicitly, with decisions about whether to assimilate, integrate, reject, or experience marginally the majority culture. On those campuses that have a sufficiently large and diverse student body, encouraging ethnic minority students to join and participate in a variety of student organizations can help them to understand and appreciate the values, attitudes, and customs of their own and the majority culture. Should the decision about one's relationship to the majority culture become a debilitating problem, many advisers might prefer to refer such students to student personnel or other competent professionals.

Ethnic minority students are just like any other students. All are interested in pursuing employment following graduation. Moreover, Puente observes in the next chapter that ethnic minority students who discover career opportunities in psychology are more likely to pursue psychology at the graduate level. Advisers' sensitivity to ethnic minority students' career needs within and outside of psychology can contribute to a richer and more diversified discipline and society.

Evaluating Advising Strategies

The evaluation of advising strategies requires identification of criteria for specific elements. These elements include the advising program (i.e., the methods of delivery and materials), advisers, and students. The following paragraphs contain illustrative cases of evaluations.

In their evaluation, Lunneborg and Baker (1986) asked department chairpersons to rate several items on how well they perceived their departments were meeting advising needs. Items included such things as

(a) policies and program information, (b) appropriate referrals, (c) students' interests and values, (d) career information, and (e) minority students.

In evaluating advisers' behavior, Kapraun and Coldren (1980) had students rate their advisers on several dimensions, including whether the adviser (a) was consistently available for appointments; (b) was aware of and had access to information that the student needed; (c) discussed academic goals and progress toward those goals; (d) referred the student, when necessary, to the proper person; and (e) was someone with whom the student had a congenial relationship. In addition to rating specific adviser behaviors, students gave an overall rating of adviser effectiveness. With such data, administrators can determine which behaviors are correlated with overall effectiveness. Ratings indicating that specific behaviors are a problem can prompt training to change those behaviors.

The evaluation can also examine how students assess changes in themselves that they attribute to advising. Examples include whether students believe the program was instrumental in helping to increase self-knowledge or in helping to make educational and career choices.

Regular evaluation permits detection of consistency and change in program effectiveness. Using evaluation data, both administrators and faculty can examine each element of the advising program and decide whether to retain, modify, or eliminate it. The choice about how to use data about faculty advisers will depend on institutional policies, but in general applications include faculty development and evaluation. Developmental applications consist of using data to reinforce advising strengths and to identify and modify advising weaknesses. Evaluation applications include using the data for salary and personnel decisions (e.g., tenure and promotion reviews). Whatever the choice, the presence of such data can exert a positive influence, increasing advising effectiveness in the department.

In the previous chapter, Halpern and her colleagues identified guidelines for establishing or improving assessment. Readers will find that many of those guidelines generalize to evaluating advising strategies.

SUMMARY AND RECOMMENDATIONS

We have organized our comments for developing and improving departmental advising programs around management issues and the themes identified in preceding sections of the chapter. We acknowledge that specific applications will vary with the specific circumstances at each institution.

1. People in leadership positions who actively advocate and promote advising constitute a central, if not prerequisite, condition for successful advising programs. Ordinarily, departmental chairs are the most likely candidates. Chairs can

promote advising by publicly communicating their commitment to it (e.g., through verbal and written communication), establishing an advising committee, requiring a minimum number of office hours during registration, attending undergraduate functions (e.g., Psi Chi meetings), and the like.

2. Assigning one or more individuals the tasks of initiating, maintaining, and revising the advising program establishes a framework for production and accountability.

3. Building viable, working relationships with students includes displaying respect for and showing interest in them as individuals, as well as informing them about the shared responsibility that they and faculty have for making advising successful. Increasing students' decision-making skills is one positive result of building an effective advising relationship.

4. The content areas of advising that we have encountered most often are academic programs (e.g., institutional regulations, requirements for the major, referral sources, study skills, etc.), career opportunities, and postbaccalaureate educational alternatives. Our analysis revealed that successful advising goes beyond simply giving information to students; successful advising challenges students to examine themselves (i.e., their values, interests, abilities, and skills) and to develop and apply decision-making skills to their educational and career choices.

5. Available resources for advising include a variety of delivery systems (e.g., one-on-one contacts, self-help, small groups, peers, and courses) and formats for materials (e.g., handouts, pamphlets, books, videotapes, and computer applications). Creation of a clearinghouse for locally produced materials could facilitate the expedient transmission of such materials. APA's Education Programs Office is one alternative to an advising materials clearinghouse.

6. Formal training in advising-related behavior and about pertinent information increases the likelihood of successful advising. Recognizing and rewarding advising activity (e.g., by adjusting work loads to include advising, giving weight to advising in promotion and tenure reviews, honoring outstanding advising in public forums, etc.) are requisite conditions for altering a system that emphasizes scholarship and teaching. Administrators above the level of departmental chairs must decide the extent to which financial resources can be applied to produce more effective advising.

7. Advising a diverse student population, consisting of larger numbers of adult learners, women, and minority group members, requires increased expertise about their specific needs

and the application of conventional and novel advising strategies. The between- and within-group variability among students requires sensitivity, flexibility, and adaptability among advisers.

8. Regular evaluation of advising programs is essential for identifying conditions to maintain or improve the programs' quality. Administrators can use data about faculty performance for development and evaluation purposes depending on institutional policies.

REFERENCES

Almanac: Earned degrees conferred, 1988–89. (1991, August 28). *The Chronicle of Higher Education,* p. 28.

American Psychological Association. (1986). *Careers in psychology.* Washington, DC: Author.

American Psychological Association (Producer). (1990). *Careers in psychology: Your options are open* [Videotape]. Washington, DC: Author.

American Psychological Association (Producer). (1991a). *Career encounters in psychology* [Videotape]. Washington, DC: Author.

American Psychological Association. (1991b). *Graduate study in psychology and associated fields, 1990 with 1991 addendum.* Washington, DC: Author.

Appleby, D. C. (1989). The microcomputer as an academic advising tool. *Teaching of Psychology, 16,* 156–159.

Bartsch, K., & Sandmeyer, L. (1979). *Skills in life/career planning.* Monterey, CA: Brooks/Cole.

Beatty, J. D. (1991). The National Academic Advising Association: A brief narrative history. *NACADA Journal, 11,* 5–25.

Betz, N. E., & Fitzgerald, L. F. (1987). *The career psychology of women.* San Diego, CA: Academic Press.

Blocher, D. H., & Rapoza, R. S. (1981). Professional and vocational preparation. In A. W. Chickering & Associates (Eds.), *The modern American college* (pp. 212–231). San Francisco: Jossey-Bass.

Cervantes, R. C. (1988). Hispanics in psychology. In P. J. Woods (Ed.), *Is psychology for them? A guide to undergraduate advising* (pp. 182–184). Washington, DC: American Psychological Association.

Chartrand, J. M., & Camp, C. C. (1991). Advances in the measurement of career development constructs: A 20-year review. *Journal of Vocational Behavior, 39,* 1–39.

Chickering, A. W., & Havighurst, R. J. (1981). The life cycle. In A. W. Chickering & Associates (Eds.), *The modern American college* (pp. 16–50). San Francisco: Jossey-Bass.

Crockett, D. S. (Ed.). (1978). *Academic advising: A resource document.* Iowa City, IA: American College Testing Program.

Crockett, D. S. (Ed.). (1986). *Advising skills, techniques, and resources.* Iowa City, IA: American College Testing Program.

Crockett, D. S., & Levitz, R. S. (1984). Current advising practices in colleges and universities. In R. B. Winston, Jr., T. K. Miller, S. C. Ender, T. J. Grites, & Associates (Eds.), *Developmental academic advising* (pp. 35–63). San Francisco: Jossey-Bass.

Daloz, L. A. (1986). *Effective teaching and mentoring: Realizing the transformational power of adult learning experiences.* San Francisco: Jossey-Bass.

Daloz, L. A. (1988). The story of Gladys who refused to grow: A morality tale for mentors. *Lifelong Learning, 11*(4), 4–7.

DeCoster, D. A., & Mable, P. (1981). Interpersonal relationships. In D. A. DeCoster & P. Mable (Eds.), *Understanding today's students* (pp. 35–47). San Francisco: Jossey-Bass.

Dunphy, P. W. (1976). Anatomy of a career decision. In P. W. Dunphy, S. F. Austin, & T. J. McEneaney (Eds.), *Career development for the college student* (4th ed., pp. 18–32). Cranston, RI: Carroll Press.

Ender, S. C., Winston, R. B., Jr., & Miller, T. K. (1984). Academic advising reconsidered. In R. B. Winston, Jr., T. K. Miller, S. C. Ender, T. J. Grites, & Associates (Eds.), *Developmental academic advising* (pp. 3–34). San Francisco: Jossey-Bass.

Engle, G. W. (1954). *William Rainey Harper's conceptions of the structuring of the functions performed by educational institutions* (Doctoral dissertation, University of Michigan, 1954). (University Microfilms No. 00–10 369).

Fretz, B. R., & Stang, D. J. (1980). *Preparing for graduate study in psychology: Not for seniors only!* Washington, DC: American Psychological Association.

Gordon, V. N. (1984). Educational planning: Helping students make decisions. In R. B. Winston, Jr., T. K. Miller, S. C. Ender, T. J. Grites, & Associates (Eds.), *Developmental academic advising* (pp. 123–146). San Francisco: Jossey-Bass.

Grites, T. J. (1984). Noteworthy academic advising programs. In R. B. Winston, Jr., T. K. Miller, S. C. Ender, T. J. Grites, & Associates (Eds.), *Developmental academic advising* (pp. 469–537). San Francisco: Jossey-Bass.

Grites, T. J. (1986). Training the academic advisor. In D. S. Crockett (Ed.), *Advising skills, techniques, and resources* (pp. 139–159). Iowa City, IA: American College Testing Program.

Harper, W. R. (1905). *The trend in higher education.* Chicago: University of Chicago Press.

Howard, A., Pion, G. M., Gottfredson, G. D., Flattau, P. E., Oskamp, S., Pfafflin, S. M., Bray, D. W., & Burstein, A. G. (1986). The changing face of American psychology. *American Psychologist, 41,* 1311–1327.

Jones, J. M. (1988). Why should Black undergraduate students major in psychology? In P. J. Woods (Ed.), *Is psychology for them? A guide to undergraduate advising* (pp. 178–181). Washington, DC: American Psychological Association.

Kapraun, E. D., & Coldren, D. W. (1980). An approach to the evaluation of academic advising. *Journal of College Student Personnel, 21,* 85–86.

Keith-Spiegel, P. (1990). *The complete guide to graduate school admission: Psychology and related fields.* Hillsdale, NJ: Erlbaum.

Knowles, M. S., & Associates. (1984). *Andragogy in action: Applying modern principles of adult learning.* San Francisco: Jossey-Bass.

Kramer, H. C., & Gardner, R. E. (1983). *Advising by faculty.* Washington, DC: National Education Association.

Kramer, H. C., & Gardner, R. E. (1984). Improving advising knowledge and skills through faculty development. In R. B. Winston, Jr., T. K. Miller, S. C. Ender, T. J. Grites, & Associates (Eds.), *Developmental academic advising* (pp. 412–439). San Francisco: Jossey-Bass.

Larsen, M. D., & Brown, B. M. (1986). Rewards for academic advising: An evaluation. In D. S. Crockett (Ed.), *Advising skills, techniques, and resources* (pp. 349–359). Iowa City, IA: American College Testing Program.

Lerner, R. M., & Busch-Rossnagel, N. A. (Eds.). (1981). *Individuals as producers of their development: A life-span perspective.* New York: Academic Press.

Lunneborg, P. W. (1988). Reentry of women and men in psychology. In P. J. Woods (Ed.), *Is psychology for them? A guide to undergraduate advising* (pp. 185–187). Washington, DC: American Psychological Association.

Lunneborg, P. W., & Baker, E. C. (1986). Advising undergraduates in psychology: Exploring the neglected dimension. *Teaching of Psychology, 13,* 181–185.

Matthews, J. R., & Ware, M. E. (1988). Promoting the adviser's role in undergraduate education. *College Teaching, 36,* 34–36.

McGovern, T. V., & Carr, K. F. (1989). Carving out the niche: A review of alumni surveys on undergraduate psychology majors. *Teaching of Psychology, 16,* 52–57.

McShane, D. A. (1988). Becoming a psychologist: A challenge for American Indian students. In P. J. Woods (Ed.), *Is psychology for them? A guide to undergraduate advising* (pp. 168–172). Washington, DC: American Psychological Association.

Merriam, S. B., & Caffarella, R. S. (1991). *Learning in adulthood.* San Francisco: Jossey-Bass.

Merriam, S. B., & Cunningham, P. M. (1989). *Handbook of adult and continuing education.* San Francisco: Jossey-Bass.

Mezirow, J., & Associates. (1990). *Fostering critical reflection in adulthood: A guide to transformative and emancipatory education.* San Francisco: Jossey-Bass.

Riesman, D. (1981). *On higher education: The academic enterprise in an era of rising student consumerism.* San Francisco: Jossey-Bass.

Schlossberg, N. K., Lynch, A. Q., & Chickering, A. W. (1989). *Improving higher education environments for adults.* San Francisco: Jossey-Bass.

Scholz, N. T., Prince, J. S., & Miller, G. P. (1985). *How to decide: A guide for women.* New York: College Entrance Examination Board.

Shipton, J., & Steltenpohl, E. H. (1981). Educational advising and career planning: A life-cycle perspective. In A. W. Chickering & Associates (Eds.), *The modern American college* (pp. 689–705). San Francisco: Jossey-Bass.

Smith, E. M. (1985). Ethnic minorities: Life stress, social support, and mental health issues. *The Counseling Psychologist, 13,* 537–579.

Suinn, R. M. (1988). Asian Americans and psychology. In P. J. Woods (Ed.), *Is psychology for them? A guide to undergraduate advising* (pp. 173–177). Washington, DC: American Psychological Association.

Super, D. E. (1990). A life-span, life-space approach to career development. In D. Brown, L. Brooks, & Associates (Eds.), *Career choice and development* (2nd ed., pp. 197–261). San Francisco: Jossey-Bass.

Titley, R. W., & Titley, B. S. (1982). Academic advising: The neglected dimension in designs for undergraduate education. *Teaching of Psychology, 9,* 45–49.

Trombley, T. B. (1984). An analysis of the complexity of academic advising tasks. *Journal of College Student Personnel, 25,* 234–239.

Vaillant, G. E. (1977). *Adaptation to life: How the best and brightest came of age.* Boston: Little, Brown.

Ware, M. E. (1987). *Career development and opportunities for psychology majors* (2nd ed.). Omaha, NE: Creighton University Press.

Ware, M. E. (1988). Teaching and evaluating a career development course for psychology majors. In P. J. Woods (Ed.), *Is psychology for them? A guide to undergraduate advising* (pp. 64–74). Washington, DC: American Psychological Association.

Ware, M. E. (1990). *Pursuing graduate study in psychology* (3rd ed.). Omaha, NE: Creighton University Press.

Ware, M. E. (1991, August). *You are majoring in what? What can you do with psychology?!* Paper presented at the 99th Annual Convention of the American Psychological Association, San Francisco.

Ware, M. E., & Millard, R. J. (1987). *Handbook on student development: Advising, career development, and field placement.* Hillsdale, NJ: Erlbaum.

Ware, M. E. (Producer), & Sroufe, P. (Producer-Director). (1984a). *Career development and opportunities for psychology majors* [Videotape]. Omaha, NE: Creighton University.

Ware, M. E. (Producer), & Sroufe, P. (Producer-Director). (1984b). *Pursuing graduate study in psychology* [Videotape]. Omaha, NE: Creighton University.

Woods, P. J. (Ed.) (With Wilkinson, C. S.). (1987). *Is psychology for you? Planning for your undergraduate years.* Washington, DC: American Psychological Association.

Woods, P. J. (Ed.). (1988). *Is psychology for them? A guide to undergraduate advising.* Washington, DC: American Psychological Association.

Zanna, M. P., & Darley, J. M. (1987). *The compleat academic: A practical guide for the beginning social scientist.* New York: Random House.

3

TOWARD A PSYCHOLOGY OF VARIANCE: INCREASING THE PRESENCE AND UNDERSTANDING OF ETHNIC MINORITIES IN PSYCHOLOGY

ANTONIO E. PUENTE, in collaboration with EVELYN BLANCH, DOUGLAS K. CANDLAND, FLORENCE L. DENMARK, CAROL LAMAN, NEIL LUTSKY, PAMELA T. REID, and R. STEVEN SCHIAVO

The title of this chapter suggests a metaphor about variability that relates psychology's goals to its own methods of investigation. Psychology uses measurement of central tendencies and variances to develop general laws of behavior and to describe similarities as well as differences within a population. Measurement of central tendencies suggests generalities about a group. Measurement of variances describes not only the boundaries of the group, but illustrates the relationship of an individual to a group.

This chapter reflects concerns about the patterns of demographic variance that exist in the general population as well as among students and teachers of psychology. An understanding of current patterns can lead to the recognition that people who are from nonmajority segments of society are underrepresented and poorly understood relative to majority groups. This pattern is scientifically, ethically, and politically undesirable. Organized psychology should actively promote the understanding and presence of ethnic minorities within the discipline. As Albert (1988) argued, culture has an important role in modern psychology.

In this chapter, we will consider the means to enrich diversification among those who study and teach psychology. In the first section, we review the recent debate over cultural diversity in American higher education, summarizing selected institutional responses to multicultural students and curricula and the research and policy literature on student retention. After establishing this overall perspective, the second section provides demographic information about psychology students and faculty. In the third section, we describe a departmental self-study that facilitates understanding, defining, and evaluating diversity issues. In the fourth section, we discuss strategies to recruit ethnic minority students to undergraduate psychology courses as well as strategies to recruit and retain these individuals to the psychology major. The chapter concludes with a discussion of the problems of recruiting and retaining ethnic minority faculty.

MULTICULTURALISM IN AMERICAN HIGHER EDUCATION

Cultural diversity is a hotly debated issue in society and on college campuses in recent years. After World War II, higher education was transformed by the admission of "nontraditional" students. First, military veterans increased the age of the traditional student population beyond that of the 18–22-year-old. Second, increasing numbers of women balanced the gender proportions on campus. Third, people of color were included rather than excluded from institutions. Hence, student diversity increased on many campuses, especially at community colleges.

For years, it was assumed that these changes in student demographics did not require changes in degree programs, faculty teaching strategies, or academic and student support services. All students were considered as essentially the same and the focus of higher education was to develop and maintain excellence in scholarship. However, when increasing numbers of admitted students became attrition statistics, administrators and researchers identified a common problem—student retention. Retention was eventually tied to a more effective matching of educational opportunities with the needs of diverse students.

A starting point in assessing and resolving retention issues is to describe the multicultural shifts in American society and the philosophical bases for building an academic community and psychological knowledge base that includes cultural diversity. Resources on the topics of retention and development of all ethnic minority students as well as particular subgroups will be presented. These descriptions establish the institutional context for efforts within psychology programs and with ethnic minority students.

Changing Demographics

The demographics of the American people are indeed changing. Cortes (1991) summarized this trend in his review of statistics from the Population Reference Bureau:

> By the year 2080, the United States of America will be approximately 24 percent Latino, 15 percent African-American, and 12 percent Asian-American. More than half of the nation's population will be "diverse." What is now referred to as "ethnic diversity" will be the majority within the next 100 years. (p. 8)

Astin (1982) provided an overview of the emergence of ethnic minority students on American college campuses. A report in the series "Change Trendlines" (Carnegie Foundation for the Advancement of Teaching, 1987) analyzed undergraduate, graduate, and professional school enrollment patterns from 1976 through 1984 by race and ethnicity for Asian Americans, African Americans, Hispanics, and Native Americans. Annual updates with similar descriptive statistics can be found in a special almanac edition of *The Chronicle of Higher Education* published every fall semester.

What is critical to fully understanding changing demographics is an understanding not only of between-group differences but of within-group differences. In many cases, within-group differences mask between-group differences because of the influence of other (and usually less understood) variables such as social class. A variety of sources have explored such differences in greater detail for African-American students (Allen, 1987; Arbeiter, 1987; Fleming, 1984; Helms, 1990), Asian-American students (Hsia & Hirano-Nakanishi, 1989; Suzuki, 1989), and Hispanic students (Carnegie Foundation for the Advancement of Teaching, 1988; De Necocchea, 1988; Estrada, 1988; Fields, 1988). Smith's (1985) review article on the stress experienced by ethnic minority individuals and their coping strategies is another excellent resource.

Institutional Responses

Responses to these changing demographics have been quite varied. Cortes (1991), Hill (1991), and Wong (1991) provided philosophical and pragmatic rationales for incorporating diversity into the academic community. Wong (1991) summarized the spirit of these efforts well when he stated, ". . . diversity without community becomes anarchy. . . . community without diversity becomes fantasy, if not anachronism" (p. 54).

Several proposals have been put forth as a means to address the changing landscape of the American population and campus demographics. For example, Astin (1985) proposed a talent development model aimed not at achieving community but at achieving increased student learning in all levels and types of institutions. Another excellent example is Green's (1989) *Minorities on Campus*, which provides a pragmatic guide for achieving the mutual goals of access and excellence.

Related efforts have focused on specific curricular issues. The curriculum has undergone major transformations on some campuses in response to new scholarship on gender, race, and class as well as in response to the new generations of students. The Carnegie Foundation for the Advancement of Teaching (1992) and Levine and Cureton (1992) analyzed the magnitude of these changes nationally. Butler and Schmitz (1992) and Schneider (1991) offered examples of how to diversify courses and academic programs.

Finally, retention has generated much attention in the literature on higher education. Astin (1975) first addressed this elusive problem. More recently, Tinto (1987) completed a comprehensive study on its "causes and cures." National organizations such as the Educational Testing Service (Clewell & Ficklen, 1986), the American Association of State Colleges and Universities (Task Force on Educational Equity, 1987), and the American Council on Education (Green, 1989) used growing empirical literature to fashion specific recommendations and to develop programmatic guidelines for improving recruitment and retention. A two-part study reported in *Change*, the magazine of the American Association of Higher Education (Richardson, Simmons, & de los Santos, 1987; Skinner & Richardson, 1988), offers insight into the practices of 10 institutions that have been very successful in these endeavors. Richardson (1989a, 1989b) has also provided a general blueprint of how academic cultures can accommodate diversity.

In the following sections, we will focus our attention more directly on these issues and their consequences for psychology students, psychology majors, and psychology faculty.

PSYCHOLOGY STUDENTS AND FACULTY DEMOGRAPHICS

By the year 2000 more than 25% of the college-age population will be African Americans or Hispanics (Kohout & Pion, 1990). U.S. Census Bureau projections indicate that by 2030, approximately 11.6% of the U.S. population will be White adolescents and young adults ages 15–24; comparable figures for African Americans will be 14.7% and for Hispanics 15.5% (Spencer, 1986). Thus, the ratio of ethnic minority adolescents to White adolescents will be approximately 3:1. Therefore, the ethnic minority population will be the population from which psychology will draw its students and the population that the field will serve.

A major problem facing psychology is that relatively few ethnic minority individuals study psychology. Despite some gains posted during the late 1970s (Howard et al., 1986), it is believed that those increases are not being realized at present. Indeed, the opposite may actually be occurring. Nevertheless, the paucity of students does not reflect decreased numbers of potential precollege students. An American Council on Education report indicated that in 1985, 20% of the school-age population was from minority groups, especially in large metropolitan areas (Green, 1989). This figure is expected to rise to 39% by the year 2020.

One explanation for few ethnic minority students in psychology may be that they are exposed to other interesting or viable disciplines first and in many cases before college, thereby committing them to other fields of study before they encounter psychology. For example, the American Council on Education noted that a large percentage of ethnic minorities enroll in 2-year or community colleges where the breadth of psychology offerings may not be as well represented as it is in 4-year programs (Green, 1989). Currently, about 55% of Hispanic and 43% of African-American students in higher education are enrolled in community colleges.

A second explanation for psychology's problems in attracting ethnic minority students is the unfair but commonly held belief that an undergraduate degree in psychology is not very marketable. A recent review of psychology alumni studies effectively disputed this expectation (McGovern & Carr, 1989). However, ethnic minority students are pursuing careers that they believe will yield higher status or pay with a baccalaureate and without pursuing additional graduate or professional study. For example, the percentages of bachelor's degrees awarded to ethnic minorities in science and engineering fields climbed from 11.5% in 1980–81 to 14.0% in 1986–87. In psychology, 15.1% of the bachelor's degrees awarded in 1980–81 were received by ethnic minorities; this number declined to 14.1% in 1982–83 and 12.8% in 1984–85 before returning to 15.5% in 1986–87 (Kohout & Pion, 1990; U.S. Department of Education, 1990). In 1987, ethnic minority individuals received 12.2% of all doctoral degrees awarded in all science and engineering fields, compared with 9.2% of all doctoral degrees awarded in psychology (Kohout & Pion, 1990). These statistics suggest that science and engineering are more successful in attracting ethnic minority students into programs leading to advanced degrees. If there is no reason to suppose that ethnic minorities should be intrinsically less attracted to psychology than to other disciplines, then the differences in percentages require attention and action.

A recent survey of psychology doctoral programs in the United States showed that slightly more than 6% of faculty were ethnic minorities: African American, 3%; Asian American, 2%; Hispanic, 1%; Native American, less than 1% (APA, 1990). Although comparable statistics for ethnic minority faculty in undergraduate institutions have not been collected, such statistics may be even worse because graduate schools can offer incentives that undergraduate institutions may not be able to afford. In contrast, the 1989–90 racial and ethnic group percentages for all full-time faculty in colleges and universities were: Asian American, 5%; African American, 4.5%; Hispanic, 2%; and Native American, less than 1% ("Almanac," 1991). Psychology appears to have fewer ethnic minorities represented at the faculty level than do other disciplines.

Kohout and Pion (1990) reported that the majority of ethnic minorities who receive psychology doctoral degrees do so in three applied fields: 57.8% of the degrees awarded between 1983 and 1987 were in the areas of clinical, counseling, and school psychology. This trend has been evident since 1975 (Howard et al., 1986). Data from the APA (1990) *Directory of Ethnic Minority Professionals in Psychology* indicate that 64.4% of the professionals registered are in these three specialties. Similarly, of the applicants for the APA Minority Fellowship Program (MFP) between 1986 and 1990, only 23.2% were research applicants; the remainder were clinical applicants (Minority Fellowship Program, 1991). The MFP has been a long-standing source and barometer of ethnic minority representation in graduate school. These figures strongly suggest that the number of ethnic minority faculty has leveled off considerably and is not keeping up with the overall growth in graduate education in psychology.

These demographics and the needs of psychological practice, research, and education suggest that psychology must promote greater diversity to enrich the field. These trends were recognized by the participants of the recent National Conference on Graduate Education in Psychology (APA, 1987). Many of the 14 resolutions developed at the graduate conference have been incorporated in one form or another into specific recommendations that serve as a foundation for the current discussions. Additional concerns and suggestions have also been raised by the National Council of Schools of Professional Psychology in *Toward Ethnic Diversification in Psychology Education and Training* (Stricker et al., 1990).

THE DEPARTMENTAL SELF-STUDY

Improving the diversity of the psychology student population is a necessary, important, and invigorating challenge. This challenge can be undertaken by a single faculty person, by a subcommittee, or by an entire department. However, it is anticipated that a greater effect will be achieved if entire departments can focus on these issues. Diversity initiatives range from simple actions built into the department's annual goals to complex, long-term strategies that are part of a collaborative, longitudinal plan.

An initial step used to increase ethnic minority representation in psychology courses is the departmental self-study. Departments establish a baseline for themselves by analyzing their current recruitment and retention statistics. The self-study fosters an appreciation for the seriousness of the challenge as well as for the commitment necessary to meet that challenge. Because the issues influencing this problem vary considerably from department to department and institution to institution, recruitment and retention issues must be considered in light of local institutional missions and circumstances and specific community interests, resources, and needs.

The departmental self-study format can vary. Discussions might take place as part of annual or periodic faculty or departmental reviews. Ideally, dedicated meeting times or retreats provide less frenetic contexts in which to explore difficult problems and generate new strategies. Some departments may want to involve outside consultants or a facilitator.

The framework for departmental discussion should be forged by the participants themselves. However, several pertinent questions may be useful. The following questions can help initiate and structure faculty exploration on attracting and retaining ethnic minority students. These questions are not exhaustive.

- Why should psychology be concerned about increasing ethnic minority student participation?
- What does this department offer in our program that holds special appeal for ethnic minority individuals?
- What are the needs and aspirations of potential ethnic minority students? How do these vary from their majority counterparts?
- What methods are successful for recruiting students to undergraduate psychology classes? To the major? To psychology careers?
- What resources (pamphlets, folders, books, videos, contact people, etc.) enhance recruiting success?
- How can interest in psychology be promoted at earlier educational levels?
- How will the effectiveness of recruitment and retention efforts be evaluated?
- What are the successful recruitment and retention models in higher education that are important to examine?

ETHNIC MINORITY STUDENT RECRUITMENT

The general public has little prior exposure to scientific psychology. Indeed the first exposure to scientific psychology for most is an introductory psychology course. This may be even more true for ethnic minorities. Psychology faculty, therefore, should consider promoting the discipline even before enrollment decisions are made. Enhancing the appeal of psychology to ethnic minority students may require even more targeted promotion efforts. Although recruitment at the graduate level is critical (Isaac, 1985), recruitment practices must begin at the undergraduate level.

Improving Outreach and Addressing Special Needs

Improving Outreach to Students and the Community

Psychology faculty can visit grammar, middle, and high schools; technical and community colleges; and community groups to discuss psychology as a scientific means to enhance human understanding and welfare. The appeal of psychology will be stronger with ethnic minority students if the speaker is a member of an ethnic minority group or if topics can be selected that have a particular importance for minorities. Local or visiting ethnic minority psychologists are strong role models. Alumni and upper-level undergraduates can be just as effective in discussing their undergraduate work in the major. Outreach efforts are not limited to on-site visits. Pamphlets and other resource materials about careers in psychology and psychological issues can also be used.

Departments can sponsor awards for behavioral science projects in science fairs to recognize emerging interest in psychology. Special recognition might be offered for projects that explore issues relevant to diversity. With assistance from a local psychology department, the media can also promote better public understanding of psychology, especially by addressing the concerns of ethnic minorities.

Potential college students can visit college campuses for a short lecture or presentation, for a classroom or a laboratory experience, or for precollege summer workshops. Interested students could become involved in summer research programs.

A theme of this chapter and others in this book (e.g., chapter 5) is the need to improve linkages among educational levels. The need to network also applies to ethnic minority recruitment. Strong local networks among high schools and high school counselors, community colleges and advisors, and colleges and universities facilitate the advising of students into programs with a well-known commitment to diversity. This commitment is made known by individual contacts, community network meetings, and summer workshops on teaching resources, goals, and strategies.

Employers of ethnic minority graduates may be encouraged to support psychology as a beneficial major for career development. For example, hospitals and community agencies may be especially receptive to collaborating with a department offering course work to improve employee performance and commitment. On-site classes, especially introductory psychology, may also interest someone to a sufficient degree that further course work in a traditional setting will be pursued.

Developing Programs Relevant to Nontraditional Needs

The decision to take courses in psychology may depend on the relevance of those courses to undergraduate students. When students do not have a history of college attendance, additional support systems need to be in place to foster a sense of belonging. Attention should be given to the scheduling and location of classes, faculty knowledge of available financial supports, and access to day care. In particular, students who are the first generation in their families to attend college may need assistance to navigate through admissions, enrollment, and financial aid procedures.

Practical application of the principles of psychology is especially attractive to beginning students of psychology. They should have the opportunity to become involved early with student interest groups. Students of all ethnic backgrounds benefit from involvement in minority community programs (e.g., volunteer assistants in public schools or with elderly people). Active learning opportunities (see chapter 7) expose psychology students to a wider population and promote understanding among different traditions.

Recruiting Ethnic Minority Students Into the Psychology Major

Psychology has personal, intellectual, and applied value for ethnic minority students with either a baccalaureate or a graduate degree. The potential, however, may not be evident to those not involved in the field. Specific strategies have to be developed to make this potential more understood. With regard to ethnic minority students, competing forces may direct them toward other disciplines and professional programs. Psychology departments need to develop more complex, long-term strategies to foster ethnic minority presence in the major.

Most psychology majors initially expect the study of psychology to assist them in understanding their lives, their families, and their communities. Because first exposure to psychology may have been through the mass media, students' career expectations may be unrealistic. This discrepancy may lead to disenchantment with the real-world opportunities available in psychology. This situation may be more of a problem with ethnic minority students, whose difficulties may be the norm and not the exception. Therefore, departments need to shape realistic career expectations and goals for their undergraduates.

Departments that successfully recruit ethnic minority students into the major still face the challenge of retaining those students. Recruiting and retaining ethnic minority psychology majors depends on a number of factors, including financial assistance, mentor support, advising, and the degree to which students participate fully with other students and faculty in departmental activities. Departmental climate and other local and community conditions influence the retention of ethnic minority psychology majors through graduation.

The following subsections offer strategies for attracting, recruiting, and retaining ethnic minority majors.

Addressing Differences in the Introductory Course

A fundamental area of attention in psychology is individual differences. In fact, diversity is an important theme throughout psychology, including the multiple theoretical perspectives that students learn as the basic content of the introductory course. The value of diversity in the science of psychology and in its theories should be underscored throughout the students' first course.

Materials in the introductory course should address questions raised by ethnic diversity. Topics can highlight psychology's contributions to social issues, ethnic minority issues, and the issue of individual differences. Bronstein and Quina's (1988) *Teaching a Psychology of People* is an effective resource for lecture ideas, course assignments, or additional readings.

In the introductory course, career opportunities in psychology should be described. Instructors can offer information about career development and include active learning exercises to assess student potential for work in psychology. These discussions are even more meaningful when current conditions and projected demographic changes are introduced as variables that will influence future needs in the discipline. *Toward Ethnic Diversification in Psychology Education and Training* (Stricker et al., 1990) provides resources for developing possible future employment projections.

Transforming the Undergraduate Psychology Curriculum

An undergraduate curriculum that incorporates the psychology of variance is critical. Such a curriculum can expand the knowledge base to include all ethnic minority issues, thereby enhancing the recruitment and retention of ethnic minority students. This emphasis on the psychology of variance need not await the arrival of minority students. Concepts of variability and individual difference serve as foundations for understanding human behavior. Although these ideas are introduced in the introductory psychology course, these concepts should be amplified and reinforced in later course work. Diversity-related problems can be analyzed in all existing and new courses, in texts, in supplemental materials, in new programs or concentrations, and in research and placement opportunities.

Information and materials about variance should be added to the curriculum. These concepts are particularly important for introductory psychology classes at the high school or college level in which students are first exposed to psychology. The inclusion of diversity issues motivates ethnic minority students to appreciate psychology more and teaches all students the effects of diversity on their own lives.

Including diversity-related topics in the curriculum can help instructors better address teaching issues that are relevant to an ethnically diverse society. Including such topics does not mean that instructors need to eliminate coverage of core concepts in psychology. Although some traditional text information may need to be omitted because of time constraints, the trade-off is likely to be enhanced student interest in more personally engaging topics. At a minimum, instructors should be encouraged to use examples that highlight diversity issues to clarify traditional psychology concepts.

There are abundant examples of content areas that involve ethnic minority interest in psychology. These include sex, gender, social class, ethnicity, culture, religion, immigration, acculturation, bilingualism, cross-cultural research, and how to cope with prejudice and discrimination.

Courses or concentration areas can be developed to focus on ethnic diversity and mutual understanding. Such courses should emphasize minority scholarship and achievement as well as minority issues. Examples of specialized courses include Cross-Cultural Psychology, Psychology of Human Diversity, African-American Psychology, and Ethnicity and Gender, among others. Special preparation and research may be required to develop such courses; it should not be assumed that faculty members are prepared to teach these courses simply because they are members of a relevant minority group.

Creating New Concentrations

Psychology can attract students who seek immediate postbaccalaureate employment by developing interdisciplinary courses and new majors oriented to the job market. For example, 2-year institutions, such as Houston Community College, offer an applied science or an associate in applied science degree in mental health; students can train to become paraprofessional counselors, geriatric workers, psychological technicians, social worker associates, and workers for residential institutions. The National Organization of Human Services Educators (NOHSE) provides information on the mental health associate degree. Some psychology departments, such as the one at Pace University in New York City, offer a bachelor of arts degree in an interdisciplinary area (e.g., human relations) that can lead to employment at business and human services agencies. At Pace University, students' advanced work emphasizes practical application and experiences in the areas of personnel, residential care, and health and human services agencies.

Interdisciplinary courses (e.g., industrial psychology, health psychology, sports psychology) can be developed with students' vocational interests in mind. For example, psychology departments could collaborate with nursing departments to develop a specialized health management concentration.

Improving Pedagogy

The classroom climate needs to provide ethnic minority students a good learning atmosphere to facilitate subject mastery and student retention. Trujillo (1986) reported that majority faculty tended to have significantly lower expectations of ethnic minority students than did their counterparts. Effective teaching can help faculty promote effective learning climates that are supportive of diversity. Instruction that encourages active involvement with a diverse student body can build a sense of community in the classroom. Exercises can be used to facilitate ethnic minority students' involvement. Diversity can also be considered when assigning group projects, developing problem-solving exercises, and forming study groups.

Critical thinking should be a cornerstone of classroom activities. Students with no previous exposure to scientific processes may have difficulty understanding psychological inquiry. Instructors need to be explicit in their expectations of students' critical thinking skills, perhaps modeling how these processes are accomplished. Underprepared students benefit from detailed, explicit instructions; all students benefit from immediate feedback. Comprehensive syllabi with complete grading requirements should be available to students to help them develop a thorough understanding of what will be required of them.

Research has indicated that students with different ethnic backgrounds vary in their responses to different teaching methods (Anderson, 1988; Murrell & Claxton, 1987). Such resources can be consulted for new teaching approaches when faculty are unsuccessful in reaching certain kinds of students.

Faculty can do classroom research with their own students (Kolb, 1976). The growing emphasis on assessment practices makes publishing research in this area a likely prospect. Classroom research also provides evidence to enhance the probability of future grant funding. (See chapter 1 for additional suggestions.)

Creating New Texts and Supplements

For curricular change to be effective, new materials on ethnic diversity need to be developed. For example, there is no current introductory psychology text that focuses exclusively on ethnic minority or cultural diversity issues. Furthermore, most of the basic introductory psychology books rarely cover diversity as a topic.

Authors, publishers, and reviewers need to be aware of APA's concern with ethnic minority issues and their inclusion in classroom materials. Publishers can employ minority speakers to promote books that effectively portray ethnically sensitive topics. They can also encourage the development of videos or other diversity-related supports to enhance existing texts and publicize them through the APA at regional and national conferences. Whenever possible, local faculty can develop supplemental materials to help increase their acceptance and use. Supplemental materials can include readings, pamphlets, posters, and videos. The best starting point when searching for this type of material can be found in sections 2 and 3 of *Teaching a Psychology of People* (Bronstein & Quina, 1988). This book provides ways to integrate diversity into existing courses and to create new courses on diversity.

Faculty release time may be needed to support the development of scholarly and instructional materials. Grant funding to underwrite such efforts is another needed support. Finally, materials need to be developed and maintained for different educational levels. Some materials should be targeted for the freshman and sophomore levels so that they can be used at community colleges as well.

Enhancing Opportunities

There are many topics in which research on variance can be conducted or discussed. Statistics, testing, and methodology courses can use topics that examine questions of diversity. Instructors can include the research findings as part of other courses as well. Ethnic concerns are appropriately synthesized with other issues such as ethics. A faculty committee can foster increased attention to ethnic diversity issues in research by encouraging research proposals to demonstrate ethnic sensitivity and fairness. They can promote diversity as an important variable and area of concern through comments on research proposals and in faculty meetings. Special summer internships have already been described in the literature and serve as an excellent way to launch research interests (Prentice-Dunn & Roberts, 1985).

Traditional vocational and pedagogical (e.g., internship) placement rosters should be screened to identify those placements offering relevant learning in diversity issues. Faculty and students can solicit additional placements that would expand students' choices and experiences. Faculty should coordinate with on-site supervisors to emphasize the importance of students experiencing ethnically relevant issues.

Out-of-class activities such as Psi Chi, Psi Beta, psychology clubs, and other departmental activities are forums where all students can network.

Ethnic minority students need explicit faculty encouragement to attend such activities and to feel welcome. Departments can also sponsor social activities that have the appreciation of cultural diversity as a theme.

Expanding Support Systems

Helping academically underprepared students to function successfully in college greatly enhances the possibility of recruiting ethnic minority students to psychology. A higher percentage of ethnic minority students are academically underprepared because of prior experiences with poor schools, low self-esteem, poverty, and low expectations. These students should not be considered intellectually inferior. Some have left school before because of family economic need, pregnancy, immigration problems, or lack of encouragement. A sense of self-respect and dignity, which can be fostered by appropriate personal support, allows students with few role models and limited encouragement to succeed as undergraduate psychology majors.

Supplemental academic support services (e.g., remediation, writing assistance, learning labs, testing services) can make the crucial difference in a student's ability to compete in the major. Retention of students is related to the quality and timeliness of the academic support services offered. Students should not be stigmatized or financially penalized for participating in these services. In addition, support services may need to go beyond academic assistance and include more personal development issues, such as assertiveness training courses, adjustment courses, and study skills courses.

In addition, departments can provide ethnic minority students with financial assistance guidance. They can pursue grants directly or can identify an advising specialist who can advise ethnic minority students about available financial support.

Departments can create climates in which ethnic minority students are valued not just for their membership in a minority group but for their contributions to the department. For example, faculty can recruit ethnic minority students to be their research assistants and can provide opportunities for coauthorship and conference presentations. Ethnic minority students can serve as peer tutors, peer counselors, or teaching assistants. These roles provide financial assistance and build self-esteem in the students, who in turn become effective role models for less advanced students. Departmental recognition of ethnic minority students for distinguished achievement serves as a powerful incentive for younger students.

The use of alumni as mentors can be effective in enhancing an undergraduate's sense of belonging. This arrangement has the additional advantages of assisting students to network for future employment opportunities while meaningfully involving former students in the department's activities.

Despite verbal attention to training ethnic minority students, many departments are not fully appreciative or committed to the educational goals of students from nonmajority backgrounds. A committed climate can be fostered through targeted faculty development activities (discussed later) as well as through departmental sponsorship of events designed for student participation.

Guest speakers, especially tenured and respected ethnic minority scholars, can be invited to student or faculty events to share their knowledge. Some faculty speakers may be from other departments or from medical schools; speakers can also be invited from private practice or from businesses or government agencies. Minority graduates should be invited to speak on departmental panels or at departmental functions, including orientation sessions for nonmajors.

Departments can establish a minority speakers' bureau and create opportunities for them to address ethnic minority issues and achievements. Lists of speakers are available from the APA as well as from regional, state, and local psychological organizations. Regional psychology programs could also collaborate on an exchange program featuring minority faculty members. (See chapter 5 for additional suggestions for building networks.)

Systematic efforts must be made to alter the environment that does not foster cultural diversity. In addition, it is often assumed that improving diversity affects scholarship. Richardson (1989a) suggested that most higher education cultures perceive undergraduate quality as maintained by high achievement, strong and specific orientation, and detailed and traditional modes of college preparation. (Taylor, 1976, discussed these concepts for psychology training.) Diversity does not appear to fit well within this contextual framework. Richardson also suggested that programs that strive for diversity are viewed as focusing on low achievement, uncertain and general orientation, nontraditional modes of college preparation and attendance, and overall low levels of scholarship. Thus, the concepts of diversity and scholarship are seen by institutional cultures as mutually exclusive. However, Richardson cogently argued that the two concepts are not mutually exclusive. In contrast, it can be argued that true scholarship encompasses, not excludes, diversity. For example, Bacchetti (1991), chair of the Accreditation Commission for Senior Colleges and Universities of the Western Association of Schools and Colleges, recently suggested that diversity is a key factor in educational quality and hence should be a factor in accreditation.

RECRUITMENT AND RETENTION OF ETHNIC MINORITY PSYCHOLOGY FACULTY

Most departments recognize that the hiring and retention of ethnic minority faculty constitute an effective means of attracting ethnic minority students to the discipline and expanding the psychological knowledge base. The presence of ethnic minority faculty offers ethnic minority students role models, possible mentors, and a sense of belonging. Active participation by ethnic minority faculty reinforces the appropriateness of including ethnic issues and concerns in the curriculum and in research programs.

A starting point from which to address the issue of ethnic minority faculty recruitment and retention is to briefly review the seminal article by Suinn and Witt (1982). This study is one of the few to address factors involved in attracting ethnic minority faculty. In order of importance, the following variables were listed by ethnic minority faculty as reasons for declining faculty position offers: higher salaries elsewhere; geographic location; higher concentration of minorities in community; teaching load; other locale perceived as more supportive; higher concentration of minority faculty at university; fringe benefits; academic rank of institution; higher concentration of ethnic minorities in the department; tenure policy; school characteristics; and ethnicity assignments. We now consider several recommendations to promote faculty diversification that are applicable at various stages of faculty recruitment and retention.

Recruiting Undergraduate Students to Academic Life

Undergraduate advisers need to foster the notion that academic and professional careers in psychology are viable, interesting, and rewarding. Such discussions can focus on the positive values and ideals that characterize academic life (e.g., autonomy, flexibility, collegiality), hopefully offsetting any economic reservations students hold. Ethnic minority students who show academic potential could be encouraged to apply to programs specializing in the training of academic psychologists. Knowledge of available financial support (e.g., Office of Minority Affairs and the Minority Fellowship Program of the APA) may enhance the attractiveness of graduate study versus the pursuit of postbaccalaureate employment.

Adopting Expanded Advertising, Recruitment, and Orientation Practices

Ethnic minority faculty may be recruited most readily through specialized newsletters and publications, such as the newsletter of the APA's Division 45 (Society for the Psychological Study of Ethnic Minority Issues) and the newsletters of ethnic minority associations (e.g., *Black Issues in Higher Education, The Hispanic Outlook in Higher Education,* etc.). In addition, successful ethnic minority academics may be in a position to promote informal networking about available positions in academic psychology.

To facilitate their entry into the department, incoming and junior ethnic minority faculty can be paired with senior faculty who have commitments to departmental diversity. Although this mentorship is likely to extend beyond issues of diversity, support for the new member should not be limited to the provision of a mentor. Departments should actively promote a sense of belonging within the department and to the larger college or university community.

Teaching assignments within the department should represent the broad spectrum of psychology. Minority faculty should not be teaching courses only on ethnic minority issues, nor should they be asked automatically to serve as the voice of their heritage in public settings. Attention should be paid to college or university and community service assignments offered to ethnic minority faculty. Inappropriate choices of service assignments (quality and quantity) can be detrimental to professional development.

Developing a Core of Committed Faculty

Central to the effectiveness of strategies to improve diversification is having a core of faculty committed to the importance of this objective. Ideally, such core faculty should include both ethnic minority and majority members. Minority issues must not be the domain of ethnic minority faculty only; these issues should be the concern of the entire faculty.

Faculty development activities can be geared toward improving the climate for diversification. Departments can encourage faculty to seek grants and foster research geared toward ethnic minority issues. Travel funds can be designated for continuing education efforts. Faculty workshops can be used to promote changes in the climate. These workshops can include information about how diversity improves teaching and learning, how to deal with controversy in classroom settings, how to facilitate a positive classroom atmosphere, how to handle difficult situations that arise in class discussions, what resources are currently available, and which topics may be most productive as stimuli for diversity issues. In addition, workshops could address classroom climate issues, including how to handle prejudiced comments in the classroom, how to manage one's own biases, how cross-cultural differences affect behavior, how to interpret nonverbal communication, and how to engage in classroom research.

If existing faculty are not prepared to teach courses related to diversity, several options are available. Continuing education training for faculty can prepare them to offer future courses. Adjunct faculty can be hired to teach specific courses. Faculty exchanges and visiting faculty are other options. Faculty from culturally diverse colleges should be recruited as visiting professors. For situations in which appropriate faculty are not accessible, a series of invited speakers or special seminars may be an alternative.

Departments can encourage collaboration on the development of ethnic minority materials. Faculty can take advantage of existing resources on ethnic minority issues or they can seek student input through questionnaires, comments, or examples to help frame the issue locally. Faculty can develop model syllabi, curriculum guides, course objectives, or other materials. These activities will encourage active learning about ethnic diversity and inclusion of such topics in their own courses. Faculty workshops can also be used to promote changes in curriculum.

Making Administrative Commitments Visible

An institutionally based community of ethnic minority scholars can be sponsored by an enterprising department. By assisting such a group to be established and by actively supporting the group, departments make their commitment to diversity visible. However, at present there may be more rhetoric than action. For example, in a preliminary analysis of a survey by the APA's Office of Minority Affairs, most psychology departments had specific recruiting and retention strategies for ethnic minority students (Guzman & Messenger, 1991). In contrast, only 26% of the responding departments indicated that specific plans for programmatic retention had been implemented.

Allocating incentives for involvement in diversity issues manifests a powerful commitment by departments. Incentives can include enhanced value toward promotion, public praise, increased research budgets, and merit pay. Such rewards can be offered for a variety of diversity-oriented activities, such as development of a new ethnicity-oriented course or workshop; improved or extended ethnic minority advising; and scholarship in areas of ethnic minority issues. The department's commitment to undergraduate diversification can be exemplified in other ways as well. Faculty intervention strategies can be formally evaluated.

One major way to support cultural competency is through tenure and promotion. However, because of a variety of factors this is often a difficult task. Suinn and Witt (1982) found that too much minority service, insufficient publications (both a result of limited data collections and poor writing); insufficient data-based publications; heavy advising, teaching, and committee loads; isolation; lack of mentoring; and poor guidance were the most common reasons cited by ethnic minority faculty who were denied tenure or promotion.

Departments can seek current information about ethnic organizations and publications. An example is a chapter by Guy-Sheftall and Bell-Scott (1989) in the book *Educating the Majority: Women Challenge Tradition in Higher Education*. In addition, the APA's Task Force on Minority Recruitment and Retention maintains ongoing investigation of this issue and publishes regular reports of its findings. There is little question that progress has been made. For example, Potter (1974) reported that doctoral programs in clinical psychology showed ambivalence to the recruitment of minorities and women. At least the concern is present today. Unfortunately, the results may still be as disconcerting as they were when Potter reported the findings of her survey almost 20 years ago.

Improving National Attention to Diversity

Because of the importance of recruiting and retaining ethnic minority faculty to the overall success of diversity initiatives, more opportunities for discussing faculty development topics related to ethnic issues should be provided at state, regional, and national conferences. Possible topics include minority mentoring programs, advising strategies for multiple ethnic groups, and grant opportunities that support ethnic issues. Finally, national, regional, and state conferences in psychology provide a platform for presenting other innovative ideas that work to improve diversification within psychology.

CONCLUSION

Psychology is dedicated to the scientific study of behavior. It is appropriate that this concept extend to the teaching of psychology. A basic assumption underlying the dissemination of psychological knowledge is that it must be empirically based and generalizable. Nowhere is this assumption further from the truth than in our understanding of the psychology of human diversity. Cultural competency should be encouraged in psychology. However, such competence should not be perceived as another version of affirmative action in education. The recommendations made in this chapter attempt to go beyond this form of redressing the wrongs of the past. The recommendations for discussion and action in this chapter should serve as the foundation for the examination of why cultural competency and diversity are critical to understanding human behavior.

REFERENCES

Albert, R. D. (1988). The place of culture in modern psychology. In P. A. Bronstein & K. Quina (Eds.), *Teaching a psychology of people: Resources for gender and sociocultural awareness* (pp. 12–18). Washington, DC: American Psychological Association.

Allen, W. R. (1987, May/June). Black colleges vs. white colleges: The fork in the road for black students. *Change, 19*(3), 28–34.

Almanac: Full-time employees in colleges and universities by racial and ethnic group, 1989–90. (1991, August 28). *The Chronicle of Higher Education*, p. 29.

American Psychological Association. (1987). Resolutions approved by the National Conference on Graduate Education in Psychology. *American Psychologist, 42,* 1070–1084.

American Psychological Association. (1990). *Directory of ethnic minority professionals in psychology.* Washington, DC: Author.

American Psychological Association. (1990). *Race/ethnicity of faculty in U.S. graduate departments of psychology: 1989–90.* Washington, DC: Author.

Anderson, J. A. (1988). Cognitive styles and multicultural populations. *Journal of Teacher Education, 39,* 2–9

Arbeiter, S. (1987, May/June). Black enrollments: The case of the missing students. *Change, 19*(3), 14–19.

Astin, A. W. (1975). *Preventing students from dropping out.* San Francisco: Jossey-Bass.

Astin, A. W. (1982). *Minorities in American higher education: Recent trends, current prospects, and recommendations.* San Francisco: Jossey-Bass.

Astin, A. W. (1985). *Achieving educational excellence.* San Francisco: Jossey-Bass.

Bacchetti, R. F. (1991, May 8). Diversity is a key factor in education quality and hence in accreditation. *The Chronicle of Higher Education,* p. A48.

Bronstein, P. A., & Quina, K. (Eds.). (1988). *Teaching a psychology of people: Resources for gender and sociocultural awareness.* Washington, DC: American Psychological Association.

Butler, J., & Schmitz, B. (1992, January/February). Ethnic studies, women's studies, and multiculturalism. *Change, 24*(1), 37–41.

Carnegie Foundation for the Advancement of Teaching (1987, May/June). Change trendlines—Minority access: A question of equity. *Change, 19*(3), 35–39.

Carnegie Foundation for the Advancement of Teaching (1988, May/June). Change trendlines: Hispanic students continue to be distinctive. *Change, 20*(3), 43–47.

Carnegie Foundation for the Advancement of Teaching (1992, January/February). Change trendlines: Signs of a changing curriculum. *Change, 24*(1), 49–52.

Clewell, B. C., & Ficklen, M. S. (1986). *Improving minority retention in higher education: A search for effective institutional practices.* Princeton, NJ: Educational Testing Service.

Cortes, C. E. (1991, September/October). Pluribus & Unum: The quest for community amid diversity. *Change, 23*(5), 8–13.

De Necocchea, G. (1988, May/June). Expanding the Hispanic college pool. Pre-college strategies that work. *Change, 20*(3), 61–65.

Estrada, L. F. (1988, May/June). Anticipating the demographic future. Dramatic changes are on the way. *Change, 20*(3), 14–19.

Fields, C. (1988, May/June). The Hispanic pipeline: Narrow, leaking, and needing repair. *Change, 20*(3), 20–27.

Fleming, J. (1984). *Blacks in college. A comparative study of students' success in black and white institutions.* San Francisco: Jossey-Bass.

Green, M. F. (Ed.). (1989). *Minorities on campus. A handbook on enhancing diversity.* Washington, DC: American Council on Education.

Guy-Sheftall, B., & Bell-Scott, P. (1989). Finding a way: Black women students and the academy. In C. S. Pearson, D. L. Shavlik, & J. G. Touchton (Eds.), *Educating the majority: Women challenge tradition in higher education.* New York: ACE/Macmillan.

Guzman, L. P., & Messenger, L. C. (1991). *Recruitment and retention of ethnic minority students and faculty: A survey of doctoral programs in psychology.* Unpublished manuscript.

Helms, J. E. (Ed.). (1990). *Black and white racial identity.* New York: Greenwood Press.

Hill, P. J. (1991, July/August). Multi-culturalism: The crucial philosophical and organizational issues. *Change, 23*(4), 38–47.

Howard, A., Pion, G. M., Gottfredson, G. D., Flattau, P. E., Oskamp, S., Pfafflin, S. M., Bray, D. W., & Burstein, A. G. (1986). The changing face of American psychology: A report from the committee on employment and human resources. *American Psychologist, 41,* 1311–1327.

Hsia, J., & Hirano-Nakanishi, M. (1989, November/December). The demographics of diversity: Asian Americans and higher education. *Change, 21*(6), 20–27.

Isaac, P. D. (1985). Recruitment of minority students into graduate programs in psychology. *American Psychologist, 40,* 472–475.

Kohout, J., & Pion, G. (1990). Participation of ethnic minorities in psychology: Where do we stand today? In G. Stricker, E. Davis-Russell, E. Bourg, E. Duran, W. R. Hammond, J. McHolland, K. Polite, & B. E. Vaughan (Eds.), *Toward ethnic diversification in psychology education and training* (pp. 153–165). Washington, DC: American Psychological Association.

Kolb, D. A. (1976). *The learning style inventory: Self-scoring test and interpretation booklet.* Boston: McBer.

Levine, A., & Cureton, J. (1992, January/February). The quiet revolution. Eleven facts about multiculturalism and the curriculum. *Change, 24*(1), 25–29.

McGovern, T. V., & Carr, K. (1989). Carving out the niche: A review of alumni surveys on undergraduate majors. *Teaching of Psychology, 16,* 52–57.

Minority Fellowship Program. (1991). *Information regarding MFP applicants.* Unpublished manuscript.

Murrell, P. H., & Claxton, C. S. (1987). Experiential learning theory as a guide for effective teaching. *Counselor Education and Supervision, 27*(1), 4–14.

Potter, N. (1974). Recruitment of minority students and women. *American Psychologist, 29,* 151–152.

Prentice-Dunn, S., & Roberts, M. C. (1985). A summer internship for psychological research: Preparation of minority undergraduates for graduate study. *Teaching of Psychology, 12,* 142–145.

Richardson, R. C. (1989a). *Institutional climate and minority achievement.* Denver: Education Commission of the States.

Richardson, R. C. (1989b). *Serving more diverse students: A contextual view.* Denver: Education Commission of the States.

Richardson, R. C., Simmons, H., & de los Santos, A. G. (1987, May/June). Graduating minority students: Lessons from ten success stories. *Change, 19*(3), 20–27.

Schneider, C. G. (Ed.). (1991). Engaging cultural legacies: A multidimensional endeavor. *Liberal Education, 77*(3), 2–7.

Skinner, E. F., & Richardson, R. C. (1988, May/June). Making it in a majority university: The minority graduate's perspective. *Change, 20*(3), 34–42.

Smith, E. M. J. (1985). Ethnic minorities: Life stress, social support, and mental health issues. *The Counseling Psychologist, 13*(4), 537–579.

Spencer, G. (1986). *Projections of the Hispanic population: 1982 to 2080* (U.S. Bureau of the Census, Current Population Reports, Series P-25, No. 995). Washington, DC: U.S. Government Printing Office.

Stricker, G., Davis-Russell, E., Bourg, E., Duran, E., Hammond, W. R., McHolland, J., Polite, K., & Vaughn, B. E. (Eds.). (1990). *Toward ethnic diversification in psychology education and training.* Washington, DC: American Psychological Association.

Suinn, R. M., & Witt, J. C. (1982). Survey of ethnic minority faculty recruitment and retention. *American Psychologist, 37,* 1239–1244.

Suzuki, B. H. (1989, November/December). Asian Americans as the "model minority": Outdoing whites? Or media hype? *Change, 21*(6), 13–19.

Task Force on Educational Equity. (1987). *Minority recruitment and retention models.* Washington, DC: American Association of State Colleges and Universities.

Taylor, D. (1976). Recruitment and training of ethnic minorities in psychology. *Personality and Social Psychology Bulletin, 2,* 142–147.

Tinto, V. (1987). *Leaving college: Rethinking the causes and cures of student attrition.* Chicago: University of Chicago Press.

Trujillo, C. M. (1986). A comprehensive examination of classroom interactions between professors of minority and non-minority college students. *American Educational Research Journal, 23,* 629–642.

U. S. Department of Education. (1990). *Digest of education statistics 1990* (Office of Educational Research and Improvement NCES 91-660). Washington, DC: U.S. Government Printing Office.

Wong, F. (1991, July/August). Diversity and community: Right objectives and wrong arguments. *Change, 23*(4), 48–54.

4

THE COMPLEAT SCHOLAR: FACULTY DEVELOPMENT FOR THOSE WHO TEACH PSYCHOLOGY

BRUCE R. FRETZ, in collaboration with ANTOINE M. GARIBALDI, LARAINE M. GLIDDEN, WILBERT J. McKEACHIE, JOHN N. MORITSUGU, KATHRYN QUINA, JILL N. REICH, and BARBARA SHOLLEY

Faculty at institutions of higher learning are expected, at a minimum, to be teachers, scholars, and contributors to the functioning of the academic environment. Faculty development programs can be designed to help faculty effectively perform these multiple roles. However, such programs have not always served this purpose:

> Until recently, faculty development entailed little more than sabbaticals, travel funds, newsletters, and inspirational workshops (Centra, 1978). But changes in academe have necessitated changes in faculty development. Campuses face problems of an aging and entrenched professorate, of a struggle to do more with less, and of shifting emphases to research and publication. . . . Increasingly, campuses want faculty development programs . . . integrating traditionally isolated activities, such as teaching, with scholarship and collegiality. (Boice, 1989, p. 97)

For more than 25 years there has been a steady stream of articles about inadequacies in the preparation of college teachers and in the assessment of instructional methods (Boyer, 1987, 1990; Sanford, 1967). The changing nature of student demographics, making for a multicultural student body, as well as the introduction of new classroom and research technology have compounded the challenges faculty members face. Psychology faculty, however, are members of a discipline that has provided leadership in developing assessment and intervention techniques to respond to such challenges (Boice, 1989).

The first section of this chapter identifies nine institutional barriers and individual resistances to faculty development. Although faculty development programs may be imperative, they are complex to implement, especially given the need for addressing the research and service roles of faculty as well as their responsibility as teachers of undergraduates. In the second section, we present three principles that are missing from previous literature on faculty development. These principles provide a framework for faculty development, rather than portray it as a corrective intervention applied to reluctant or unproductive faculty members. Equally important, these principles can facilitate a department-wide or individualized set of faculty development strategies. As has been well documented in the literature on counseling and psychotherapy interventions (Kiesler, 1966; Krumboltz, 1966), the search for a single, best intervention is never as fruitful as an intervention specifically designed to meet the needs of the individual. After discussing our three principles, we describe the who and what of faculty development. Faculty development strategies must address not only the needs of individual faculty members but also the broader concerns of a department. Can faculty be assisted in their revisions of curricula, their sharing of innovative teaching methods, or their decisions about how teaching, scholarship, and service are to be defined, assessed, and rewarded?

The remaining sections of this chapter are devoted to describing faculty development strategies suitable for a wide range of situations. Many strategies can be implemented by self-motivated individuals, by entire departments, by universities, or by the profession of psychology at large. To assist psychology departments in designing meaningful faculty development programs, a schematic model with illustrations is provided. Given the limited theoretical and empirical bases that exist for current faculty development initiatives, the concluding section of this chapter addresses the unique contributions psychologists can make by using psychological theory and psychometric strategies to establish these efforts on a more scientific foundation.

MEETING THE CHALLENGE: BARRIERS AND RESISTANCES

Faculty development needs have been articulated for several decades (Eble & McKeachie, 1985; Schuster, Wheeler, & Associates, 1990); it is only recently that writers have begun to make clear the institutional barriers and individual resistances that limit faculty development (Boyer, 1990; Carnegie Foundation for the Advancement of Teaching, 1989). Although any individual faculty member could produce a litany of such barriers and resistances, the following nine would probably appear on most faculty, department chairs', or deans' lists. Each of these nine, briefly described below, should be viewed as a challenge that can be met by a well-designed faculty development program.

Instructional Training

Probably the most prominent barrier to faculty development is that "the college teaching profession does not recognize the need for instructional training . . . the large majority of veteran faculty members, though able to produce transcripts documenting coursework in virtually every aspect of their content specialty, cannot point to one class that addressed instructional issues" (Weimer, 1990, p. 9). In their national survey, Lumsden, Grosslight, Loveland, and Williams (1988) found few psychology programs that provided more than a few hours of orientation to instruction.

New Student Demographics

Compounding the lack of exposure to instructional methods and technology for most faculty is their lack of knowledge about the rapidly changing characteristics of the students whom they now teach. Chapters 2, 3, and 6 in this book document those changes and their implications for understanding students, their advising needs, and curricular changes that faculty need to consider.

Teaching Versus Research Activity

One of the most resistant barriers for faculty in research-oriented institutions is the bifurcation of research/scholarship and teaching. Whether the issue is promotion and tenure, salary increases, or the focus of faculty development, tensions emerge around whether dichotomous or complementary roles are being considered. It is beyond the scope of this chapter to review the extensive literature regarding this issue. However, it is our position that, for effective teaching of undergraduates in psychology, all faculty need to give continual attention to their intellectual vitality through their own research and scholarship, through critical reading of contemporary writing on topics they teach, and through the pursuit of lifelong learning that they espouse for their students. Moreover, continual attention to the communication of psychological theory and research through teaching is needed.

Teaching Versus Research Rewards

Closely related to the bifurcation of teaching and research is the imbalance of incentives and rewards for teaching versus research. There is relatively meager institutional support for developing new teaching strategies compared with the support given for initiating new research endeavors. Almost every article or book we reviewed on college teaching lamented this imbalance.

Demands to Assess Teaching Outcomes

From the faculty member's viewpoint, the institution may be adding "insult to injury" when, in the current age of accountability, increased demands are made to assess outcomes of teaching. The demands come at a time when resources for improving teaching are sparse and decreasing. Despite psychologists' skills in assessment, the discipline has had a limited involvement in the measurement and evaluation of what we teach in psychology (Halpern, 1989). However, as chapter 1 in this book describes so well, demands for student and program assessment can be transformed into opportunities and resources for faculty development.

Assumptions About Teaching

Weimer (1990) described additional factors leading to faculty resistance. There are assumptions such as "If you know it, you can teach it," or "Good teachers are born, not made." Add to those assumptions the threats that come from changes in the status quo. With an ever-increasing number of faculty now staying in the same positions and teaching the same courses (Chait & Ford, 1982), there is an understandable comfort in and allegiance to what is familiar. Motivating faculty to change their usual styles, especially if they have "good teachers are born" views about teaching skills, constitutes a major challenge.

Reaching the Neediest Faculty

We need to develop the knowledge base to understand what kinds of faculty development programs to provide for whom and under what conditions if we are to reach broader segments of the faculty who teach psychology undergraduates. As Centra (1978) and Boice (1989) made clear, faculty development program evaluations often show that the faculty served are the ones least in need of help. Moreover, they found that the tendency of developers to rely primarily on faculty members' requests for developmental activities often resulted in offering little more than ways of doing less teaching.

Part-Time Instructors

As reductions in higher-education funding require increased use of part-time faculty, there is the question of what kinds of faculty development are needed for both new and experienced part-time faculty members. Part-time faculty are used extensively in 2-year and community colleges and in colleges and universities whenever the latter institutions experience increases in enrollment without concomitant staffing increases in full-time faculty. Departments rarely provide developmental resources for part-time faculty, although they may be the faculty who teach the largest number of undergraduates in lower-level and service-oriented courses.

Individual Versus Departmental Missions

Finally, there is the challenge of how faculty decide what kinds of developmental activities are needed to accomplish the mission of the department. Most programs focus on individual needs with little consideration of whether those needs are congruent with the mission of the whole department. If faculty development programs are to serve students indirectly and faculty members directly, then department-wide considerations need to become an integral part of faculty development planning. As Halpern and her colleagues suggest in chapter 1, faculty are well served to discuss their overall goals before initiating development projects in assessment, curricular reform, or faculty development.

THE SEARCH FOR MEANINGFULNESS IN FACULTY DEVELOPMENT: THREE PRINCIPLES

Is faculty development a euphemism for revitalizing "dead wood" (or at least reawakening dormant life)? Does faculty development mean anything more than a focus on teaching skills? These limited conceptions of faculty development are all too evident in the existing literature. If the barriers and resistances reviewed in the preceding section are to be overcome, then a reconceptualization of faculty development is needed. We want to reframe faculty development within the following three principles:

1. Faculty development is a lifelong process.
2. Faculty development should address all roles of the academic psychologist; these roles should be seen as complementary and integrative.
3. Faculty development is most effective in an academic culture characterized by the following values:
    a. Recognition and affirmation of individual differences

among faculty in the content of their intellectual inquiry and in their styles of teaching

b. Openness to issues of student diversity (e.g., content and strategies for teaching may vary according to diversity of the students being taught)

c. Encouragement of continual development of skills, building on strengths and expanding on expertise (e.g., support and resources regularly provided to enhance both traditional and innovative teaching)

d. Acknowledgment of a reward system that gives explicit recognition to teaching and service, as well as to research, in hiring, promotion, tenure, and merit pay

e. Acceptance of a view of undergraduate education as the intellectual foundation (i.e., more than a set of courses) for the development of both "informed citizens" and academic and professional psychologists.

The first principle affirms that faculty development is not a one-time event. Becoming an effective teacher begins during one's undergraduate years and continues throughout one's career. Although certain skills are common to all instruction (e.g., styles of communication, intellectual openness, and curiosity), other skills are tied to career stage and function as a level of experience, personal goals, and differential roles and responsibilities. For academics and their organizational environment, Chartrand and Camp (1991) reviewed the past 20 years of research on career development. Of particular note is a recent emphasis on organizational development and changes in individuals' career commitments. Menges (1985) provided a description of career-span faculty development. Belker (1985) described the education of mid-career professors. Baldwin (1984) described the changing developmental needs of an aging professoriate. Thus, faculty development as a lifelong process should become an inherent part of being a faculty member. It is the right and responsibility of every faculty member to be regularly engaged in faculty development activities. It is the right of students to have faculty committed to continued development. Students and faculty should expect that academic institutions will facilitate faculty development.

The second principle clarifies faculty development as comprehensive and integrative of the multiple roles of faculty (i.e., teachers, advisers, researchers, clinicians, and professional leaders). Faculty development should address all roles, and the teaching role is inextricably linked to all others. Teaching provides stimulation for new scholarship and new practice, which, in turn, stimulates learning by faculty who contribute to the teaching of such scholarship and practice.

The third principle acknowledges the environmental context and climate in which faculty development occurs. In fact, the absence of any of the five listed values may undermine both the processes and outcomes of faculty development strategies implemented in accordance with the first two principles. The literature on the need for teaching strategies to take into account diversity in our multicultural population and differences in students' cognitive styles continues to grow (Anderson, 1988). Just as important, faculty have a wide range of individual differences that need to be recognized, such as personal characteristics, individual skills, and stylistic preferences.

FACULTY DEVELOPMENT: THE WHO

Because faculty development is a lifelong process, some faculty development programs may need to be designed as early as the undergraduate years for some students aspiring to faculty careers. Undergraduate students, ideally, can gain the perspective that their formal education is only the beginning step in the life of an active, academic mind. Faculty role models engaged in new endeavors and taking on new challenges are as critical to prospective young academics as the content and methodology of the formal curriculum. Faculty development needs to become more systematic during graduate school and needs to include programs to meet the content and pedagogical needs of faculty. After graduate training, faculty development should include full-time faculty, part-time faculty, postdoctoral students, clinical affiliates, high school teachers, and academic administrators. Only when a full spectrum of psychologists are included can the benefits of the lifelong and encompassing components of these three principles be fully realized.

FACULTY DEVELOPMENT: THE WHAT

As mentioned earlier, the second principle states that faculty development is comprehensive and integrative, affecting all parts of the professional life of a faculty member. In planning a personal, departmental, or institutional program, there are 16 identifiable target areas (see Exhibit 1) addressed by the activities described in the later sections of this chapter.

Obviously, neither an individual nor an institutional faculty development program can focus on 16 areas simultaneously. An effective plan for each developmental stage (e.g., graduate student versus midcareer faculty) will focus on parts of each area through different programs. Programs may be relatively short but intensive or may include a sequence of activities over a full year. Almost all of these areas can be addressed initially by a 2- or 3-hour workshop; other topics need an entire semester.

For those areas directly concerned with teaching, the obvious one

EXHIBIT 1
Target Areas for Faculty Development Program Content

Content area	Use of more sophisticated
Instructional methods	technology
Assessment of learning outcomes	Self-assessment methods
Ability to respond to diverse students	Academic life coping skills
(demographics)	Time management
Ability to respond to diverse students	Career development
(cognitive backgrounds and styles)	Ethical standards
Advising	Service
Improved faculty relationships with	Ability to change the department
students	environment
Research and scholarship	

involves *content area* to be taught. This is the focus of most traditional faculty development programs such as sabbaticals. As described later in this chapter, summer institutes and brief workshops provide intensive exposures to new knowledge in content areas as well. Content area appears first in this list because, with rapidly increasing emphases on the other topics on this list, it could well be overlooked.

The most rapidly increasing focus of faculty development in the past two decades has been in the area of *instructional methods*. As noted above, most faculty have little or no preparation in pedagogy. Innovative teaching for active learning and critical thinking outcomes, described in detail in chapter 7 in this book, are just two of the many workshop topics that focus on teaching methods.

As elaborated in chapter 1 in this book, the call for increased accountability in undergraduate education also demands better understanding of how to assess learning outcomes. Probably all faculty can acknowledge shortcomings in their current examinations, but few may have readily available alternatives, at least given the number of students they are expected to teach and to assess. *Assessment of learning outcomes* will be a fruitful area for future attention.

The next two topics are related to the need for faculty to respond to the diversity of students now enrolled in college and university classrooms. This *ability to respond to diverse students* refers to the ability of faculty to respond to (a) students with diverse demographics such as ethnicity and age and (b) students with diverse cognitive backgrounds and styles. Although such cognitive differences may sometimes be significantly related to multicultural differences (Anderson, 1988) between and within cultural groups, students display a wide variety of learning styles and levels of prior learning. Since World War II, we have been educating students from increasingly heterogeneous educational backgrounds and are slowly learning that something more is needed to gain the interest and commitment of talented but nontraditionally prepared students (McGovern, Furumoto, Halpern, Kimble, & McKeachie, 1991).

The topic of *advising* and related needs for faculty development are described in chapter 2 in this book. There is a need for faculty development on how to relate to students within and outside of the classroom. Discrepancies between the tastes and values of old and young people have been lamented in literature since the days of the Greeks, but they may become increasingly important as the professoriate ages. Institutional retention studies almost always result in identifying the need for *improved faculty relationships with students*.

The remaining nine topics for faculty development are less related to teaching but are part of the multiple roles faculty face. These topics begin to focus on continual revitalization for keeping abreast of and producing *research and scholarship*. Rapidly changing technology makes faculty *use of more sophisticated technology* a high priority. Four additional areas are closely related to what might be seen as self-management of an academic career: *self-assessment methods, academic life coping skills, time management,* and *career development*. These areas are all too rare in faculty development programs. They are essential for achieving a lifelong, comprehensive, integrative process. Without training in these areas, many faculty will neither see the relevance of nor feel they have the time for faculty development activities.

Another topic for faculty development that has been ignored in the past is a heightened sensitivity to *ethical standards* for teaching and research relationships. Keith-Spiegel and Koocher (1985) and Tabachnick, Keith-Spiegel, and Pope (1991) noted the paucity of material on ethics in teaching at a time of increasing concern about specific teaching behaviors. These concerns became agenda items for the APA Ethics Committee, resulting in specific sections of the revised APA Code of Ethics on Teaching, Research, and Publishing ("Draft of APA Ethics Code Published," 1991). Dual relationships (including but not restricted to those involving intimacy), definitions and understanding of harassment, and what to do about impaired colleagues have all become critical issues for teachers of undergraduates.

Of topics listed thus far, *service* generates the fewest faculty development offerings despite many faculty having distinguished records of service contributions. In community colleges and state universities, where increasing amounts of service are expected, institutional support may be related to provision of service beyond traditional teaching.

Finally, there is the topic of the *ability to change the department environment*. Although troubled departments hire consultants to help them evaluate and redirect their programs, faculty are seldom schooled in how to become their own change agents. Ironically, psychology, with its studies of social and organizational dynamics, includes much of the knowledge from which effective change consultation derives. We propose that a faculty development program include explicit preparation for faculty to become their own change agents.

FACULTY DEVELOPMENT: A SCHEMATIC MODEL

Given the potential participants and content areas of faculty development, we found it useful to create a flowchart. Figure 1 presents a chart including the elements we propose for a comprehensive plan for faculty development at either the individual or organizational unit level.

Establish Program

Figure 1 is built on the assumption that faculty development is a lifelong and comprehensive process (Principles 1 and 2). Any approach to faculty development should be placed within this programmatic context, whether designed by an individual faculty member or by a department or college. If this context does not exist in a department, then the chairperson must take a leadership role, explaining the need and supporting the process. The program must also be established in the context of values and norms of the institution's academic culture (Principle 3). If the goals and the activities are too inconsistent with the institution's norms, neither participation nor change will occur.

Establish Vision/Mission

Within this programmatic context, the unit—whether individual, department, or institution—must establish a vision or mission. In its most general form, faculty development addresses all the roles of the psychologist (Principle 2). Yet at any one time, some visions or missions are more apparent than others. We use the terms vision and mission to connote two levels of a similar factor. Namely, a *vision* is a general set of ideas or direction, whereas a *mission* reflects a more in-depth statement including relevant goals, objectives, and strategies. Faculty initiating this process might best begin with a vision and work through the model once or twice, leaving for later iterations the development of a mission statement with all of its attendant parts.

Assess Needs

With a direction set, needs assessment must follow. One precaution based on the frustrating experiences of many faculty is to remember that there are many methods appropriate for assessing needs. It is often best to

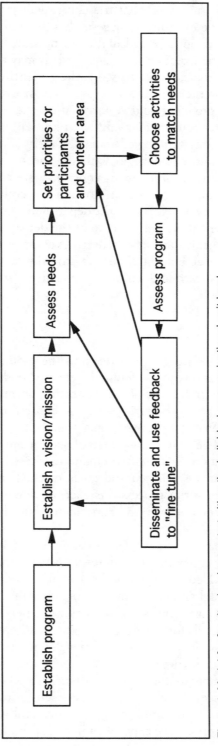

Figure 1: Model for faculty development at either the individual or organizational unit level.

begin with a simple survey of what the constituent group reports to be its needs. Our collective experience suggests that psychology faculties can get sidetracked by their sophisticated ability to measure needs, then wander aimlessly through the forest of data generated. It may be helpful for faculty to consider the 16 topics we discussed earlier. Identifying what the group considers critical is crucial to the success of any program.

What faculty groups should be targeted for the needs assessment? As we discussed earlier, there are many different kinds of faculty. For example, to incorporate an understanding of human diversity into the undergraduate curriculum, a program could begin with (a) the teaching assistants who meet with the majority of students in undergraduate courses, (b) part-time faculty who teach many students in community colleges but are distant from the central policy developers of the department, or (c) full-time college faculty who represent the teaching core of the department. It is important to recognize that faculty are at different developmental levels personally and professionally, (see Exhibit 2), each with priorities and needs that will affect motivation to learn and willingness to participate in particular kinds of programs.

Set Priorities

After identifying needs, priorities must be established as to (a) who shall participate in and (b) who should be covered under the program. The priorities chosen are indicators of the values and norms of the department. In setting priorities for both participants and content areas, it is important to plan their implementation over some time (e.g., an academic year or perhaps 2 years). The major advantage of such a programmatic approach to faculty development is that participants can establish a time line on which activities can be planned and goals reached, emphasizing the developmental nature of the process. As each planned phase is completed, the results will affect not only the participants but also the departmental culture.

In establishing an action plan for content, it is useful to organize priorities into three categories: (a) what is possible without added resources; (b) what requires added resources; and (c) what requires both resources and approval by some higher administrator or organization. Generating options in every category assures that some activities can begin immediately while resources and approvals for others are obtained. When setting priorities, it is also useful to consider the range of development and career levels of participants. Although there may be those who are more or less ready for change, it may be more useful to begin with programs oriented toward those most likely to change, thereby building a consensus for faculty growth and development. Finally, in establishing priorities and an action plan, it is important not to overlook the expertise among current faculty. For example,

EXHIBIT 2
Strategies for Developing the Scholar Across Career Levels

The Developing Scholar: Undergraduate Students

Take courses to develop written and oral communication skills
Participate in peer teaching and tutoring
Receive active mentoring
Receive instruction in teaching

The Apprentice: Graduate Students

Participate in teaching assistant and fellows training
Use master teachers as models and mentors
Take courses in teaching
Use resource centers

Basic Survival: Beginning Faculty Member

Participate in orientation programs on multiple roles of faculty
Master time management skills
Network through newsletters, discussions, and support groups
Analyze evaluation processes and academic culture

Expanding and Experimenting: Midcareer Faculty Member

Receive acknowledgment for contributions
Become a mentor and retain previous mentors
Use colleagues (national and local) to expand knowledge and skills
Participate in continuing education programs

Revitalization/Renewal: Senior Faculty Member

Develop new knowledge and skills
Network with colleagues at all levels
Use retired faculty as mentors
Take motivational workshops (for plateaued professors)

---

a department may not need to bring in a consultant on time management outcomes assessment when there are faculty members on campus specializing in these areas already.

Choose Activities

There are numerous ways to offer faculty development. Some activities are suited for groups, whereas others work better for individuals. Some activities require established and structured centers, whereas others need only the participating group's approval. In choosing which activities best meet identified needs, consider both the targeted people and the targeted topics. Given the previously discussed range of targets and topics, a department may want to work at several levels. Activities aimed at different levels might include, for example, a mentoring system for new faculty to build their "survival skills," a workshop for midlevel faculty ready to learn new computer techniques, and a series of travel subsidies to local or regional seminars for senior faculty who have drifted away from the excitement of seeking new knowledge.

Assess Program

Whatever path is chosen, it is essential to map progress and to use feedback not only for "in-flight" corrections, but to acknowledge the time and effort of the participants and to reward their contributions. Rewards (or lack thereof) indicate to the whole group (i.e., department, institution, and discipline) how much these activities are really valued. Reward structures are perhaps the major way in which cultures are transformed. In today's academic culture, activities in support of teaching can be an impetus toward recognizing teaching as an integral component of the compleat scholar.

Disseminate and Use Feedback

As with any dynamic process, feedback leads to a fresh look at the vision or mission underpinning the program. With the system in place, the chairperson may not need to be the one to take the lead in the next round. In fact, faculty ownership of the program is integral; the more their ownership is encouraged, the stronger the program will be. With each iteration of this model, the department is further on its way to developing the faculty and building a culture that nurtures effective teachers and scholars.

FACULTY DEVELOPMENT: THE HOW

Structures

The structures we describe are architectonic frameworks to assist faculty members in their development. That is, they facilitate, but are not essential to, implementing faculty development programs. They include committees, centers for instruction, and formalized external reviews of departmental programs. Structures may be at the institutional or departmental level, may be of relatively permanent or temporary duration, may be focused on the individual or the organization, or may vary on a number of other dimensions. They may have a variety of titles. For example, the Media Resources Center at Iowa State University provides services that include not only instruction in media, but also solutions to other problems related to the broader domain of college teaching (Albright, 1988).

Centers and Committees

A *center* is a physical place with a relatively permanent institutional commitment; a *committee* is a group of individuals engaging in a process.

Although centers can be born and die, they are of relatively long duration. Committees may also be long-standing, but because they are less likely to require a large commitment of resources, they probably have a shorter life. They may be created ad hoc at either the departmental or institutional level to fulfill a particular need. For example, computer technology holds potential for revolutionizing classroom instruction. This potential, however, will not be realized unless there is continuing education of faculty in advanced technology. In some academic settings, this training has become the province of existing centers. In other universities, special committees were formed to oversee and guide the process.

Centers and committees have a variety of organizational features. They may be entirely faculty owned. Alternatively, they may be centers staffed by full-time administrators whose professional affiliations are with other faculty developers. And, of course, their missions are varied. At large research-oriented universities, centers and committees serve constituencies of part-time or full-time teachers or potential teachers, ranging from undergraduates planning academic careers to late-career faculty members. At teaching-oriented institutions, the faculty is more likely to be full-time and permanent, but with diverse needs. Regardless of these differences, issues of course development, instructional improvement, and a climate in which faculty development is an expected role throughout one's career should be paramount and pervasive.

Although faculty development is frequently conceptualized as the development of individuals, committees and centers play a role in development at other levels. The constituencies might be the department (intradepartmental), the college (interdepartmental), the learned society or professional organization (e.g., APA), or the academic community (interuniversity). Although all of these constituencies may be able to address multiple areas pertinent to faculty development, each is uniquely positioned to address particular areas. However, no matter what level of action is in place, attention must be paid to ensuring faculty ownership of the goals, needed materials, processes, and outcomes.

The resources for centers and committees can be both tangible and intangible. Two intangible resources are credibility and leadership. Credibility is dependent on many features and is established over time. As a committee or center builds a record of success, it will accrue credibility. Leadership, as the social and industrial–organizational psychology literatures tell us, can manifest itself in diverse ways. It is most desirable that the center or committee's leadership provide a dynamic balance between generating some new initiatives and responding to identified needs.

Tangible resources are important also. A center or committee can provide those or can help identify people, places, or organizations that provide money, personnel, bibliographic materials, space, and so forth. A valuable role for a center or committee is in the creative use of resources.

When money is not available, it may be possible to find ways to achieve the same goals without money. For example, a "Center for Teaching Excellence" may need computers for distribution to faculty to assist them in their efforts to introduce computers into their classroom instruction. The university may not have the money to purchase the machines, but it may have the space to accommodate them. A computer company may be willing to invest hardware or software resources into such a broad-based, faculty-initiated project. Such collaboration may be of benefit to both parties. The change agent for this effort could be at any level: an individual faculty member, a faculty development committee, a center staff member, or the off-campus computer company. Regardless of origin, the faculty development committee or center will play a crucial role in bringing parties together for planning and implementation.

Organizations such as the APA can facilitate activities that vitalize the work of committees or centers. For example, the APA can set goals, models, or guidelines for the composition of faculty development programs in the discipline. Recognizing the importance of teaching by establishing an APA teaching fellows program or by sponsoring a summer institute on teaching would illustrate a commitment to undergraduate education. It would certainly be appropriate for the APA to build expertise in this area by linking with other professional organizations dedicated to issues of faculty development. Chapter 5 in this book provides ample suggestions on the rationale and methods for linkages. And finally, as a highly visible national organization, APA could support faculty development activities through public education; lobbying efforts; and other efforts designed to facilitate efforts by individuals, departments, and institutions.

Establishing a committee, a center, or any faculty development program involves long-range planning. Sorcinelli (1988) described valuable lessons that she learned in the evolution of a program at Indiana University at Bloomington. She cited the importance of faculty ownership and the encouragement of collegiality, the need for collaboration and a range of opportunities, the necessity of balancing individual with institutional needs, and the integration of teaching and research. Finally, she emphasized the critical role of structure, stating that the dean's creation of a permanent position for a director of faculty development was essential. This person develops the program, maintains and evaluates services, and assumes ultimate responsibility for the program's effectiveness.

Formal External Review

External review occurs at a departmental or institutional level for two primary purposes: quality control and program development. For psychology, external review of programs provides feedback that can stimulate faculty development efforts. For example, external reviewers have the credibility and objectivity needed to facilitate institutional change. They may be able to advocate for resources both at individual faculty levels and at departmental levels in a way that would be impossible for people within the institution. By bringing a different and presumably broader perspective to the process, periodic external review can be an important supplement to the continuing internal work of centers or committees. To meet the developmental framework advocated in Principle 1, it is critical to have external review teams return periodically to evaluate a program's progress toward agreed-on goals. Chapter 1 on assessment offers more specific recommendations for planning and implementing such a review.

Methods

There are many methods of providing instruction and assistance to teachers at all stages of development (preservice, beginning of a career, midcareer, and late career). This section describes six methods for achieving effective faculty development: courses, orientation programs, workshops and seminars, summer institutes, conferences, and retreats. As content- or skill-focused activities of specific duration, these methods require planning and resources. However, as the illustrations demonstrate, each can be adapted to a range of resources, efforts, and needs.

The specific formats adopted by a department or institution may vary, but the benefits of these activities may lie well beyond the content or skills learned. In the long run, the opportunities to gather and to learn in a cooperative, positive way reinforce collegiality and help build a climate of enthusiasm for faculty development. Sharing of ideas and resources and mutual assistance are, regrettably, not everyday activities in most departments because of fears of peer evaluation and because of time pressures. After a seminar presented to long-time faculty colleagues, some of the most frequent comments were "We ought to do this more often. I haven't talked to him so much in years!" and "I didn't know you did that in your class. That's a great idea!"

Courses

Some universities have instituted programs to train their graduate students in basic teaching techniques. Lumsden et al. (1988) identified a number of such programs. A format being adopted by some graduate programs in psychology is the required or recommended semester-long course in the teaching of psychology. In one such offering, students choose a specific course (e.g., introductory or social psychology) for development, select a faculty mentor who teaches that course, and spend the semester developing the course as well as deliberating issues related to academic careers.

Another type of graduate course in teaching addresses instructional goals and objectives, a variety of teaching and evaluation techniques, and audiovisual and computer technologies. Students practice lecture skills with videotaped feedback. Values and ethics are discussed, as are career-related issues. Traditional resources for such a course include *Teaching Tips* (McKeachie, 1986); issues of the Division 2 journal, *Teaching of Psychology;* the *Journal of Educational Psychology;* and an increasing number of books and articles related to developing instructional objectives and student evaluation (Gabelnick, MacGregor, Matthew, & Smith, 1990; Lucas, 1989; Weimer, 1990) (Jossey-Bass frequently publishes books on college teaching.) Departments offering such courses give preference for the best teaching assistantships to those who have completed the course. Teaching assistantships thus increase in value among the students, and individuals are more knowledgeable and prepared when they enter the classroom.

Orientation Programs

Just as students require familiarization with their new academic setting, new teachers can benefit from an orientation program. Many schools offer a brief introduction to personnel benefits and faculty dining halls; some also include a component on teaching and instructional resources. One orientation option is a week-long, presemester program offering training in writing syllabi, setting objectives, planning classroom activities, and leading a class. These workshops can be geared to all faculty levels: graduate assistants, new faculty members, or experienced faculty members wishing to take a refresher workshop. Larger institutions offer more extensive orientation programs for foreign students with teaching responsibilities, addressing American customs as well as language and other needs.

For an even more extensive orientation, community colleges and an increasing number of universities such as the University of Maryland and James Madison University have offered new faculty members a series of workshops during their first semester on topics such as critical thinking skills and active learning. An important result is that new faculty members meet peers from other disciplines and subsequently form a support system. The Lilly Foundation has funded such faculty development programs for faculty across disciplines.

An orientation program requiring fewer resources can pair a new instructor with a more experienced colleague. When new faculty members are hired, they are contacted by an experienced colleague well before arriving on campus. Ongoing communication is established before the new person's arrival, easing the transition into the new setting. Meetings are scheduled before the semester begins, at midsemester, and at the end of the semester. Issues related to teaching and faculty roles are discussed, and help is provided in whatever areas the new faculty member judges necessary.

Workshops and Seminars

Probably the most common method of reaching faculty members and other teachers are workshops and seminars presented in brief formats, typically lasting from 3 hours to 3 days. The 3-hour workshop format is accessible to a wide range of instructors, including those who teach part-time. It involves a relatively small investment of the participants' time with the potential for immediate applications. A variety of offerings can be targeted for the differing needs and levels of faculty experience. If resources are available, then outside experts can be hired to stimulate thinking in a new area. For example, an expert in writing across the curriculum or in multicultural issues may be hired to work with psychology faculty members to modify their courses.

However, when resources are limited, there are experienced faculty members on every campus who have expertise in particular skills or techniques of teaching. For example, a department could use a portion of its monthly meeting for teaching approaches to diversity, with a different faculty member being responsible for each chapter of Bronstein and Quina (1988).

Continuing education workshops on teaching are offered at national meetings of the APA and the American Association of Higher Education. One highly successful program has been a workshop sponsored by the APA's Division 35 on teaching the psychology of women. The workshop features at least two major authors of textbooks on the psychology of women, who discuss the approaches and techniques they use in their classes. Similar workshops have been offered on teaching introductory psychology and on integrating ethnic minority scholarship into courses.

Summer Institutes

The summer months offer an opportunity for in-depth developmental training. Participants at all levels of teaching psychology can come together to update course content in a changing field, learn new approaches to student diversity, and develop advanced teaching skills. An outcome beyond obtaining new knowledge is the opportunity to establish networks with those interested in teaching. Several examples illustrate the broad range of applicability of such summer programs.

The Society for Research in Child Development sponsored 2-week national summer institutes in integrating social policy into research and teaching. In another summer program partially funded by the National Science Foundation, high school psychology teachers gathered to have experts update their knowledge on a range of topics in psychology. The goal was for these high school teachers to prepare students for the College Board's Advanced Placement Examination in Psychology. Many colleges offer summer courses appealing to psychology teachers at all levels. Because schoolteachers often need credits for recertification, courses addressing effective ways to teach psychology could be provided as an optional way to earn credits.

Universities and departments are increasingly sponsoring their own summer institutes and workshops to address teaching needs. Such programs offer faculty the tremendous advantage of participation without leaving home and family. The institution's administration commitment, after providing staff and stipends, is minimal.

The University of Richmond invited members of its faculty from various disciplines to participate in a summer institute on "The Brain and Behavior." The material enriched their courses and strengthened interdisciplinary links across the campus. The University of Maryland and Virginia Commonwealth University offered summer institutes on transforming the curriculum to incorporate issues of gender and ethnicity, with stipends provided for participating faculty. Faculty from several campuses of the Maricopa Community College in Arizona used summer opportunities for faculty to develop interdisciplinary capstone courses on "ways of knowing," with psychologists' contributions as one element of the program. Psychology faculty may also find attractive offerings in the summer institutes provided by the National Science Foundation or the National Endowment for the Humanities.

Conferences

There are several conferences that address the teaching of psychology. Some of these are at the national level (e.g., National Institute on the Teaching of Psychology), and some are at the regional level (e.g., Eastern Conference sponsored by James Madison University and the Mid-American Conference sponsored by the University of Southern Indiana). All offer presentations by nationally known authors and teachers. A more modest option can be found in regional association meetings. The New England Psychological Association, for example, specifically focuses part of its annual meeting on undergraduate teaching, offering a low-cost, daylong experience that is accessible to faculty from the area.

Retreats

One of the strongest motivations for effective teaching is an institutional or departmental culture supportive of excellence in teaching. One method of stimulating such a climate is a retreat for all faculty or for a substantial group of them. Such retreats deal with major educational issues facing the institution or department, such as curriculum revision or program reorganization. Inevitably, as faculty discuss the goals of the curriculum or program, some may find that teaching methods are inextricably related to the solutions. When a department is able to afford them, outside consultants and off-campus sites are valuable. However, the same goals can be achieved with a competent facilitator from within the institution and in a comfortable, relaxed, local site such as a faculty center.

Techniques

There are several techniques for implementing faculty development that can be incorporated as part of the structures or methods just reviewed. These techniques also can be used independently. Six techniques deserve special mention and description: mentoring, teaching pairs, teaching circles, apprenticeship programs, peer teaching, and microteaching. All these techniques are elements of a long-term and ongoing development process. All are relevant to the range of involvement from individual faculty to a department to the national level. All are aimed at increasing the quality and quantity of faculty and student conversations about teaching.

Mentoring

There is a long tradition of mentoring in various professional fields, and, in general, the outcomes appear positive (Daloz, 1986). Mentoring plays an important role in faculty development. It is often seen as an integral part of the complete academic role. Mentoring is an affective professional relationship that has cognitive and evaluative components as well. Mentoring entails a sharing of skills, knowledge, and traits by someone who is emulated and who possesses pertinent wisdom and experience. Mentoring is a special, two-way relationship that reflects honest praise, protection, criticism, support, and direction, always with an underlying concern for personal and professional development. The relationship is one of temporary inequality in which the mentor's purpose is to provide a climate in which the protégé will flourish. Although a mentor may induct or orient, a good mentor listens closely and learns from the protégé while teaching. As a faculty member passes from one career stage to another, mentors may change or multiply. For example, a new faculty member may have different mentors for research opportunities, teaching enhancement, and political savvy.

Some individuals may be more skilled in developing mentor relationships. Recognition of these special skills needs to be acknowledged and valued by those in higher administration. Administrators also need to be alert to individuals who may have limited possibilities for finding a mentor; some potential protégés may be more isolated on the basis of gender or ethnic minority status and may need active assistance in finding suitable mentors.

A formal mentoring program could rather easily be developed by the APA's Division 2 to parallel a task force of Division 35 that acts as a mentor. In this program, mentors and protégés are sought through the

Division 35 newsletter. Interested faculty complete questionnaires that address areas of need (for protégés), expertise (for mentors), possibilities for meetings, and special interests. A coordinator oversees a match by first selecting several mentor files, sending these to the protégé for ranking, contacting the potential mentor for confirmation, and then coordinating the contact.

Several components are critical to a successful mentoring relationship: (a) it should be an emerging relationship, not a mandated one; (b) each relationship is individual and unique; (c) the protégé should have the right to select the mentor and should have the mechanisms for making an informed choice (e.g., interviews); (d) the mentor should have the right to turn down a possible protégé; and (e) periodic reviews of the program could allow an "escape" from an unsatisfactory relationship. It is especially important that clear expectations exist on both sides.

Informal mentoring relationships can also develop readily between a faculty member and either graduate or undergraduate students when the student finds common grounds with a faculty member to share academic interests, hone research skills, examine graduate programs, define life plans, or work to clarify goals. The mentor offers guidance, support, and appropriate criticism with the goal of developing a future colleague.

Teaching Pairs

In contrast and as a companion to the mentoring concept, teaching pairs usually consist of individuals at the same level and might be more appropriate for those who are at midcareer. The concept of this program is that people are paired by personal choice for classroom observation and comment, usually for one semester; then roles are reversed in the second semester. The New Jersey Master Faculty Program is a prototype for this activity. Pairs can be from the same department, different departments, or different institutions. However, because one of the long-term benefits of pairing is a sustained relationship, there is some argument for working with people within smaller units, such as the department or division.

Teaching Circles

Getting a group of people together to talk about teaching on a regular basis with no absolute agenda is the purpose of teaching circles. The effect of a teaching circle is that individuals may modify their individual practices and solve teaching problems while developing group cohesion and finding connections among colleagues. For instance, circles could be composed of all the faculty who teach introductory courses, faculty across disciplines who wish to discuss feminist theory, or administrators and faculty who interact about classroom innovation.

One possible offshoot of such circles is that a department organizes one day of activities on "teaching talk." Although regularly scheduled ongoing conversation provides a better forum for active commitment to teaching, any dedicated time is better than none. Techniques like teaching circles can be implemented with limited resources, although some small funds for food and drink help bring people together.

Apprenticeship Programs

To increase the number of college psychology instructors, apprenticeship programs for juniors and seniors could enable them to serve as teaching and research assistants to faculty mentors, so that these students have a more thorough taste of academic life. Students could be placed as interns in summer academic programs at major graduate institutions as has been done at all of the Big Ten schools and several smaller institutions such as Xavier University, University of Delaware, and Loyola University of Chicago. In those programs, minority students are apprenticed to a researcher with the specific objective of adding cultural diversity to the research program. The apprentice learns research skills, and the master researcher can gain the knowledge and means to be more inclusive in research inquiry.

Peer Teaching

Closely related to apprenticeship programs are variations of peer teaching models in which students have the opportunity to practice the skills of teaching and the opportunity to learn how much more one learns when one is expected to teach. Peer teaching can be done at every level from high school psychology courses to postgraduate courses.

Microteaching

Finally, there are a variety of more specific techniques that are available to improve teaching. *Microteaching*, that is, teaching a single unit of information for the purpose of receiving feedback from peers, is one of the most widely practiced and researched of these techniques (Aubertine, 1967; Authier & Gustafson, 1982). Microteaching can be a useful tool at all levels of experience, especially when trying out a new strategy or presenting new content.

Many faculty and graduate students interested in learning about their teaching have also benefited from observing a videotape of their teaching. A consultant assists with the analysis of the videotape of the lecture so that a richer perspective is gained. Important guidelines for providing constructive videotape feedback are found in the work of Kagan (1984) on interpersonal process recall. From a developmental viewpoint, it is recommended that the instructor retape the same lecture material at the next opportunity (e.g., next semester) to have visible proof of the outcomes of any changes attempted.

PSYCHOLOGISTS' POTENTIAL FOR UNIQUE CONTRIBUTIONS TO FACULTY DEVELOPMENT

Although much of this chapter focused on faculty development for psychologists, this brief section focuses on what psychologists can do for the faculty development of their own discipline and other disciplines. As Bardon (1979) and Boice (1989) have written, psychologists may be ideally suited for contributing to the development and evaluation of faculty development programs. The potential for contributions becomes evident if one reviews the basic premises and foci of psychology. The scientist–practitioner model in applied psychology has always ascribed to the concept that the best interventions are built on a combination of sound theory and empirical results. In the theoretical areas of developmental, social, learning, and organizational psychology, one finds the basic principles that underlie almost every area of faculty development discussed in this chapter. The relevance of psychometric theories and the value of methodological strategies for evaluating intervention programs are also potential major contributions to faculty development.

What has been missing is a more widely held and practiced view that faculty development is an appropriate target area for the application of psychological theory and empirical research. Just as there have been case and small-group studies of innovative teaching, as well as more traditional research programs, when there is interinstitutional teaching collaboration, so too can there be similar designs for the study of the development and evaluation of faculty development programs. What is needed is the leadership of national organizations, major colleges and universities, and faculty advocates to facilitate these studies. Some of the theoretical and empirical foundations for such studies may be found in a special issue of the *Journal of Educational Psychology* (1990, Volume 82, Number 2).

RECOMMENDATIONS

The issues, principles, and broad range of faculty development programs described in this chapter lead to a number of recommendations. The first two recommendations are fundamental to establishing faculty development as a significant endeavor that will make contributions not only to the well-being of faculty themselves but also to the effectiveness of their research, teaching, and service. These first two recommendations can be achieved only with the active support of national organizations or at least coalitions of psychologists.

Recommendation 1

Model guidelines for undergraduate education should be developed and disseminated to all psychology departments. These guidelines should include specific items on faculty development and should be based on the three principles described earlier:

1. Faculty development is a lifelong process.
2. Faculty development addresses all roles of a psychologist; these roles should be seen as complementary and integrative.
3. Faculty development is most effective in an academic culture that (a) recognizes the individuality of faculty members, (b) incorporates the diversity of cultural perspectives of students, (c) encourages continued development, (d) uses a reward system that recognizes the importance of teaching and service, and (e) sees undergraduate education as the foundation for the development of future psychologists.

The guidelines for undergraduate education in psychology should include a description of the following features that characterize effective programs:

- Clear expectations of continued development and maturation of teaching skills and course content throughout a faculty member's career
- Coordination and planning of faculty development programs from the beginning of each faculty member's career, with periodic reviews for feedback and adjustment of goals and objectives
- Ownership by the faculty of their own developmental process as evidenced by their initiation of programs, their involvement in the planning process, and their active participation in available activities
- Explicit designation of departmental and individual responsibilities for faculty development
- Sensitivity to individual faculty member needs and institutional resources
- Provision of incentives and rewards for faculty development
- Incorporation and dissemination of new resource information throughout the department
- Flexibility and dynamism built into the system of development so that programs are sensitive to changing faculty and institutional and broader environmental needs
- Faculty development viewed as a positive attribute contributing to appointment, promotion, tenure, and merit pay

Recommendation 2

Because there is a pressing need for new theoretical models and empirical evidence to expand an understanding of the effective processes and outcomes of faculty development, it is recommended that at the departmental, institutional, and professional discipline levels, explicit attention be given to (a) ensuring the role of faculty development in undergraduate education, (b) developing a theoretical base to guide further research, (c) expanding empirical knowledge about faculty development, and (d) seeking funds to support these activities.

A number of other relevant recommendations for the profession of psychology regarding faculty development appear in appendix D of this handbook. Finally, there are four recommendations that are specifically designed for implementation by psychology department chairs.

Recommendation 3

Faculty development programs need to be built into the annual calendar of departmental events and become line items in departmental budgets.

Recommendation 4

Evidence of faculty development activities on the part of an individual faculty member should become part of the portfolio of material submitted for appointment, promotion, tenure, and merit pay.

Recommendation 5

College and university departments should explore with their institutional development offices the possibilities of obtaining private contributions for the support of faculty development programs.

Recommendation 6

To become fully informed about the needs and opportunities for implementation of faculty development programs, chairs should become acquainted with the Professional and Organizational Network in Higher Education and other networking sources described in chapter 5.

CONCLUSION

The quality of both present and future undergraduate education in psychology can be greatly enhanced by attention to faculty development.

As described in this chapter, there are numerous challenges to overcome in establishing and maintaining the diverse kinds of faculty development programs that are required to meet the varying needs of beginning versus experienced faculty and part-time versus full-time faculty. However, over the past 10 years, there has been an increasing number of new programs and models that can be adapted to meet these diverse needs. An individual faculty member, a department, or an entire college or university can create effective faculty development plans using many of the structures, methods, and techniques described in this chapter. Finally, for psychologists, the unique opportunity in faculty development is the application of psychological theories and empirical strategies to expand our understanding of the most effective means for achieving the desired outcomes of faculty development.

REFERENCES

Albright, M. J. (1988). Media resources center. In G. R. Erickson (Ed.), *A collection of brief descriptions of faculty, instructional, and organizational development programs in higher education* (p. 8). Lincoln, NE: Professional & Organizational Development in Higher Education.

Anderson, J. A. (1988). Cognitive styles and multicultural populations. *Journal of Teacher Education, 39,* 2–9.

Aubertine, H. (1967). The use of microteaching in training supervising teachers. *High School Journal, 51,* 99–106.

Authier, J., & Gustafson, K. (1982). Microtraining: Focusing on specific skills. In E. K. Marshall, P. D. Kurtz, & Associates (Eds.), *Interpersonal helping skills* (pp. 93–130). San Francisco: Jossey-Bass.

Baldwin, R. G. (1984). The changing developmental needs of an aging professorate. In C. M. N. Mehotra (Ed.), *Teaching and aging* (pp. 45–56). San Francisco: Jossey-Bass.

Bardon, J. (1979). Educational development as school psychology. *Professional Psychology, 10,* 224–233.

Belker, J. S. (1985). The education of mid-career professors: Is it continuing? *College Teaching, 33,* 68–71.

Boice, R. (1989). Psychologists as faculty developers. *Professional Psychology: Research and Practice, 20,* 97–104.

Boyer, E. L. (1987). *College: The undergraduate experience in America.* New York: Harper & Row.

Boyer, E. L. (1990). *Scholarship reconsidered: Priorities of the professoriate.* Princeton, NJ: Carnegie Foundation for the Advancement of Teaching.

Bronstein, P. A., & Quina, K. (Eds.). (1988). *Teaching a psychology of people: Resources for gender and sociocultural awareness.* Washington, DC: American Psychological Association.

Carnegie Foundation for the Advancement of Teaching. (1989). *The condition of the professorate: Attitudes and trends, 1989.* Princeton, NJ: Author.

Centra, J. A. (1978). Types of faculty development programs. *Journal of Higher Education, 49,* 151–152.

Chait, R., & Ford, A. (1982). *Beyond traditional tenure.* San Francisco: Jossey-Bass.

Chartrand, J. M., & Camp, C. C. (1991). Advances in the measurement of career development constructs: A 20-year review. *Journal of Vocational Behavior, 39,* 1–39.

Daloz, L. A. (1986). *Effective teaching and mentoring: Realizing the transformational power of adult knowing experiences.* San Francisco: Jossey-Bass.

Draft of APA ethics code published. (1991, June). *APA Monitor,* pp. 30–35.

Eble, K. E., & McKeachie, W. J. (1985). *Improving undergraduate education through faculty development.* San Francisco: Jossey-Bass.

Gabelnick, F., MacGregor, J., Matthew, R. S., & Smith, B. L. (1990). *Learning communities: Creating connections among students, faculty, and disciplines.* San Francisco: Jossey-Bass.

Halpern, D. (1989). Assessing student outcomes for psychology majors. *Teaching of Psychology, 15,* 181–185.

Kagan, N. (1984). Interpersonal process recall: Basic methods and recent research. In D. Larson (Ed.), *Teaching psychological skills: Models for giving psychology away* (pp. 229–244). Monterey, CA: Brooks/Cole.

Keith-Spiegel, P., & Koocher, G. P. (1985). *Ethics in psychology.* New York: Random House.

Kiesler, D. J. (1966). Some myths of psychotherapy research and the search for a paradigm. *Psychological Bulletin, 65,* 110–136.

Krumboltz, J. (Ed.). (1966). *Revolution in counseling.* Boston: Houghton Mifflin.

Lucas, A. F. (Ed.). (1989). *The department chairperson's role in enhancing college teaching.* San Francisco: Jossey-Bass.

Lumsden, E. A., Grosslight, J. H., Loveland, E. H., & Williams, J. E. (1988). Preparation of graduate students as classroom teachers and supervisors in applied and research settings. *Teaching of Psychology, 15,* 5–9.

McGovern, T. V., Furumoto, L., Halpern, D. F., Kimble, G. A., & McKeachie, W. J. (1991). Liberal education, study in depth, and the arts and sciences major—Psychology. *American Psychologists, 46,* 598–605.

McKeachie, W. J. (1986). *Teaching tips* (8th ed.). Lexington, MA: Heath.

Menges, R. J. (1985). Career-span faculty development. *College Teaching, 33,* 181–184.

Sanford, N. (1967). *When colleges fail.* San Francisco: Jossey-Bass.

Schuster, J. H., Wheeler, D. W., & Associates. (1990). *Enhancing faculty careers: Strategies for development and renewal.* San Francisco: Jossey-Bass.

Sorcinelli, M. D. (1988). Encouraging excellence: Long-range planning for faculty development. In E. C. Wadsworth (Ed.), *A handbook for new practitioners* (pp. 27–34). Lincoln, NE: Professional & Organizational Development in Higher Education.

Tabachnick, B. G., Keith-Spiegel, P., & Pope, K. S. (1991). Ethics of teaching: Beliefs and behaviors of psychologists as educators. *American Psychologist, 46,* 506–515.

Weimer, M. (1990). *Improving college teaching.* San Francisco: Jossey-Bass.

5

FROM ISOLATION TO COMMUNITY: INCREASING COMMUNICATION AND COLLEGIALITY AMONG PSYCHOLOGY TEACHERS

WAYNE WEITEN, in collaboration with STEPHEN F. DAVIS, JANE A. JEGERSKI, RICHARD A. KASSCHAU, K. BATES MANDEL, and CAROLE WADE

Colleges and universities have been viewed traditionally as communities devoted to learning, and academic disciplines such as psychology have been characterized as communities of scholars. According to a variety of sources, the collegiality in these overlapping academic communities appears to be eroding. A recent Carnegie report commented on the fragmentation in higher education today:

> The administrative structure has grown more and more complex, the disciplines have become increasingly divided, and academic departments are frequently disconnected from one another. The curriculum is fragmented, and the educational experience of students frequently lacks coherence. Many are now asking: How can the work of the nation's colleges and universities become more intellectually coherent? (Boyer, 1990, p. 2)

This fragmentation has contributed to the intellectual isolation reported by many faculty. Feelings of professional isolation may be magnified by disparities that exist between faculty members' graduate training experiences and their subsequent professorial work (Geertz, 1983). In graduate school, earnest students are immersed in vital social networks on the basis of shared experiences, interests, and goals. These rewarding, collegial experiences are seldom replicated when new professors embark on teaching careers. Gabelnick, MacGregor, Matthews, and Smith (1990) commented on this contrast effect:

> Many colleges cannot hope to duplicate the specific, disciplinary richness of graduate education nor does graduate training equip most faculty to step comfortably outside disciplinary boundaries. The result is often a kind of intellectual isolation. . . . The lack of local opportunities for community building, professional development, and experimentation may increase the sense of disengagement on the part of the faculty. The infinite variety of colleges and universities further increases the lack of communication and dissipates any sense of shared goals among institutions. Ironically, both within and among colleges, faculty lack opportunities to learn from one another at precisely the moment when increasing communication among diverse faculty has become a necessity. (p. 7)

Today, enhanced communication and collegiality among faculty is a necessity because the professoriate is currently going through a host of difficult transitions. Schuster (1990b) described trends that are reshaping the academic landscape. He asserted that faculty have witnessed a deterioration in their working conditions, clerical support, funding for travel and sabbaticals, compensation, mobility, and morale. He also asserted that faculty are buffeted by shifting values and conflicting expectations and pressures:

> Tight budgets, the demands for efficiency and accountability, and shifting campus values result in faculty members sometimes being asked to juggle a bewildering variety of roles: to deepen their own research and scholarship, to enliven their teaching, to restore cohesion and integrity to a curriculum pulled asunder by the twin forces of rampant specialization and student fixation on careerism, to link instruction more closely to industry's needs for a trained workforce, to expand access and fashion curricular remediation for marginally prepared students while at the very same time imposing more rigorous academic standards. (Schuster, 1990b, pp. 8–9)

Our charge was to identify solutions that might enhance communication and esprit de corps among psychology teachers across all institutional levels. We were guided by the following assumptions:

1. Psychology teachers need to continue learning to continue to teach effectively.

2. Psychology teachers need to maintain the lively spirit of inquiry that is crucial to intellectual vitality.

3. Students' educational experiences are enhanced when they are taught by faculty who continue learning and who maintain a healthy spirit of inquiry.

4. Psychology teachers' efforts to realize these goals can be facilitated by communication and professional collaboration with colleagues from diverse specialties and from different levels of instruction.

Our committee attended to the following questions:

1. What are the potential benefits of increased communication and collegiality among psychology teachers?

2. What are the principal problems that limit networking and the sense of community among psychology teachers and that promote feelings of professional isolation?

3. What types of professional development opportunities should be created or expanded to increase communication among psychology teachers at all levels of instruction?

4. What can be done to improve the dissemination of information about available professional development opportunities for psychology teachers? What can be done to increase the number and diversity of faculty who avail themselves of these opportunities?

5. What can individual faculty, departments, and educational institutions do to foster increased communication and collegiality among psychology teachers? How can the APA, Division 2 of the APA (Teaching of Psychology), regional associations, or other interested organizations contribute to this effort?

We will address these questions in this chapter. Three themes will be apparent in our analyses and suggestions. First, we believe that the problems, issues, tasks, and challenges facing psychology teachers at different levels of instruction, from high school to graduate school, are more similar than is widely believed. Faculty across all levels can learn from each other. Hence, we discuss approaches to improving vertical integration (interaction across levels of instruction) as well as horizontal integration (interaction within a particular level of instruction). Second, we believe that programs to increase communication and collegiality among psychology teachers should be organized both from the bottom up and the top down. Initiatives should be launched at the grass-roots level by individual faculty and departments, as well as by the APA, Division 2 of the APA, and other national and regional organizations. Third, we believe that different approaches to increasing communication and collegiality are appropriate to different situations. We propose a range of possible strategies, including local consortia, academic alliances, institutes, workshops, faculty exchange programs, student research conferences, regional teaching conferences, teaching programs at national and regional conventions, computer bulletin boards, and direct-mail campaigns. In addition, we spotlight case histories of specific linkage efforts made by teachers, departments, and organizations across the country.

BENEFITS OF INCREASED COMMUNICATION AND COLLEGIALITY

Why should we be concerned about enhancing the community among psychology teachers? What are the potential benefits of increased communication and collegiality among psychology faculty? Before considering various approaches to forming linkages or networks among psychology teachers, we will examine the potential benefits that result from fostering communication and collaboration among psychology teachers. Given the paucity of relevant research on this topic, our analysis must be based more on intuition, logic, and experience than on empirical data. In our discussions, four potential benefits emerged: the enhancement of the professional lives of faculty members, improved motivation among psychology teachers, a better educational experience for students, and more successful institutional programs.

Professional Benefits for Faculty

Interactions with colleagues in psychology can improve participants' teaching skills. Although effective teaching techniques are acquired through learning (Eble & McKeachie, 1985), graduate training places little emphasis on the acquisition of teaching skills. As Schuster (1990a, p. 69) noted, "There is little evidence that graduate schools (or for that matter, individual graduate programs—that is, academic departments) normally see the preparation of professors as one of their more important roles." The topic of teaching did not even merit an index entry in the volume summarizing the proceedings of the 1986 APA-sponsored National Conference on Graduate Education in Psychology (Bickman & Ellis, 1990). It is apparent that psychology teachers are left to their own devices in their efforts to improve their teaching. Thus, programs that bring faculty together to exchange ideas about teaching methods foster the development of more effective teaching techniques and the application of collective wisdom to pedagogical and other classroom problems.

Professional interactions provide opportunities for psychology teachers to upgrade and update their knowledge of the research literature in psychology. The volume of published research in psychology has increased dramatically in recent decades, making it difficult for faculty to stay abreast of progress in the field. As Mahoney (1987, pp. 165–166) noted, "The modern scientist sometimes feels overwhelmed by the size and growth of the technical literature relevant to his or her work." This problem is acute for faculty who teach introductory survey courses because they have to keep up with developments in so many different areas of psychology. Programs that facilitate the sharing of knowledge help faculty stay current in areas related to their teaching responsibilities.

As the United States grows more culturally diverse and more cognizant of its diversity, psychologists must increase their sensitivity to multicultural issues (Bronstein & Quina, 1988; Myers, 1990). The importance of this goal as it relates to undergraduate education is discussed at length in chapter 3 of this book. Increased communication and collegiality may help psychology teachers to realize this goal. Opportunities to meet and to learn from colleagues of different racial, ethnic, or cultural backgrounds can broaden teachers' perspectives, improve their understanding of diversity, and enhance their ability to relate to students.

Faculty linkages across institutions provide opportunities to set up cooperative networks for sharing media, library, and computer resources. High schools, community colleges, small liberal arts colleges, comprehensive universities, and research-oriented universities have different strengths and resources. Given typical budgetary constraints in education, it makes sense for institutions in a particular geographic area to share their resources (Maeroff, 1983).

Faculty linkages across institutions can expand the number of subjects available for participation in research projects. Psychology departments in research-oriented universities depend heavily on subject pools, although doubts have been raised about the ethics and external validity of this practice (Miller, 1981). These concerns may be partially remedied by soliciting volunteer subjects from psychology classes in other types of institutions in a particular area. Access to high school and community college populations can increase the heterogeneity of researchers' samples and the number of "naive" subjects available.

Increased networking among faculty from different schools promotes the development of collaborative research projects (Osberg & Raulin, 1989). In many psychology departments, it is difficult to find colleagues who share specific research interests. This problem is acute in smaller departments in which every faculty member may have a different area of expertise.

A sense of community gives psychology teachers new avenues to address increasing political tensions in academia. Freedom of expression, sexual harassment, racial tension, economic retrenchment, and public accountability are sources of concern on many campuses (Carnegie Foundation for the Advancement of Teaching, 1990). Working in concert, faculty may exert more influence over how their institutions deal with these important problems.

Motivational Benefits for Faculty

As discussed in chapter 4 of this book and elsewhere (Boice, 1984), faculty development activities maintain the professoriate's intellectual vitality. Valuable interactions with colleagues foster renewed commitment to teaching and improved morale. Sharing common experiences and giving and receiving ideas regarding common educational problems can be emotionally rewarding. Collegial interactions may inspire faculty to aspire to new levels of excellence in teaching and scholarship.

Gathering with other psychology faculty affords the opportunity to reaffirm one's identity as a psychology teacher. This benefit is crucial for faculty who, because of their work in small departments in rural areas, may be more prone to suffer from professional isolation.

According to Centra (1985, p. 155), "If maintaining faculty vitality is a critical goal for institutions, then faculty burnout is a clear symptom that we are falling short of achieving that goal." Increased communication and collegiality may help prevent professional burnout (Kahill, 1986). Meeting with other teachers stimulates feelings of reinvigoration, of enthusiasm for teaching, and of renewed eagerness to invest in one's professional duties. The intellectual, motivational, and emotional support of fellow teachers offers a first line of defense against burnout.

Educational Benefits for Students

Schuster (1990b, p. 3) asserted that "the quality of higher education and the ability of colleges and universities to perform their respective missions is [sic] inextricably linked to the quality and commitment of the faculty." Insofar as increased communication and collegiality help psychology teachers to become more caring, competent, and committed, they should also result in improved educational experiences for students.

Increased communication and collegiality among psychology teachers lead to opportunities for students to participate in research activities, attend professional meetings, and present papers and projects. Increased opportunities of these sorts are a natural consequence of networking and collaboration among faculty members.

The strengthening of professional relationships among faculty at different institutions in a local area can result in increased opportunities for students to use facilities not ordinarily available to them. For example, high school and community college students gain access to laboratories and equipment available at neighboring senior institutions.

In chapter 2 of this book, Ware and associates make an eloquent case for the need to improve academic advising for students. This objective is yet another goal that can benefit from increased communication and collegiality among psychology teachers at all institutional levels. As faculty across institutions talk to each other more, they are likely to improve their knowledge of their students' options for further education and training. Increased faculty interactions across institutional levels can lead to improved opportunities for students to progress to the next stage of their education because of contacts made through mentors who network with one another.

Benefits for Institutions

Many colleges and universities are concerned about declining enrollments and their ability to recruit competent students (Riesman, 1980). For many postsecondary schools, enhanced interinstitutional relations among faculty offer a significant advantage in recruiting students. Increased contacts with faculty and students from feeder schools should make students at these schools better informed about opportunities at higher-level institutions.

Improved communication and collegiality among psychology teachers can result in better educational experiences and better advising for students. These outcomes should be viewed as institutional benefits. In an era of increasing criticism about the quality of undergraduate education in the United States (Bloom, 1987; D'Souza, 1991; Hirsch, 1987; Sykes, 1988), such benefits are particularly important.

Bemoaning the lack of interinstitutional dialogue across levels of instruction, Hodgkinson (1985, p. 1) pointed out that "the only people who see these institutions (nursery schools through postgraduate institutions) as a system are the students." This problem can be remedied in part by increased vertical integration among psychology teachers so that students can develop more coherent plans of study.

In recent years, we have witnessed increased discussion of curricular models in psychology (McGovern, Furumoto, Halpern, Kimble, & McKeachie, 1991). Vertical and horizontal linkages among faculty foster coherence in curriculum as professional development activities bring faculty together to discuss duplication or overlap between courses, gaps in prerequisite courses, and other curricular matters.

In summary, enhanced communication and collegiality among faculty at all levels of instruction promote a host of benefits for faculty, students, and institutions. Unfortunately, there are many obstacles to overcome. We examine these barriers in the next section.

BARRIERS TO INCREASING COMMUNICATION AND COLLEGIALITY

In this section, we describe factors that contribute to the lack of community among psychologists. We discuss barriers that exist in higher education in general and in the discipline of psychology in particular and salient problems at specific levels of instruction—in university departments, community colleges, and high schools.

Barriers in the Educational System

Reduced Funding for Higher Education

Financial crises exist at many colleges and universities (Anderson & Meyerson, 1990). Budgets are being scrutinized and administrators are attempting to prune any nonessential expenditures. These financial constraints make it difficult for colleges to underwrite faculty travel, participation in professional development activities, and new programs designed to increase interinstitutional communication.

Low Morale Among Faculty

Our era appears to be one of discontent among professors in virtually every discipline. In their in-depth examination of the professoriate, Bowen and Schuster (1986) reported that job satisfaction declined noticeably in the 1970s and 1980s. They described an aging, immobile, and frequently demoralized faculty who reported feeling underpaid and underappreciated. Boyer (1987) reported that nearly half of the nation's professors said they would leave academia if they had the opportunity to do so. Job dissatisfaction undermines job commitment, making many faculty apathetic about pursuing opportunities for more linkages with their colleagues. Some faculty exhibit a "factory mentality" that makes them unwilling to engage in activities for which they are not directly compensated.

Decline in Student Commitment to Education

Job commitment among professors is influenced by the educational commitment that they find among their students, and this commitment seems to be declining. In one recent survey, only 23% of students reported spending more than 15 hours per week on study outside of class (Carnegie Foundation for the Advancement of Teaching, 1990). In another survey, 55% of faculty respondents endorsed the statement "Most undergraduates at my institution only do enough to get by" (Carnegie Foundation for the Advancement of Teaching, 1989). Many of today's students have full-time jobs and parental responsibilities, and they must juggle divided commitments. Unfortunately, apathy among students breeds apathy among faculty.

Heavy Teaching Loads

Heavy teaching loads that absorb enormous amounts of time and energy can be found at all levels of instruction. According to a National Education Association survey, 51% of faculty at 4-year colleges and 54% of faculty at 2-year colleges indicated that reductions are needed in their teaching loads (Bowen & Schuster, 1986). Teaching responsibilities place severe constraints on the time available for professional development and networking.

Negative Attitudes About Collaboration With Faculty at Lower Levels in the Educational System

There is a "pecking order" among educational institutions (Maeroff, 1983). Efforts to increase vertical integration among faculty working at different levels of instruction are met with various attitudinal barriers related to this pecking order. Many faculty in research universities express doubts about the value of collaborating with colleagues in baccalaureate institutions. Faculty in baccalaureate schools may feel that they have little in common with community college faculty, who in turn may have limited interest in collaborating with high school faculty.

Barriers in the Discipline of Psychology

The Clinical–Academic Schism

Antagonism between the scientific and applied arms of psychology has mounted in the past decade or two (Spence, 1990). Psychologists find themselves with two national organizations that purport to represent them: the APA and the recently formed American Psychological Society (APS). This rift, symptomatic of the waning sense of community among academic psychologists, will probably make it more difficult to organize and execute programs designed to increase collegiality among psychology teachers.

Increased Specialization in Psychology

Graduate education in psychology has become increasingly specialized, with fewer and fewer generalists being trained. Two or three decades ago, psychologists had more exposure to subfields outside their own (Altman, 1990). This increased fragmentation of the field of psychology can undermine the sense of kinship and mutuality among academic psychologists.

Decline in Professional Identification With Psychology

As the field of psychology diversifies, more and more people trained in psychology will identify with disciplines such as neuroscience, cognitive science, or behavioral medicine (Altman, 1990; Scott, 1991). Although there are benefits to interdisciplinary affiliations, divided loyalties are antagonistic to the goal of increasing the sense of community and collegiality among academic psychologists.

Lack of Information About Innovative Approaches to Increasing Collegiality

Some disciplines (e.g., education) have done an excellent job of compiling and disseminating information about innovative approaches to increasing collaboration and community among faculty (Wilbur & Lambert, 1991). Unfortunately, psychology has fallen short in this regard. The vast majority of psychology faculty are uninformed about the range of options available for enhancing communication and collegiality.

Barriers in University Departments

Inadequate Emphasis on Teaching

A recent Carnegie Foundation report (Boyer, 1990) asserted that teaching is undervalued in most research universities and in many ostensibly teaching-oriented universities as well. Boyer (1990, p. xi) noted, "It's futile to talk about improving the quality of teaching if, in the end, faculty are not given recognition for the time they spend with students." In institutions where excellence in the classroom has negligible impact on one's career progress and where outstanding teaching is neither championed nor recognized, faculty have little incentive for seeking linkages with other faculty to improve their teaching.

Pressure to Publish

In many universities, psychology faculty are required to participate in the highly competitive "publish or perish" sweepstakes, and their publication record is the prime determinant of whether they earn tenure or promotion (Mahoney, 1987). This pressure exists even at many universities that traditionally emphasize teaching (Bowen & Schuster, 1986). Moreover, most departments expect faculty to publish particular types of articles and books—on basic research and theory—and place little value on publications related to teaching. Hence, even when they feel motivated to do so, academic psychologists have little if any time left to pursue collaborative activities with other faculty to enhance their teaching.

Increased Class Size

Large classes with hundreds of students are the norm at many universities (Carnegie Foundation for the Advancement of Teaching, 1986). Although active learning strategies can be adapted to large classes, the rule of thumb is simple: The larger the class, the more likely the traditional lecture format will dominate (Benjamin, 1991). By placing limits on instructors' pedagogical options, large classes discourage interest in educational innovations gleaned from interactions with one's colleagues.

Barriers in Community Colleges

Multidisciplinary Organizational Arrangements

Community college psychology faculty are affiliated often with multidisciplinary social or behavioral science divisions rather than with psychology departments. This organizational arrangement may undermine faculty members' identification with the field of psychology and their motivation to gather with other psychology teachers.

Second-Class Status in Professional Organizations

In his profile of community college faculty, Seidman (1985, p. 11) noted that "there is a nagging, pervasive sense . . . that being at a community college means being near the bottom of the higher education totem pole." Although the ratio is changing, the majority of community college faculty do not hold a doctoral degree (Seidman, 1985). This may deter community college faculty from seeking membership in professional organizations, some of which require additional review for nondoctoral members or relegate them to associate status.

Dependence on Part-Time Faculty

Community colleges depend on part-time faculty far more than universities do (Price & Goldman, 1981). These part-time faculty tend to be on the fringes of institutional communication networks. In comparison to full-time faculty, they are less likely to participate in professional development activities or get involved in professional organizations.

Barriers in High Schools

Professional Isolation

In many high schools and even high school districts, there is only one person who teaches psychology. Unlike members of mathematics, science, or English departments, high school psychology teachers have relatively few opportunities for interacting with colleagues to expand and enhance their professional networks.

Lack of Discretionary Professional Time

Unlike their counterparts in higher education, high school teachers have little flexibility in scheduling classes, and it is much more difficult for them to attend professional meetings. They almost universally teach a large number of classes with very limited preparation time (Boyer, 1983). These realities constrain their ability to engage in collaborative work with other psychology teachers.

Lack of Identification With the Discipline

High school psychology teachers come from diverse educational backgrounds. Many have limited training in psychology, and the majority teach other subjects besides psychology (Griggs, Jackson, & Meyer, 1989). Hence, high school psychology teachers probably do not identify strongly with the field of psychology and are reluctant to pursue opportunities for interaction with colleagues in psychology.

Perceptions of Disinterest Among College Faculty

Many high school psychology teachers express the belief that college-level educators are not concerned about the teaching of psychology at the high school level. This perception of disinterest, which may not be entirely inaccurate, discourages them from seeking interactions with college faculty.

In summary, a host of obstacles stand in the way of increased communication and collegiality among psychology teachers. Fortunately, such obstacles are not insurmountable. In the next section, we consider strategies to enhance communication and collaboration among psychology faculty at all levels of instruction.

APPROACHES TO INCREASING COMMUNICATION AND COLLEGIALITY

What types of professional development opportunities should be created to increase communication and collegiality among psychology teachers at all levels of instruction? Our suggestions are not radically new ideas. Most strategies that we endorse have some history of sporadic or local use in psychology, but they have not been used to their fullest potential.

In outlining approaches to increasing communication and esprit de corps among psychology teachers, we will describe case histories of specific programs. These cases will clarify the form that programs may take, illustrate the problems that are likely to be encountered, and highlight the benefits to be realized. We begin by focusing on local strategies and then examine regional and national programs.

Local Consortia

Local consortia of psychology departments can be developed to facilitate horizontal linkages among instructors in a geographical area. These organizations may receive external sponsorship or funding but need not do so. They offer a way for psychology teachers to become acquainted and meet on a periodic basis. Consortia are a mechanism for setting up cooperative enterprises such as teacher exchanges, guest lectures, student research conferences, collaborative research projects, sharing of subject pools, sharing of transportation expenses to regional meetings, and so forth. Both of the case histories described here involve collections of colleges that have banded together; the same strategies could be applied at the departmental level.

Case History: The Associated Colleges of the Chicago Area

The Associated Colleges of the Chicago Area (ACCA) was started in 1966 to establish a cooperative arrangement between the member colleges and universities and Argonne National Laboratory, a major federal science research and development institution located in the suburbs of Chicago. ACCA's primary objective was to promote college-level education and training in biology, chemistry, computer science, mathematics, and physics by opening the facilities of Argonne National Laboratory to students and faculty at 15 educational institutions, most of them 4-year liberal arts colleges. In 1985, a division for psychology teachers was added. In 1992, approximately 65 psychologists at member schools were eligible to participate, and on average, 20–25 of these psychologists attended ACCA meetings.

Each college belonging to the consortium contributes $600 annually to ACCA's budget. Each division can apply for funds for various activities on a yearly basis and use Argonne's extensive laboratory facilities and meeting rooms. The psychology division has compiled a membership directory that lists each faculty member's affiliation, courses taught, research interest, special teaching interests, and committees served on. Faculty meet over a gratis dinner three times a year to share new resources and solutions to problems in teaching undergraduates. Visiting lectureships are open to faculty within the consortium. The lecturer gives a colloquium at a host school and is taken to dinner by host faculty who share common academic interests. These informal interactions set the stage for subsequent professional collaborations. Participating faculty report an intellectual excitement from their experiences in ACCA and establish invaluable professional contacts.

One of the major activities of ACCA is an annual student conference that gives faculty-sponsored students an opportunity to present papers describing research, literature reviews, and field experiences. All papers submitted are accepted, so that as many students as possible can have the experience of giving a professional presentation. Audiences are small, allowing for maximum interaction. The role of faculty as mentors for student participants contributes to their own professional development in many ways. Moreover, this event brings faculty together on both a social and a professional level. Currently, about 40–50% of the ACCA Annual Student Conference consists of presentations by psychology students. For more information about ACCA, contact the Psychology Department, Elmhurst College, Elmhurst, IL 60126.

Case History: North Texas Community/Junior College Consortium

The North Texas Community/Junior College Consortium (NTC/JCC) was established in 1989 in cooperation with the University of North Texas. It initially consisted of 16 two-year institutions in the area, and it is continuing to grow. Faculty from all disciplines belong to the consortium, which is funded by membership fees paid by the participating college districts. The consortium is devoted to improving undergraduate education at its member institutions through a variety of staff development and research projects. The consortium focuses on low-cost, high-yield approaches to improving teaching, emphasizing better use of resources through interinstitutional collaboration.

The NTC/JCC sponsors professional development opportunities for faculty—including a fall conference, spring workshops, and a summer retreat—that would not be feasible for a single college district. The consortium has also sponsored research on developmental education, classroom assessment, honors programs, and core curricula. For more information, contact the NTC/JCC at P.O. Box 13857, Denton, TX 76203.

Informal Local Interinstitutional Meetings

Local interinstitutional interactions can be initiated even when formal organizational structures for such exchange do not exist. All that is required is for a host department to invite faculty from other nearby schools to attend a meeting to discuss issues of mutual concern. Usually the focus is on a particular issue, such as facilitating transfer from feeder 2-year colleges to a local 4-year college or university. These meetings may be one-time events, or they may be arranged on a periodic basis. They may bring together faculty from similar types of schools (such as all the liberal arts colleges in an area) or from diverse institutions (such as a university and the community colleges located in the vicinity).

Case History: Informational Exchanges at the College of DuPage

At the College of DuPage, a community college in the Chicago area, the school's Psi Beta chapter annually invites psychology faculty and Psi Chi students from neighboring 4-year institutions to discuss the transfer process. A typical meeting begins with an open forum in which the faculty and students from the 4-year schools talk about their departments and field questions from students at the 2-year institution. Afterward, the visiting Psi Chi students from the 4-year schools meet with the Psi Beta students from the host school and the visiting faculty meet with the host faculty. Faculty meetings involve discussions of curricular goals, teaching strategies, transfer parameters, and advising issues. For more information about this program, contact the Psychology Department, College of DuPage, Glen Ellyn, IL 60137.

Case History: The Speaker Series at Houston Community College

Approximately six times per year, a speaker from one of the universities in the Houston area lectures to the psychology faculty at Houston Community College (HCC). Occasionally, the speaker is drawn from a government agency or from private practice. The invited speakers meet with the full-time faculty for about 1½ hours, giving a seminar in their area of expertise. This forum provides the psychology faculty at HCC an opportunity to enhance their knowledge and to make contacts with faculty at 4-year schools in the vicinity. It also permits faculty from the 4-year schools to become more familiar with the programs, teachers, and educational issues at HCC. For more information on this program, contact the Psychology Department, Houston Community College, 22 Waugh Drive, Box 7849, Houston, TX 77270.

Case History: Indianapolis-Area Colleges

The psychology departments at five Indianapolis-area colleges and universities have been engaging in informal cooperation since 1983 when Drew Appleby, the department chair at Marian College, invited the chairpersons from the other four schools to a lunch at Marian. This informal alliance of departments (Butler University, Indiana University–Purdue University at Indianapolis, Franklin College, the University of Indianapolis, and Marian College) has been instrumental in the initiation of a jobs in psychology conference and in the continuation of a student research conference originally begun in Evansville, Indiana.

At the Central Indiana Jobs in Psychology Conference, alumni from the departments make presentations on their career progress to current students. They discuss how the attitudes and skills that they acquired as psychology majors helped them in their careers. Since 1990, the departments have taken turns hosting the Mid-America Undergraduate Psychology Research Conference, which was formerly hosted by the University of Southern Indiana in Evansville. Although the conference was highly successful in Evansville, the move to a larger metropolitan area has led to a substantial increase in attendance and participation. For more information about this informal consortium, contact the Psychology Department, Marian College, 3200 Cold Spring Road, Indianapolis, IN 46222.

Academic Alliances

In recent years, the American Association for Higher Education (AAHE) has taken an active role in promoting the concept of academic alliances. As defined by the AAHE, *academic alliances* are local collaborative groups of college and high school (and sometimes middle school) teachers from the same discipline or interdisciplinary area of study who meet regularly to discuss issues of mutual concern. Modeled after county medical societies and bar associations, these alliances are intended to remedy academic isolation and to enrich the intellectual lives of their members. Unlike summer institutes or workshops, academic alliances create ongoing, long-term professional relationships within a permanent structure.

Most of the early academic alliances were formed in the disciplines of foreign language and literature. Gradually, however, the concept caught on in other disciplines and local alliances emerged in biology, chemistry, English, geography, geology, history, mathematics, multicultural studies, physics, political science, and women's studies. Typically, an academic alliance consists of 12–65 faculty who hold monthly or bimonthly meetings or scholarly forums. At these meetings, members share resource materials; explore new technologies; review textbooks, journals, and abstracts; work on common administrative and curricular problems; and sponsor scholarly activities for their students. The activities are determined by the members of the local organization.

Academic alliances are structured in a democratic, not hierarchical, manner. They are guided by a steering committee whose composition represents the local membership. According to the AAHE, a key ingredient in the success of academic alliances has been their continuing effort to ensure a sense of equality among members from different levels of instruction. Postsecondary faculty should not dominate the organization in either number or perceived importance.

The AAHE's National Project in Support of Academic Alliances was established to contribute to the vitality of existing alliances, to foster the development of new alliances, to broaden the advocacy base for academic alliances, and to encourage more participation from underrepresented groups. As part of this project, the AAHE attempts to maintain a list of existing local alliances. As of May 1990, there were no academic alliances for psychology teachers. Academic alliances have enormous potential for enriching linkages and professional development among psychology teachers, and we strongly urge the formation of such groups.

To assist in the formation of academic alliances, there are various possible external sources of start-up funds, including the National Science

Foundation, the Woodrow Wilson National Fellowship Foundation, and the AAHE's National Project in Support of Academic Alliances. Although some external funding is available, there is nothing to prevent college and school personnel in an area from forming their own self-funded, grass-roots alliance. According to the AAHE, one appealing aspect of academic alliances is that they can operate on very limited financial resources.

Case History: The Milwaukee-Area Academic Alliance in English

The Milwaukee-Area Academic Alliance in English was founded in 1988. As described in Wilbur and Lambert (1991), it serves all high school and college English teachers in the six-country area surrounding Milwaukee. Its purpose is not to bring in outside experts for in-service programs, but rather to provide a forum for members to share ideas about teaching English. There are three meetings per year, held on Saturdays, that are attended by 35–40 faculty. At a typical meeting, there are two or three short presentations by individual members, followed by general or small-group discussion. The alliance has no membership dues. Minimal expenses are absorbed by the College of Letters and Sciences at the University of Wisconsin–Milwaukee.

The benefits to members of this alliance, summarized in Wilbur and Lambert (1991), include the following:

> It provides a natural way to effect smooth school–college articulation, since college teachers and high school teachers both learn what goes on in the others' classrooms. In addition, and very important, it provides a major psychological benefit to teachers who feel overworked, underappreciated, and isolated in their own schools. Evaluations of the meetings held so far are overwhelmingly positive. Teachers report coming away from the meetings with a sense of renewal and professionalism. (p. 126)

For more information on academic alliances, contact the AAHE, One DuPont Circle, Suite 360, Washington, DC 20036.

Institutes and Workshops for High School Faculty

Institutes for high school teachers that are hosted by colleges and universities are excellent ways for high school teachers to be informed about current developments in psychology. These workshops facilitate vertical linkages between high school and college faculty. Institutes for high school faculty have been offered in a variety of time formats, ranging from 1 day to 6 weeks. Some are advertised nationally, but most concentrate on drawing high school faculty from a limited geographic area. Many are scheduled for summer, when high school teachers have more discretionary time.

Case Study: The Summer Institute for High School Teachers at Texas A&M University

In 1991, the psychology department at Texas A&M University sponsored a month-long summer institute for 32 high school psychology teachers. Funded by a grant of $125,000 from the National Science Foundation, the workshop helped teachers to prepare to offer honors psychology courses that would approximate the college-level introductory course. Part of the impetus for the program was the development of the College Board's Advanced Placement Examination in Psychology, which commenced in 1992. The expenses of the 32 participants, who came from 13 states, were paid by the National Science Foundation grant. The attendees were experienced teachers with extensive backgrounds in psychology.

The institute, directed by Ludy T. Benjamin, Jr., focused on the organization and content of the college introductory course, with an emphasis on experiments, demonstrations, active learning exercises, and the use of microcomputers in the classroom. During the institute, participants had the opportunity to interact with 25 faculty from institutions in seven states. This highly successful program is a superb example of how college psychology departments can reach out to high school psychology teachers. For more information, contact the Psychology Department, Texas A&M University, College Station, TX 77843.

Case Study: Annual Workshops Sponsored by the North Carolina Association of Psychology Teachers

In 1988, the North Carolina Center for the Advancement of Teaching (NCCAT), an independent unit of the University of North Carolina, sponsored a special seminar for high school psychology teachers in North Carolina. The seminar included three components: (a) lectures intended to upgrade participants' content knowledge; (b) discussions of educational issues; and (c) sessions to share instructional materials, demonstrations, and active learning exercises. At the end of the week, the participants devised plans for a continuing statewide organization—the North Carolina Association of Psychology Teachers (NCAPT)—to sponsor future meetings and a newsletter.

Since 1988, NCAPT has sponsored annual workshops that have followed the format of the original seminar. Each workshop is attended by 45–60 high school faculty. This program has received extensive support from NCCAT and the Western Carolina University Psychology Department, but it has proved difficult to get support from other universities in North Carolina. Nonetheless, these annual workshops continue to provide high school psychology teachers in North Carolina with excellent opportunities for professional development. For more information about this program, contact the Psychology Department, Western Carolina University, Cullowhee, NC 28723.

Cooperative Educational or Administrative Ventures

There are many ways in which colleges and departments can cooperate to deliver educational programs or to coordinate administrative decision making. Team teaching by faculty from different institutions is one such option. Another option involves inviting faculty from one school to serve on a committee at another school. These cooperative ventures are undertaken usually by schools that are located in close proximity, but this is not always the case. For instance, Marietta College in Ohio and Stillman College in Alabama have explored ways to offer cooperative educational programs to their students in psychology and engineering.

Case History: Interinstitutional Team Teaching Sponsored by the Association of American Colleges

The Association of American Colleges (AAC) has promoted an innovative approach to course delivery. The program grew out of the association's efforts to improve matriculation between 2-year and 4-year colleges. Funded by a Ford Foundation grant, this program brings community college students to a 4-year school for a series of interdisciplinary courses during the summer. The students' tuition, room, and board are paid for by the grant. The teaching team for each course consists of a faculty member from the 2-year school and another from the 4-year school; the two are from different disciplines. The 5-week courses for this summer program are designed by the two participating faculties.

Faculty from Vassar College and LaGuardia Community College collaborated on their first venture of this sort. The model has been used by five additional pairs of 2-year and 4-year colleges. These cooperative ventures have been beneficial to the participating schools in a variety of ways. Faculty at the 4-year and 2-year schools learn more about the normative expectations at each other's school. The interdisciplinary collaboration is an enriching intellectual challenge for the participating faculty members. The program also builds a bridge between the two institutions that can facilitate smoother student transfers from the 2-year to the 4-year school. For more information about this program, contact the Association of American Colleges, 1818 R Street, NW, Washington, DC 20029.

Case History: Committee Input From Community Colleges at San Jose State University

To improve linkages with its feeder schools, the San Jose State University (SJSU) Psychology Department arranges for faculty from nearby community colleges to sit on its undergraduate curriculum committee. The two community college psychology teachers selected for the committee are drawn from 14 two-year schools in the vicinity of SJSU. Although the teachers are nonvoting members of the committee, they have ample opportunity for input regarding the department's curricular decisions. Once a year, SJSU hosts a luncheon for the psychology faculty representatives of all 14 community colleges.

These interactions have permitted SJSU and some of the community colleges to design special curricular programs for transfer students that are variations on SJSU's normal requirements for the psychology major. These programs take advantage of the unique strengths of the psychology department at each school and smooth the transfer process for students. From SJSU's perspective, these cooperative agreements help the psychology department to attract better students. Moreover, these agreements are beneficial to both SJSU and the community colleges in that they facilitate coherent educational programs for their transfer students. For more information, contact the Psychology Department, San Jose State University, Washington Square, San Jose, CA 95192.

Faculty Exchanges

Another way to enhance interinstitutional communication is to encourage psychology departments to use personnel resources from other types of institutions. Teachers can be invited to give one or a series of guest lectures, or teachers can arrange to exchange classes for one or more sessions both within and across institutions. Another option is to bring teachers from different levels of instruction to teach courses for a semester or a year. Some high school psychology teachers have a master's degree in psychology and are qualified to teach in 2-year colleges. Community colleges could make a concerted effort to hire more of these faculty to teach courses on a part-time basis. Similarly, some community college faculty have a doctoral degree and are qualified to teach in 4-year schools. These faculty could probably be used more frequently as adjunct faculty and as sabbatical replacements. Many community colleges could easily replace the faculty member and would view the 1-year appointment as a worthwhile professional development opportunity. Universities could obtain experienced teachers for whom the 1-year appointment would not be a problem.

It would also be helpful if university departments would extend visiting scholar privileges to community college faculty on sabbatical. The psychology department at the University of California, Los Angeles (UCLA) has sponsored community college psychology faculty as visiting scholars. The faculty were given an office, library privileges, access to laboratories and computers, and opportunities to participate in seminars and to collaborate on research. The visiting faculty enjoyed intellectually stimulating sabbaticals and networked with UCLA faculty.

University teachers could also enrich their professional development by teaching part-time at community colleges or by spending sabbaticals teaching in 2-year colleges. These experiences would expose them to more diverse student populations and provide enriching teaching challenges. Of course, traditional faculty exchanges within the same level of instruction are another option. These exchanges already occur at the community college level, through the Community College Exchange Program, and we encourage their extension to other levels of psychology instruction. Finally, some institutions may want to develop international faculty exchange programs, such as the one at the University of North Carolina, which we will profile in a case history.

Case History: The Teaching Apprentice Program at Florida State University

Grosslight (1979) reported on a successful program at Florida State University in which the psychology department placed its graduate students in teaching positions at community colleges in the region. The carefully selected students, with a minimum of a master's degree, were assigned to the community colleges for a full semester. They assumed the roles and duties of regular college faculty to allow for a thorough immersion in teaching responsibilities. While on these apprenticeships, the students were paid as faculty members by the community college. Their teaching efforts were supervised to some extent by senior faculty at the community college and by Florida State University faculty who made site visits.

According to Grosslight (1979), this program strengthens the participants' teaching skills and career preparation. Furthermore, faculty at Florida State University witnessed a dramatic improvement in the quality of preparation and presentation in subsequent courses, seminars, and colloquia by the returning apprentices. Obviously, this program also allows the community colleges to tap into a diverse pool of highly trained subject-area specialists. The principal problems noted by Grosslight are that the program breaks the continuity of the graduate students' training and that some returning apprentices have difficulty reassuming the usual graduate student role after being a professor for a semester.

Case History: International Exchanges at the University of North Carolina

Calhoun, Selby, and Macfarlane (1980) reported on a program that arranges faculty exchanges between the psychology departments at the University of North Carolina and the University of Stirling in Scotland. The program was developed in response to declining sabbatical funding. The direct, one-for-one exchange of faculty allows participants to take a sabbatical in another country at a minimal cost to their institutions. The program provides cultural enrichment for the exchanged faculty members and a periodic infusion of new viewpoints and ideas into the participating departments. There are complexities in executing such a program, including financial considerations, housing, transportation, calendar compatibility, and teaching responsibilities, but these usually can be handled through careful planning. For more information on this program, consult Calhoun, Selby, and Macfarlane (1980) and Calhoun, Toner, and Selby (1980).

Regional Student Research Conferences

Activities that bring students together can also bring teachers together and provide opportunities for increased communication and collegiality. Regional student research conferences appear to be particularly valuable in network building (Smith, 1988), although locally organized science fairs and research competitions may yield similar benefits.

Undergraduate psychology research conferences have been described in detail by Carsrud, Palladino, Tanke, Aubrecht, and Huber (1984). They have a rich history; the oldest currently active conference was founded more than 40 years ago. These conferences follow a similar format, with faculty members serving as moderators for panels of 15-minute student presentations on related topics. The presentations typically report on empirical research, although some conferences also accept theoretical papers. All the conferences have a featured speaker and a group meal or general social event.

Student research conferences enrich students' educational experiences in a variety of ways (Carsrud, 1975; Carsrud et al., 1984). They enhance students' knowledge, research skills, communication skills, and self-confidence. Although these conferences were designed with students' needs in mind, they also can yield valuable benefits for the faculty in attendance. Carsrud et al. (1984) noted that many faculty participants "exchange ideas about the problems and pressures of teaching, thus creating a valuable support network to work cooperatively toward improving undergraduate education in the behavioral sciences" (p. 144).

Case History: The Arkansas Symposium for Psychology Students

The Arkansas Symposium for Psychology Students was founded in 1985 by Randolph Smith (Ouachita Baptist University) and Ralph McKenna (Hendrix College). The conference draws participants from four states and has grown from 20 papers a year to more than 100. The 2-day conference always begins on a Friday afternoon with concurrent paper sessions, followed by an invited speaker and a banquet Friday evening, and additional paper sessions on Saturday. The student presentations include literature reviews as well as empirical reports. On the basis of his experience at these conferences, Smith (1988) asserted that "the student research conference may be as valuable for the faculty members involved as it is for the students. In particular, the student conference can serve to decrease the professional isolation that seems to affect many psychology faculty who teach at small colleges" (p. 1). For more information, contact the Psychology Department, Hendrix College, Conway, AR 72032, and the Psychology Department, Ouachita Baptist University, Arkadelphia, AR 71923.

Regional Psychological Association Conventions

Regional psychological association meetings hold special potential for facilitating communication among psychology teachers at all levels because, although they have traditionally drawn university-based research psychologists, they are affordable and convenient for community college and high school faculty as well. In recent years, thanks in significant part to the work of the Council of Teachers of Undergraduate Psychology (CTUP), the program time allocated to teaching topics has increased noticeably at some of the regional conventions. These programs have included presented papers, symposia, and teaching activity exchanges.

Although much has been accomplished, much more can still be done. We believe that the Education Directorate of the APA should sponsor a Distinguished Teacher Lecture Series at regional conventions analogous to the Distinguished Lecturer Series currently sponsored by the Science Directorate of the APA. We also urge the regional associations to become more proactive in sponsoring teaching-related presentations and in soliciting the participation of high school and community college teachers.

Case History: CTUP Sessions at Southwestern Psychological Association (SWPA) and Midwestern Psychological Association (MPA) Conferences

CTUP is a national organization whose objective is to enhance education in psychology. This organization was founded (as the Council of Undergraduate Departments) in 1968. Membership is open to anyone interested in the teaching of undergraduate psychology. There is an inexpensive, one-time, lifetime membership fee. CTUP's primary activity is to sponsor programs and workshops on teaching at the seven regional psychology conventions held annually in the United States. These programs are organized by CTUP regional coordinators who issue annual calls for papers.

In recent years, CTUP has been particularly successful in setting up teaching programs at the annual conventions of the SWPA and the MPA.

The SWPA has offered teaching activities exchange poster sessions that have been well received (Matthews & Jacobs, 1986). At the MPA annual conventions, the "creative classroom" sessions have combined actual teaching demonstrations with teaching activity posters. CTUP has also sponsored an array of symposia at the MPA conventions on topics such as ethics, advising, and specific courses. For more information on CTUP programs at regional meetings, contact the Psychology Department, Alverno College, Milwaukee, WI 53215.

Case History: The Growth of Teaching-Related Programs at the Western Psychological Association (WPA) Conference

Since 1986, the WPA has taken a leadership role in providing teachers from all levels with up-to-date scholarly information and mechanisms for exchanging ideas and methods. In addition, the WPA has increased student involvement in its annual convention.

Like the MPA and the SWPA, the WPA has incorporated CTUP sessions into its annual meeting, but its commitment to teaching-related programs has gone far beyond this concession. In 1988, WPA Executive Officer Robert A. Hicks encouraged the formation of a WPA Committee for Undergraduate Teachers and Students (CUTS). The committee, chaired by Lisa Gray-Shellberg, was asked to coordinate the efforts of Psi Chi, CTUP, and other constituencies concerned with undergraduate education and to plan a stimulating program for faculty and students from diverse institutions.

At the 1988 and 1989 WPA meetings, CUTS sponsored roundtable discussions to learn how the WPA could meet the needs of teachers and students more effectively. Through the efforts of CUTS, the CTUP teaching activities exchange was made a formal part of the WPA's call for papers. In addition, at its annual conference the WPA now provides a hospitality suite, hosted by Psi Chi and Psi Beta members, where teachers from all institutional levels and their students can interact on an informal basis. The WPA initiated a student membership category that encourages students to become fully and independently involved in the association (they do not need to be sponsored by a faculty member) and developed a *Student Guide to the WPA Convention.* As the participation of teachers and students in the WPA has grown, the portion of the convention program devoted to their interests has increased. As a result, the association has added a co-ordinator for teaching and student activities to its executive board.

A variety of trends suggest that the WPA's efforts to reach out to teachers and students have been beneficial for these groups and for the association. For example, Psi Chi participation has grown by more than 50%, support for a student scholarship program has increased more than 10-fold, membership and convention participation among community college faculty is expanding steadily, and teachers from all levels are increasingly using the WPA as a focal point for their professional activities. For more information, write WPA, Psychology Department, San Jose State University, San Jose, CA 95192.

Regional Teaching Conferences

A highly successful context for teaching exchanges and networking is the regional teaching conference. Currently, there are five such conferences. The Mid-America Conference for Teachers of Psychology was founded in 1984 by Joseph Palladino at the University of Southern Indiana. The four other conferences are: the Annual Conference for the Teaching of Psychology, founded in 1986 at the State University of New York at Farmingdale; the Eastern Conference for the Teaching of Psychology, founded in 1988 at James Madison University; the Southeastern Conference on the Teaching of Psychology, founded in 1989 at Kennesaw State College; and the Southwestern Conference for the Teaching of Psychology, founded in 1991 at Texas Wesleyan University.

Regional teaching conferences have special advantages. First, attendance is diverse, but the size of the group usually is held to a maximum of about 125, a size that is manageable and that permits people to get to know each other. Second, the conferences are devoted solely to teaching, so in only 2 days a great deal of information is exchanged. Third, the conferences are inexpensive, so many teachers who might not be able to afford more distant or costly meetings can attend. All poster submissions are accepted. The atmosphere at these conferences is friendly and encouraging. We strongly recommend the continued development of new regional conferences, particularly in areas where none are presently available. Guidelines for establishing regional teaching conferences can be found in Palladino (1988).

Case History: The Mid-America Conference for Teachers of Psychology

The primary model for the regional teaching conference is the one established by the Mid-America Conference for Teachers of Psychology (Davis & Smith, 1992). Palladino (1988) noted that this conference was begun in 1984 in response to the lack of teaching-related professional development sessions at the regional conventions. The goals of the conference are: (a) to provide faculty with an opportunity to exchange ideas about undergraduate courses, (b) to discuss issues such as curriculum and the use of computers in teaching, (c) to share ideas for stimulating students' interest in psychology, and (d) to assist in the development of a supportive network of psychology teachers.

The conference is scheduled for a Friday and Saturday in October. The program includes three major addresses to all attendees and 12–15 sessions on specific topics that run concurrently (two or three at a time). Thus, participants can select the concurrent sessions that are most relevant to their interests and tailor the meeting to their special needs. The presentations typically fall into four types. One type focuses on a particular course (or group of closely related courses) and the presenter discusses course goals, organization, syllabi, textbooks, and teaching methods. A second type focuses on what faculty can do to help students or to deal with classroom problems. For example, sessions have been devoted to cheating in the classroom, study skills, and time management. Roundtable panel discussions on the curriculum, the introductory course, and other courses represent a third type of session. A fourth type is designed to assist faculty in other aspects of their professional development (e.g., writing, breaking into publishing).

Attendance at the Mid-America Conference has increased steadily since its inception, and participants' evaluations indicate that the conference meets their needs. In particular, the conference provides invaluable opportunities for networking. As Palladino (1988) noted, "The end-of-conference evaluations have indicated that perhaps the most desirable element of the conference has been the opportunity to talk about teaching and learning with others who teach similar courses" (p. 173). For more information, contact the Psychology Department, University of Southern Indiana, 8600 University Boulevard, Evansville, IN 47712.

National Teaching Conferences

National conferences devoted to the teaching of psychology constitute another way to bring teachers together to interact and acquire new knowledge. Like regional teaching conferences, national conferences are usually sponsored by a college or university. The format features invited presentations by outstanding teachers and may also include submitted paper presentations and poster sessions. National conferences tend to be larger and more expensive than regional conferences, but they typically can attract more prominent speakers, thus allowing attendees to interact with more nationally recognized authorities in the field of psychology.

Case History: The National Institute for the Teaching of Psychology

One model of a national conference is the National Institute for the Teaching of Psychology, which is cosponsored by the University of Illinois and the University of South Florida and is held annually in Florida. This conference, which is designed for psychology teachers at all levels of instruction, extends over 4 days and draws as many as 300 attendees. Funded in part by grants from textbook publishers, it offers general sessions of interest to all participants, alternating with concurrent sessions covering specialty topics. The program includes poster sessions, which allow for presentations by the conference participants; problem-solving sessions that focus on specific courses; discussion sessions that provide informal opportunities for exchanging ideas; and publishers' roundtables, which allow participants to meet directly with representatives of companies that publish psychology textbooks. Other features include a teaching materials "swap meet," a computer software fair, a display of textbooks, and a variety of social activities.

The 20–25 faculty for the institute change each year. Collectively, they constitute a "who's who" of outstanding psychology teachers, prominent researchers, and leading textbook authors. The presentation formats are diversified, and there is ample opportunity for interchange among the participants and the faculty. The institute provides an extremely positive experience for networking. Many faculty who rarely make it to the APA or regional conventions attend the institute, which provides for intensive interaction. For more information, contact the Psychology Department, University of Illinois, 603 East Daniel Street, Champaign, IL 61820.

Case History: National Conference on Instructional Applications of Critical Thinking

Another national conference model involves a specific issue of interest to teachers at many different levels. In 1991, the Miami-Dade Community College District organized a National Conference on Instructional Applications of Critical Thinking. Teachers from the elementary school level through the university level attend and hear invited speakers and paper presentations. The emphasis is on practical classroom applications. For more information, contact Miami-Dade Community College, Wolfson Campus, 300 N.E. Second Avenue, Miami, FL 33132.

DISSEMINATING INFORMATION ABOUT OPPORTUNITIES FOR NETWORKING AND PROFESSIONAL DEVELOPMENT

Opportunities for increased networking among psychology teachers will accomplish little unless individual faculty are aware of these opportunities and motivated to pursue them. In this section, we discuss our fourth set of questions: (a) What can be done to improve the dissemination of information about available professional development opportunities for psychology teachers? and (b) What can be done to increase the number and diversity of faculty who avail themselves of these opportunities?

Newsletters for Teachers of Psychology

Currently there are two newsletters for psychology teachers, one published by the APA and one by CTUP. *Psychology Teacher Network* is an APA publication, published five times a year, that contains articles contributed by high school and college faculty on topics of interest to their peers. Included are briefings on substantive issues in psychology as bases for lectures; book and audiovisual material reviews; activities and demonstrations for use in the classroom; news relevant to psychology teachers; and descriptions of innovative academic programs. The publication is sent as a benefit of affiliation to high school teacher affiliates, and upon request, to APA members. Nonmembers and nonaffiliates may subscribe. Since 1989, CTUP has published a biannual newsletter entitled *Significant Difference*. It contains brief articles and extensive announcements about meetings for psychology teachers and upcoming CTUP programs at regional conventions.

These periodicals have filled important needs not addressed by other publications. However, the specialized newsletters published by the APA may perpetuate the impression among 4-year college and university faculty that their own concerns are quite different from those of high school and community college faculty. Therefore, we see a need for a general APA newsletter addressed to teachers at all levels of instruction.

This newsletter, which would presumably replace the two existing APA newsletters, could be an effective vehicle by which vertical linkages might be increased. For instance, joint authorship of articles by people teaching at different levels would promote collegiality and demonstrate shared concerns. The same goals could also be accomplished by single-author articles from people at different types of institutions. We recommend a bimonthly publication that could include timely information on teaching events. There also would be material of interest to all psychology teachers, such as book, video, and software reviews; topical research updates; teaching demonstrations; discussions of issues such as critical thinking and ethnic diversity; and news of teaching awards and student competitions. There is no reason why a general newsletter could not include separate sections to address concerns specific to high school, community college, and 4-year college instructors. In particular, high school faculty might benefit from a section that focuses on their special concerns.

Computer Networks and Electronic Mail

There are two computer networks that might be used to facilitate communication among psychology teachers—BITnet and Internet. BITnet is a worldwide computer network linking academic institutions and research centers. Each institution in the network is called a *site*, and each individual computer at the site is called a *node*. BITnet supports the transmission of messages, electronic mail, and files. Messages are analogous to telephone conversations in that they are interactive as long as both parties are logged on to the network. Electronic mail (E-Mail) differs from messages in that the recipient of the transmission does not have to be logged on to the network to receive a communication. The transmitted message is stored for retrieval at a later time.

Internet is another worldwide computer network that links government, military, commercial, and nonprofit institutions, as well as academic centers. The strengths of Internet include the high speed of its transmissions, its access to research libraries throughout the world, and its capability for accessing supercomputers.

Special electronic mailboxes, called *mail reflectors,* exist on both BITnet and Internet. When mail reflectors receive a transmission, they send it to a list of other electronic mailboxes. The result is the creation of "discussion groups" in which subscribers see all the messages from the mail reflector and then make comments as they wish. Mail reflectors may be a particularly effective way to link psychology teachers who want to discuss issues of mutual interest.

Computer networks have rich potential for enhancing communication among psychology teachers. The chief limitation is that many faculty, especially those in high schools and community colleges, currently do not have access to such networks. However, this problem may diminish in the future.

Computer Bulletin Boards

Computer bulletin boards represent another powerful method for facilitating communication among psychology teachers across geographic areas as well as across levels of instruction. The requirements to establish a bulletin board are a personal computer, a modem, bulletin board software, linkage to some on-line service such as BITnet or Internet, and a person dedicated to maintaining the bulletin board (the system operator). A bulletin board can be installed on a local, regional, or national basis.

When people register to access a bulletin board, they receive a password and instructions regarding the scope of activities supported. These activities include exchanging announcements concerning meetings, queries, discussion topics, and the downloading of programs. To support these activities bulletin boards often charge user fees.

We recommend the establishment of a national teaching exchange bulletin board for psychology teachers. However, bulletin boards need not be national. A number of local educational bulletin boards have been developed on the basis of shared interests. Computer bulletin boards can be used in a number of ways to facilitate networking efforts. National bulletin boards linked to databases can be accessed for information on various teaching and research topics. Individual users can leave queries, present ideas, and ask for feedback on various teaching strategies. One advantage of a computer bulletin board is that a single query could result in a number of responses and begin a series of ongoing relationships with colleagues who would never have been accessed under normal circumstances. Other uses include announcements of regional and local conferences, calls for papers, cooperative efforts among colleagues to develop course materials, the sharing of test items, and so forth.

Video Networks

Another way to use current technology to facilitate linkages might be to take advantage of video networks, such as Channel One. High schools throughout the nation have been wired with satellite dishes, monitors, and video recording equipment to receive telecasts from Channel One. Channel One is a privately funded network whose purpose is to expose high school students to a newscast that includes various types of educational programming as well as commercial messages. A rival network, CNN Newsroom, does not have commercials.

Although the use of commercials on Channel One has made it controversial, thousands of high schools have signed on to this network. Thus, video networks may become a mainstay in high schools in the near future. It may be possible to use these video networks to send public service announcements to promote faculty linkages. Psychology teachers should also consider developing educational programming for these networks.

Direct-Mail Campaigns

Direct-mail campaigns can be an effective method of disseminating information on professional development opportunities. Mail campaigns can target key individuals and make them more aware of organizational activities and conferences. To be successful, a mail campaign must have access to the most up-to-date and complete mailing list for the target market. There are different strategies for establishing such mailing lists. In 1990, the APA compiled a list of 7,500 high school psychology teachers. This list was compiled from a series of lists purchased from several vendors. The APA reports that as a result of direct mailing from this list, the number of APA high school affiliates has increased.

Division 2 of the APA significantly increased the enrollment of community college faculty through a targeted mailing campaign. This campaign was accomplished by purchasing a mailing list from a marketing company and sending letters specifically tailored for community college faculty. The letters, which were sent to more than 3,000 faculty, were signed by three prominent community college psychology teachers who described, "teacher to teacher," the benefits they had derived from Division 2 membership. This campaign resulted in the addition of more than 400 new members for Division 2.

Organizations may be able to compile their mailing lists of faculty at high schools, community colleges, or state-affiliated colleges by contacting the department of education in each state. Usually the state department of education will make these lists available gratis or for a minimal fee. Another strategy includes contacting the APA and requesting their mailing lists for specific periodicals or for entire divisions. Although it may require some initial effort, once a mailing list is established it can be an effective method for disseminating information and it can be used again and again.

Personal Advocacy

Nothing is more effective in establishing links between professionals than face-to-face efforts. Psychology teachers at all levels attend conferences, belong to committees, present papers, and are active in organizations. Often an individual is the only member of a department to attend a conference or symposium. In this situation, it would be helpful for a faculty member to approach a colleague unfamiliar with a specific event and personally invite that colleague to attend. Establishing a "friendship network" can link professionals within and across levels. We recommend that organizations concerned with teaching urge their members to personally invite friends and colleagues to participate in activities.

Continuing Education

Continuing education programs administered at the departmental or institutional level can increase the number and diversity of faculty who avail themselves of professional development opportunities. The key to this challenge is to convince psychology teachers that taking advantage of these opportunities is of real value and in their own self-interest. In high schools and community colleges, salaries often depend on the amount of education completed by faculty members. At many high schools and community colleges, attendance at conferences, workshops, and symposia may count in evaluations of teachers' educational attainments. We endorse this approach as a useful way to get more faculty involved in potentially enriching professional development activities.

Continuing education requirements could also be valuable in 4-year colleges and universities. Many institutions consider a variety of factors in evaluating the teaching component of the faculty member's duties. Departments may want to devise merit systems of evaluation that reward faculty members' attendance at professional meetings, conventions, and symposia.

At Emporia State University, for example, merit salary adjustments are determined in part by such factors.

Assistance From Publishing Companies

It is in the interest of textbook publishing companies to encourage a thriving profession of psychology teachers with strong links between the various levels of instruction. The textbook industry has become more active recently in its support of professional development opportunities for psychology teachers. Examples include the sponsoring of refreshment breaks during regional and national meetings, financial contributions to psychology teaching awards, and the underwriting of authors' expenses when they are invited to speak at teaching conferences. A recent development has been the inclusion of free advertisements for the APA's Division 2 in textbook-advertising brochures and catalogs.

There are obvious advantages to having publishing companies assist in networking efforts. Publishing companies have access to extensive mailing lists of psychology teachers and are continually contacting these teachers. Textbook companies also possess discretionary funds that could be tapped to assist in networking efforts, although psychology educators must be cautious about the ethical implications of such assistance. Division 2 of the APA has established a set of ethical guidelines for faculty and departments relating to the solicitation of financial assistance from publishing companies.

Diverse Target Groups

A goal of any networking effort is to diversify the population of faculty who avail themselves of professional development opportunities. Efforts are needed to reach target groups that are not reached effectively by the usual recruitment strategies, including women, minorities, high school teachers, community college teachers, graduate students, and master's-level professionals.

Aside from the previous strategies discussed, contacts may be made through specific APA divisions such as Division 35 (Psychology of Women) and Division 45 (Society for the Psychological Study of Ethnic Minority Issues). Another approach might be to contact graduate student organizations such as the American Psychological Association of Graduate Students (APAGS).

RECOMMENDATIONS

The expansion of programs for improved linkages among psychology teachers cannot be accomplished without the support of faculty, departments, schools, and various organizations concerned with precollege and undergraduate education in psychology. Hence, here we address our fifth set of questions: (a) What can individual faculty, psychology departments, and educational institutions do to foster increased communication and collegiality among psychology teachers? and (b) How can the APA, Division 2 of the APA, the APS, CTUP, the National Science Foundation, regional associations, or other interested organizations contribute to this effort? Our discussions yielded an extensive list of recommendations. Our suggestions for faculty, departments, and schools are outlined in this section. Our suggestions for the APA and other national and regional organizations, along with other groups' recommendations for these organizations, are summarized in appendix D of this book.

Individual Faculty

Our suggestions for individual faculty consist of exhortations to put a higher priority on networking with colleagues.

1. Psychology teachers can benefit from joining various organizations dedicated to the enhancement of undergraduate education in the field, such as Division 2 of the APA and CTUP. At present, far too few faculty are involved in these organizations.

2. Psychology teachers should increase their efforts to attend teaching conferences, regional and national conventions, and other meetings that devote attention to undergraduate education. Although it is often difficult to find the time or the money to attend, participation in such meetings can yield a host of benefits.

3. Psychology teachers should strive to be open-minded about the potential value of sharing ideas with faculty from other levels of instruction. Negative attitudes among faculty are probably the major barrier to increased vertical integration in the field.

Psychology Departments

Our suggestions for psychology departments emphasize the importance of developing organizational structures that facilitate networking among faculty.

1. Local consortia and local interinstitutional meetings are probably best organized at the departmental level. Department chairs should provide leadership in exploring the possibilities

for cooperation and collaboration with faculty from other schools in their geographic areas.

2. Undergraduate psychology departments should increase their efforts to reach out to high school psychology teachers. Departments can make major contributions to the establishment of academic alliances in psychology and to the development of more workshops for high school faculty.

3. Although faculty exchanges can create administrative headaches, department chairpersons should strive to improve opportunities for such exchanges. Exchange programs can contribute to participants' professional development and morale, and they can increase communication and collegiality among faculty.

Educational Institutions

Our suggestions for educational institutions focus on the need to devote more institutional resources to programs that promote increased faculty networking.

1. Although often inexpensive, programs to increase faculty communication and collegiality require more financial support than they receive at present. We urge deans and other academic administrators to allocate more funds to faculty travel, faculty exchanges, and other programs that promote linkages across institutions.

2. Some programs that increase networking, such as partnerships that reach across disciplines and schools, are best organized at the institutional level. We urge deans and other administrators to explore new approaches to interdisciplinary and interinstitutional collaboration.

3. Efforts to bring faculty together for discussions and interactions intended to enhance the quality of undergraduate education will enjoy limited success at institutions that place little emphasis on quality teaching. We urge college and university administrators to heed the recent call for new definitions of scholarship and new reward systems for faculty that recognize the importance of teaching excellence.

CONCLUSION

Our call for increasing communication and collegiality among faculty in psychology may seem somewhat quixotic, especially when one considers the practical and attitudinal barriers that must be overcome. Still, we believe that psychology teachers can achieve an enhanced sense of community, which will result in better educational experiences for undergraduates. After all, as educator Parker Palmer (1983) noted, teaching and learning are communal activities.

REFERENCES

Altman, I. (1990). Centripetal and centrifugal trends in psychology. In L. Bickman & H. Ellis (Eds.), *Preparing psychologists for the 21st century: Proceedings of the National Conferences on Graduate Education in Psychology* (pp. 39–64). Hillsdale, NJ: Erlbaum.

Anderson, R. E., & Meyerson, J. W. (1990). *Financing higher education in a global economy.* New York: Macmillan.

Benjamin, L. T., Jr. (1991). Personalization and active learning in the large introductory class. *Teaching of Psychology, 18,* 68–74.

Bickman, L., & Ellis, H. (1990). *Preparing psychologists for the 21st century: Proceedings of the National Conference on Graduate Education in Psychology.* Hillsdale, NJ: Erlbaum.

Bloom, A. (1987). *The closing of the American mind.* New York: Simon & Schuster.

Boice, R. (1984). The relevance of faculty development for teachers of psychology. *Teaching of Psychology, 11,* 3–8.

Bowen, H., & Schuster, J. (1986). *American professors: A national resource imperiled.* New York: Oxford University Press.

Boyer, E. L. (1983). *High school: A report on secondary education in America.* New York: Harper & Row.

Boyer, E. L. (1987). *College: The undergraduate experience in America.* New York: Harper & Row.

Boyer, E. L. (1990). *Scholarship reconsidered: Priorities of the professoriate.* Princeton, NJ: Carnegie Foundation for the Advancement of Teaching.

Bronstein, P., & Quina, K. (1988). *Teaching a psychology of people: Resources for gender and sociocultural awareness.* Washington, DC: American Psychological Association.

Calhoun, L. G., Selby, J. W., & Macfarlane, I. B. (1980). Faculty exchange in psychology: Faculty development without most of the costs. *Teaching of Psychology, 7,* 185–186.

Calhoun, L. G., Toner, I. J., & Selby, J. W. (1980). International exchange of faculty: Specific problems of implementation. *Teaching of Psychology, 7,* 111–112.

Carnegie Foundation for the Advancement of Teaching. (1986). *College: The undergraduate experience.* New York: Author.

Carnegie Foundation for the Advancement of Teaching. (1989). *The condition of the professoriate: Attitudes and trends.* Princeton, NJ: Author.

Carnegie Foundation for the Advancement of Teaching. (1990). *Campus life: In search of community.* Princeton, NJ: Author.

Carsrud, A. L. (1975). Undergraduate psychology conferences: Is good research nested under PhDs? *Teaching of Psychology, 2,* 112–114.

Carsrud, A. L., Palladino, J. J., Tanke, E. D., Aubrecht, L., & Huber, R. J. (1984). Undergraduate psychology research conferences: Goals, policies, and procedures. *Teaching of Psychology, 11,* 141–145.

Centra, J. A. (1985). Maintaining faculty vitality through faculty development. In S. M. Clark & D. R. Lewis (Eds.), *Faculty vitality and institutional productivity* (pp. 141–156). New York: Teachers College Press.

Davis, S. F., & Smith, R. A. (1992). Regional conferences for teachers and students of psychology. In A. E. Puente, J. Matthews, & C. L. Brewer (Eds.), *Teaching psychology in America: A history* (pp. 311–323). Washington, DC: American Psychological Association.

D'Souza, D. (1991). *Illiberal education: The politics of race and sex on campus.* New York: Free Press.

Eble, K. E., & McKeachie, W. J. (1985). *Improving undergraduate education through faculty development.* San Francisco: Jossey-Bass.

Gabelnick, F., MacGregor, J., Matthews, R. S., & Smith, B. L. (1990). *Learning communities: Creating connections among students, faculty, and disciplines.* San Francisco: Jossey-Bass.

Geertz, C. (1983). *Local knowledge: Further essays in interpretive anthropology.* New York: Basic Books.

Griggs, R. A., Jackson, S. L., & Meyer, M. E. (1989). High school and college psychology: Two different worlds. *Teaching of Psychology, 16,* 118–120.

Grosslight, J. H. (1979). The teaching apprentice: A community college–university program. *Teaching of Psychology, 6,* 111–112.

Hirsch, E. D. (1987). *Cultural literacy: What every American needs to know.* Boston: Houghton Mifflin.

Hodgkinson, H. (1985). *All one system: Demographics of education—Kindergarten through graduate school.* Washington, DC: Institute for Educational Leadership.

Kahill, S. (1986). Relationship of burnout among professional psychologists to professional expectations and social support. *Psychological Reports, 59,* 1043–1051.

Maeroff, G. I. (1983). *School and college: Partnerships in education.* Princeton, NJ: Carnegie Foundation for the Advancement of Teaching.

Mahoney, M. J. (1987). Scientific publication and knowledge politics. *Journal of Social Behavior & Personality, 2,* 165–176.

Matthews, J. R., & Jacobs, K. W. (1986). Teaching activities exchange: A regional report. *Teaching of Psychology, 13,* 88–89.

McGovern, T. V., Furumoto, L., Halpern, D. F., Kimble, G. A., & McKeachie, W. J. (1991). Liberal education, study in depth, and the arts and sciences major—Psychology. *American Psychologist, 46,* 598–605.

Miller, A. (1981). A survey of introductory psychology subject pool practices among leading universities. *Teaching of Psychology, 8,* 211–213.

Myers, R. A. (1990). Student issues: Recruitment and retention. In L. Bickman & H. Ellis (Eds.), *Preparing psychologists for the 21st century: Proceedings of the National Conference on Graduate Education in Psychology* (pp. 175–176). Hillsdale, NJ: Erlbaum.

Osberg, T. M., & Raulin, M. L. (1989). Networking as a tool for career advancement among academic psychologists. *Teaching of Psychology, 16,* 26–28.

Palladino, J. J. (1988). A faculty development conference: Psychology as a model. *Journal of Staff, Program, & Organization Development, 6,* 169–174.

Palmer, P. J. (1983). *To know as we are known.* New York: Harper & Row.

Price, A. R., & Goldman, M. (1981). Improving part-time faculty instruction. *Teaching of Psychology, 8,* 160–162.

Riesman, D. (1980). *On higher education: The academic enterprise in an era of rising student consumerism.* San Francisco: Jossey-Bass.

Schuster, J. H. (1990a). Strengthening career preparation for prospective professors. In J. H. Schuster, D. W. Wheeler, & Associates (Eds.), *Enhancing faculty careers: Strategies for development and renewal* (pp. 65–83). San Francisco: Jossey-Bass.

Schuster, J. H. (1990b). The need for fresh approaches to faculty renewal. In J. H. Schuster, D. W. Wheeler, & Associates (Eds.), *Enhancing faculty careers: Strategies for development and renewal* (pp. 3–19). San Francisco: Jossey-Bass.

Scott, T. R. (1991). A personal view of the future of psychology departments. *American Psychologist, 46,* 975–976.

Seidman, E. (1985). *In the words of the faculty: Perspectives on improving teaching and educational quality in community colleges.* San Francisco: Jossey-Bass.

Smith, R. A. (1988, April). *Avoiding academic isolation through student research conferences.* Paper presented at the 34th Annual Meeting of the Southwestern Psychological Association, Tulsa, OK.

Spence, J. T. (1990). Centrifugal versus centripetal tendencies in psychology: Will the center hold? In L. Bickman & H. Ellis (Eds.), *Preparing psychologists for the 21st century: Proceedings of the National Conference on Graduate Education in Psychology* (pp. 25–29). Hillsdale, NJ: Erlbaum.

Sykes, C. (1988). *Profscam: Professors and the demise of higher education.* Washington, DC: Regnery Gateway.

Wilbur, F. P., & Lambert, L. M. (1991). *Linking America's schools and colleges.* Washington, DC: American Association for Higher Education.

6

CURRICULUM

CHARLES L. BREWER, in collaboration with J. ROY HOPKINS,
GREGORY A. KIMBLE, MARGARET W. MATLIN, LEE I. McCANN,
OGRETTA V. McNEIL, BARBARA F. NODINE, VIRGINIA NICHOLS
QUINN, and SAUNDRA

Psychologists have studied the psychology curriculum for several decades; reports of their studies reveal consistencies and changes both in program objectives and in how best to accomplish them. Although these past reports provided historical perspective, they did not determine our approach to curriculum in this chapter. Because psychology is taught in a variety of undergraduate programs with different missions, we studied the curriculum and formulated our recommendations in light of the present milieu for higher education in general and for psychology in particular. A brief overview of five previous reports will illustrate the evolution of psychologists' thinking about the curriculum and will highlight the challenges of planning a program for students with increasingly diverse backgrounds, abilities, academic commitments, and career goals.

HISTORICAL BACKGROUND FOR STUDYING THE CURRICULUM

The Cornell Conference Report

After lengthy debate at Cornell University in the summer of 1951, six psychologists (chaired by Dael Wolfle and called the Wolfle Committee) published *Improving Undergraduate Instruction in Psychology* (Buxton et al., 1952). Their report identified four objectives that different psychologists might have for their courses:

> (1) Intellectual development and a liberal education; (2) a knowledge of psychology, its research findings, its major problems, its theoretical integrations, and its contributions; (3) personal growth and an increased ability to meet personal and social adjustment problems adequately; (4) desirable attitudes and habits of thought, such as the stimulation of intellectual curiosity, respect for others, and a feeling of social responsibility. (pp. 2–3)

They recognized that all of these objectives cannot be achieved in one or a few courses and that the psychology curriculum should be planned to promote accomplishment of the institution's overall goals.

The Wolfle Committee emphasized the teaching of psychology as a scientific discipline in the liberal arts tradition and recommended one model curriculum. To follow the introductory course, they proposed a series of intermediate core courses: statistics, motivation, perception, thinking and language, and ability. These were to be followed by advanced courses in specialized areas such as social, learning, comparative, and physiological psychology. Experimental methodology was stressed in all substantive courses rather than in a separate one-lab-project-per-week experimental psychology course. As integrative or capstone courses for seniors, they recommended (a) history and systems and (b) personality. Stressing that the core and advanced courses were not for majors only, they also suggested a group of special interest courses designed for nonmajors (e.g., educational psychology, industrial psychology, and the psychology of religion).

Furthermore, the Wolfle Committee proposed two possible organizational schemata and foci (developmental and cross-sectional) for the introductory course, and they highlighted some topics that other courses should cover. They specifically excluded a course for improving adjustment because the topic lacked sufficient empirical evidence to be considered a bona fide academic offering. They also excluded applied courses with a vocational slant, preferring that such training come after the bachelor's degree, and suggested that students seeking jobs after completing a baccalaureate degree might learn vocationally oriented skills in special summer institutes.

The Cornell group explicitly recognized that local conditions precluded specifying the exact content of the major for all psychology programs. In a final note, they indicated that no research supports any particular curriculum, and they urged psychologists to conduct research on curricular issues.

The Michigan Conference Report

On the basis of one such curricular research project, the University of Michigan group concluded that some departments had adopted the Cornell Conference curriculum and that many others had incorporated certain of its features (McKeachie & Milholland, 1961). After discussing the different sources of pressures on the curriculum, the Michigan report devoted a chapter to special problems arising from the needs of three groups of undergraduates: (a) preprofessional students who are not psychology majors, (b) psychology majors who use the bachelor's degree as preparation for vocational employment, and (c) psychology majors preparing for graduate study in psychology. This chapter explicitly recognized that undergraduates with different career goals might need different emphases and that there is no one sacred set of psychology courses for all majors.

Among the important assumptions of the Michigan group were that

> the basic curriculum would be at heart a liberal arts curriculum suitable for all undergraduates. It would be diverse and flexible and, within the college potential, would offer at the advanced level alternate paths for different interests. But it would be firmly anchored in the liberal arts, rejecting undergraduate vocational training as a primary goal. (McKeachie & Milholland, 1961, p. 33)

Essentially, the Michigan group reaffirmed the Wolfle Committee's general objectives.

Unlike the Cornell group, the Michigan group could not agree on one model curriculum; instead, it presented three exemplars. All models from both groups emphasized a common core of courses, but the Michigan group was divided on the nature of the core. Another important difference between the two reports is that the Michigan group suggested four types of advanced courses:

1. They suggested integrative courses, such as senior seminar, history and systems, or advanced general psychology.
2. They suggested theory or research courses especially valuable for students planning to enter graduate school, if these courses are not included in the department's core. In order of preference, they mentioned learning, social, personality, perception, motivation, measurement, developmental, abnormal, physiological, thought and language, and comparative psychology.
3. They suggested courses with a preprofessional or vocational orientation, such as tests and measurements, industrial psychology, human relations, survey research, and group dynamics. They mentioned that only large universities may be able

to offer many of these courses without diluting the basic core. If a choice must be made, they favored nonvocational courses.

4. They suggested courses representing faculty members' special interests, to add some excitement to the curriculum.

Throughout their conference, the Michigan group hoped to agree on one ideal curriculum but could not. Instead, they concluded,

> What is ideal, we now believe, depends upon the staff, the students, the total college curriculum, and other factors. Our recommendations are intended merely to illustrate some alternatives as starting points for the individual decisions each psychology department must make for itself. (McKeachie & Milholland, 1961, p. 103)

In summary, participants at the Cornell and Michigan conferences "concluded that the psychology curriculum should be basically designed for liberal education, and that special courses or tracks need not be designed for special purposes—preparation for graduate school, job training, or self-development" (Kulik, 1973, p. 3).

The Kulik Report

Study of the curriculum took a dramatically different turn in the Kulik (1973) report published by the APA. Following the frenetic decade of the 1960s, when faculty in all disciplines were challenging existing curricula, the Kulik report expressly recognized the impossibility and undesirability of stipulating what the curriculum should be. Not wanting to threaten "diversity and the accompanying freedom to innovate, experiment, and do one's own thing" (p. v), the Kulik report did not recommend a model curriculum. Instead, it summarized results of a national survey of schools that grant bachelor's degrees with a major in psychology, 4-year schools that do not offer a psychology major, and 2-year schools. Their survey data were supplemented by site visits to 17 schools, with emphasis on 10 of them.

This purely descriptive report highlighted the increasing diversity of undergraduate psychology programs and asked, "Is it conceivable that for some students occupationally oriented programs may provide a better road to personal soundness than the traditional curricula of liberal arts colleges?" (Kulik, 1973, p. 202). Kulik related his group's findings to some of the recommendations from the Cornell and Michigan reports, especially the latter, and concluded that "the diverse goals of students in psychology courses suggest that pluralism may be a valuable concept in the design of programs in psychology" (Kulik, 1973, p. 203).

The Scheirer and Rogers Report

Scheirer and Rogers (1985) reported results of another national survey sponsored by the APA. Also purely descriptive, this report summarized information from respondents at 2-year and 4-year schools about educational settings, selected characteristics of faculty and students, the introductory course, the psychology major, courses for nonmajors, special characteristics of courses, independent work, and other facets of the curriculum. Scheirer and Rogers found a staggering array of psychology courses being taught, and they compared some of their findings with those from the Kulik report.

The Association of American Colleges Report

As part of a national project sponsored by the Association of American Colleges, an APA committee studied the undergraduate psychology major. Their report (McGovern, Furumoto, Halpern, Kimble, & McKeachie, 1991) illustrated both the continuing tensions in psychology discussed by Kimble (1984) and how conflicts are reflected in undergraduate curricula. After enumerating their basic assumptions, McGovern et al. (1991) described changing student demographics in American psychology and identified eight common goals for the major. The goals concern knowledge base, thinking skills, language skills, skills for gathering and synthesizing information, skills in research methods and statistics, interpersonal skills, the history of psychology, and ethics and values.

Stressing that no one structure will best serve all undergraduate programs, McGovern et al. (1991) described four curricular models. Their generalist model is most similar to a traditionally structured major. Their three thematic models depict programs that feature developmental, biological, and health psychology, but other models could emphasize other themes (e.g., social or cognitive psychology). Despite their differences, all four models have some common features. For example, each model requires statistics and research methodology; a survey course followed by a specialized course with laboratory work; and a senior-year integrative experience, which might include work in an applied field setting or capstone courses (e.g., history and systems, advanced general psychology, or special topics).

McGovern et al. (1991) also recommended some unique features. For example, they suggested that "an interpersonal skills and group process laboratory to develop students' ability to work in groups" (p. 603) be required in all four models and that, "whenever possible, . . . this laboratory (or the senior-year applied project) be combined with a community-service component" (p. 603). Two noteworthy themes concern: (a) the importance of good teaching and advising aimed at promoting students' self-education as a lifelong process and (b) systematic assessment of educational outcomes, especially in individual courses. Expressing no preference for any one model, they concluded, "We see both the generalist and the thematic models as worthy of consideration because they reflect what is now happening and what we believe could be designed to facilitate students' integrated learning" (McGovern et al., 1991, p. 603).

THE LIBERAL ARTS TRADITION AND THE PSYCHOLOGY MAJOR

As noted earlier, previous reports on the undergraduate curriculum—most notably the reports of the Wolfle Committee and the Michigan conference—placed psychology within the liberal arts tradition. The St. Mary's conference reaffirmed the symbiotic relation between psychology and the liberal arts. That is, the rest of the curriculum relates to and provides value for the psychology major, just as the psychology major enhances the liberal arts curriculum.

Both psychology and the liberal arts have changed. Only vestiges remain of the *trivium* (grammar, rhetoric, and logic) and the *quadrivium* (arithmetic, music, geometry, and astronomy), which constituted the liberal arts curriculum during the Middle Ages (Wagner, 1983). In this last quarter of the 20th century, more than 2,100 institutions of higher learning grant baccalaureate degrees in the United States, and more than 12 million students pursue some form of postsecondary education in a variety of academic programs (Boyer, 1987).

The millions of students in liberal arts programs are enrolled in institutions that emphasize in different ways the overarching goals of (a) thinking critically and (b) exercising broad analytical skills such as forming abstract concepts and making appropriate judgments about particular phenomena through integration of abstractions; evaluating evidence and revising hypotheses; communicating abstract concepts; and comprehending the logic governing relations among concepts (Winter, McClelland, & Stewart, 1981). Corollary goals include learning how to learn; thinking independently; examining one's assumptions; exercising leadership; demonstrating mature social judgment; expressing egalitarian and antiauthoritarian values; and participating in cultural experiences (Winter et al., 1981). We have come a long way from the trivium and the quadrivium.

Beginning in the last quarter of the 19th century, significant changes in higher education reshaped the liberal arts curriculum. One notable change was the growth of departments and academic specialties. The result was a "kind of division of labor in the interest of getting the work done—a diversity of subject matters, areas of investigation, or, in terms of the identity of the participants, specializations and specialists" (Wegener, 1978, p. 67).

Within the academy, debates about the nature and importance of liberal arts education continue, as students and their parents worry increasingly about job preparation as a goal of college education. According to Bok (1986), three issues permeate these debates, and they can be framed as questions: (a) How is breadth in education best achieved? (b) How much of the curriculum should be prescribed, and how much should be left to free choice? and (c) How is educational integration best achieved, so that students can synthesize what they have learned?

In addition to structural changes within colleges and universities, society as a whole has changed in ways that challenge liberal education (Bok, 1986). Knowledge itself has become more complex, with an explosion of information beyond the mastery of even the most devoted scholar. The democratic ideal of educational opportunity for all citizens has come closer to realization as students have become increasingly diverse.

The goal of diversity, and the recognition of its importance in the curriculum, is one of the most obvious differences between our report and reports from the Cornell and the Michigan conferences. Attaining some sense of community from diverse elements remains a goal of liberal education. The community should respect differences in backgrounds and values and should seek to advance knowledge without homogenizing the culture. As Boyer (1987) wrote:

> We emphasize this commitment to community not out of a sentimental attachment to tradition, but because our democratic way of life and perhaps our survival as a people rest on whether we can move beyond self-interest and begin to understand better the realities of our dependence on each other. (p. 8)

Education should broaden the horizons of all undergraduates, including psychology majors. Thus, students should take courses in a variety of disciplines in an effort to understand the approaches and perspectives of many specialists. Ultimately, these liberating experiences should help students to analyze and synthesize the components of their education.

Psychology courses introduce students to scientific methodologies and analytic thinking that characterize the discipline, thereby contributing to the breadth of experience inherent in liberal education. In turn, students in psychology experience the benefits of the liberal arts in their courses outside the major. A strong liberal arts curriculum helps to prepare students for the major curriculum in psychology. For example, the study of composition and speech provides a basis for learning effective communication in psychology, the study of mathematics prepares students for statistics courses, and the study of natural sciences provides preparation in scientific methodology and analytic skills that transfer to and enhance psychology courses.

Not all institutions require general education courses that prepare students who major in psychology. In separate surveys, Lewis and Farris (1989) and Perlman and McCann (1991) reported that average general education requirements of institutions in the United States include roughly two courses in English, one in mathematics, and two in the natural sciences. Many institutions require even fewer courses in these areas, and some have no general education requirements. In such cases, psychology departments may wish to identify specific courses in other departments that augment the psychology major. Perlman and McCann (1991) reported that a number of departments take this approach. Some departments specify courses that students must take from the choices allowed under institutional requirements, or they require courses beyond the general education requirements. These strategies aim to increase success in classes both within and outside the major and to improve the college experience for each student.

Students completing a psychology major nested within a strong liberal arts structure can be expected to possess a sound general education, to be intelligent consumers of the scientific literature, and to be well prepared to pursue diverse postbaccalaureate goals. They can also be expected to enjoy the fruits of the cultivated mind described by Mill (1861/1979):

> A cultivated mind—I do not mean that of a philosopher, but any mind to which the fountains of knowledge have been opened, and which has been taught, in any tolerable degree, to exercise its faculties—finds sources of inexhaustible interest in all that surrounds it; in the objects of nature, the achievements of poetry, the incidents of history, the ways of mankind, past and present, and their prospects in the future. (pp. 13–14)

GOALS FOR EDUCATION IN PSYCHOLOGY

One major challenge for education is to provide students with the understanding they will need to make the world a better place in which to lead productive and satisfying lives. People in some places are starving; elsewhere they are killing themselves and one another with automobiles, handguns, cholesterol, and cigarettes. White-collar crime is rampant. Many children are abused and abandoned. Some elderly people lead boring, hopeless lives in nursing homes, and others have no homes at all. Portrayal of aggression by the media blunts the horror of some people's reactions to crime and violence. Pollution threatens to make the world uninhabitable. Bitter controversy marks relationships between diverse groups in every segment of our society.

These are problems of behavior. They will not be solved by physical science, medicine, or engineering alone. Moral indignation will not make them go away. New laws will not correct them because attitudes and values cannot be legislated. The unique contribution that psychology offers for solving problems comes from its scientific knowledge of behavior. The overarching aim of education in psychology should be to communicate the understanding that scientific psychology offers ways of thinking and knowing that have great potential value for helping people to cope with the world's problems.

Scientific Thinking About Behavior: The Primary Educational Goal

The fundamental goal of education in psychology, from which all the others follow, is to teach students to think as scientists about behavior. The scientific way is not the only way to think about behavior. Poets, preachers, and philosophers all have their ways of knowing, but their criteria of truth are different. For the scientist, truth derives from publicly observable facts; for the poet, it comes from personal experience and intuition; for the preacher, it is the authority of holy books and the language of the church; for the philosopher, it is the product of intellect and reason. All of these truths are valid within their own domains, and an educated person may subscribe to more than one of them. For solving problems, however, scientific truth has the advantage of being in contact with external reality, which is where the problems are.

The first element of scientific thinking that students should master is the empirical criterion of truth. They should learn that the final authority for factual statements in psychology is evidence and not affect; how they feel about a topic has no bearing on its truth. Their understanding of the empirical approach should include a recognition of the distinction between facts and inferences drawn from facts (e.g., the difference between IQ, a measure based on factual observation, and the concept of intelligence). They should understand that naming is not explaining (e.g., that it is no explanation to say that someone hears nonexistent voices because he or she is schizophrenic). More generally, they should recognize that every explanation that attributes causation to inherent characteristics of human beings commits this error; conspicuous examples are "explanations" that ascribe human action to gender or to race. To supplement such understanding, students should learn the role of psychological theories as synthesizers of factual information.

The person who understands these things is an informed consumer and evaluator of the psychological and quasi-psychological information reported in the media and a knowledgeable and independent decision maker on problems that involve behavior. As with other education in the liberal arts tradition, such an education in psychology has lasting value. It provides the student with a basis for lifelong involvement with psychology.

Specific Goals

Teaching students to think as scientists about behavior has important implications for academic programs in psychology. As explained in the following paragraphs, these implications suggest special qualities that should characterize graduating psychology majors.

Attention to Human Diversity

Education in psychology should help to prepare students for life in a heterogeneous society. Scientific understanding requires a recognition of ethnic, cultural, social, and gender diversity. Students should learn, for example, that data obtained from samples that fail to represent this diversity will have limited generalizability. Courses throughout the psychology curriculum should emphasize the sociocultural context of human behavior. In addition, students should learn about the experiences of underrepresented groups in the discipline and about their contributions to psychological scholarship.

A Broad and Deep Knowledge Base

The psychology curriculum need not take the student into every nook and cranny of the discipline, but it should be broad enough to represent the diversity of the field. Students should understand materials in both the social science and natural science aspects of psychology. Specific courses and overall requirements may reflect the strengths of a particular program's faculty, but balance is essential. In addition to breadth of content, psychology majors should pursue at least one topic in some depth. Through additional courses or independent study projects, students should have an opportunity to do advanced work that builds on knowledge gained in their previous courses.

Methodological Competence

Students receiving a bachelor's degree in psychology should have knowledge of statistics, research design, and psychometric methods. Courses in statistics should cover descriptive and inferential aspects of the subject, as well as correlational and hypothesis-testing methods. Students should understand the circumstances under which various measures are appropriate. They should also be alert to the many ways in which statistics are abused, such as using the mean when the median would be a better measure of central tendency; failing to distinguish between statistical significance and practical importance; treating between-group differences as generalizations of within-group differences (e.g., treating racial differences in IQ as hereditary differences on the basis of the knowledge that, within groups, inheritance contributes to individual differences in IQ); and failing to realize that, with biased samples, there is no safety in large numbers—the larger the biased sample size, the more certainly it yields erroneous information.

In the area of research design, students should understand a variety of methods, including experimental, correlational, and case-history techniques. They should know the strengths and weaknesses of these methods and develop the expertise required to detect misuses of them. For example, single case histories are valuable as sources of hypotheses, but they cannot prove a general point because they have no degrees of freedom; effects produced in experiments without control groups are always suspect; sometimes statistically reliable effects result from the unintentional manipulation of a confounded independent variable; without appropriate controls, we may mistake regression to the mean for a true experimental effect; and correlation is not causation.

Because behavioral assessment is ubiquitous, a knowledge of psychometric methods (e.g., tests, measurements, and behavioral assessment) is as important for the educated citizen as a knowledge of statistics and research design. Tests are used to assess one's acceptability for college or a job; evaluations of accomplishment determine salary, promotion, and retention in employment; lie detectors contribute to decisions about one's guilt or innocence of crime; clinical diagnoses, which are behavioral assessments, determine whether a person receives drugs or psychological treatment as therapy.

Students in psychology should understand the contributions of psychometric methods to society and develop the ability to detect abuses of these methods. They should be aware that the so-called tests that appear in popular publications and that purport to assess the reader's most intimate and personal attributes are utterly without psychometric merit. In popular publications and elsewhere, the media often confuse the concepts of validity and reliability. Similar confusion has prompted radical proposals to abandon all tests for selecting students and job applicants. Most important, perhaps, ignorance about psychometric methods has left the understanding of cultural bias in a cloud of ambiguity.

Practical Experience and Application

Students in psychology should learn to generalize a scientific style of thought to the realm of application. The curriculum should provide opportunities for them to integrate research, theory, and practice by applying their knowledge and skills both in the laboratory and in real-life situations. As part of this aspect of their education, students should learn about various professional careers in psychology and associated fields. Such learning will help some students to choose careers that best suit their aptitudes and interests; it will help other students to make intelligent use of the services of different professionals.

Effective Communication Skills

Psychology majors should be able to read and understand the discipline's books and journals. They also should acquire the skill of effectively communicating their knowledge and ideas to an audience of their peers or to an audience with no special background in psychology. Oral reports, term papers, literature reviews, research reports, case histories, personal notes, journal or log entries, and other assignments are strong allies in the mission of teaching students to think scientifically about behavior. These exercises help students learn that effective communication requires precision, both in their thinking and in the expression of their thoughts. Attaining precision usually requires revision, which, with appropriate feedback, helps to teach the skills and standards of effective communication in psychology and elsewhere.

Sensitivity to Ethical Issues

Psychology students should learn about the ethical standards of psychologists, including those that apply to the treatment of human and animal participants in research, and those that govern relationships with colleagues, students, and the recipients of psychological services (APA, 1982, 1984, 1990). Sometimes these standards will apply to students as experimenters, as participants in practica, or as authors. More often, a knowledge of ethical standards will be important for the judgments that students make as undergraduates and later as consumers of the research and practice of psychology.

CURRICULUM FOR A PSYCHOLOGY MAJOR

This section describes the characteristics of an undergraduate curriculum designed to meet the seven goals described in the preceding section. A single course or a set of courses may specifically emphasize only one particular goal, but the complete curriculum should address all seven goals.

Structure of the Major

The psychology major should be organized into four groups of courses, reflecting increasing levels of knowledge and skills, to be taken sequentially when possible. The four groups are: (a) the introductory course, (b) methodology courses, (c) content courses, and (d) integrative experiences.

The Introductory Course

The required introductory psychology course should provide a survey of psychological topics and methodological approaches that reflect breadth of the field, including various concepts, theories, and subspecialties. This course is usually taught in one academic term, but the ever-expanding content is well suited to a two-term format, if departments can accommodate that arrangement.

The introductory course provides a basic foundation in psychological principles, and it allows students to make informed decisions about selecting subsequent courses in psychology and in other departments. Also, it should address other educational goals by providing opportunities for reading, writing, and critical thinking about psychological concepts.

Psychology departments debate the question of whether to offer separate introductory courses with different emphases for majors and nonmajors. Having two separate courses may be an advantage for students who plan to major in psychology when they enroll in the introductory course. The disadvantage is that during their first 2 years of college students are considering various majors and are shifting among them. Alternative courses for nonmajors may be less theoretical, more applied, or narrower in scope. For some psychology majors, the traditional survey course is the necessary first course; for others, first courses with a different focus may be acceptable. In planning such courses, teachers should remember that the introductory course may be the only formal study of psychology for most students.

Methodology Courses

Research methods courses are especially important because they foster analytical skills and encourage critical thinking. In addition, they inspire students to ask appropriate questions when they discuss the design of studies they encounter in later courses, when they attempt to explain a psychological observation, and when they read the often erroneous reports of research in the mass media. Skills developed in methodology courses are essential because psychology has few established facts that are consistently replicated and thoroughly reliable. Instead, we have phenomena that hold true in limited circumstances, depending on the subject population and the situation. Skills in research methods can transcend isolated research findings or specific topics, and they can enhance lifelong learning.

Students who major in psychology should be well acquainted with three methodological domains: statistics, research methods, and psychometrics. These topics may be covered in separate courses devoted to each area, they may be combined with one another, or they may be interwoven with other subject matter. For example, a department may combine statistics and research methods into one or more courses. Another department might teach psychometrics in combination with a general tests and measurements course or an applied course.

Statistics. Instruction in statistics provides basic skills necessary for methods courses, and it helps prepare students to be critical in analyzing and interpreting research. Students should study both descriptive and inferential statistics and both parametric and nonparametric methods. They should understand the situations in which various statistical tests are appropriate as well as common misuses of statistics and the consequences thereof.

Research Methods. Courses in research methods are usually taken in the second or third year of study. These courses should familiarize students with the principal research approaches, including experimental, correlational, and case-study techniques. Students should understand each method's strengths and limitations. Methodology courses should cover other important topics, such as operational definitions, sampling, ecological validity, longitudinal and cross-sectional methods, and limited generality of findings (e.g., inadequate representation of different ethnic groups, restricted age range, or single-gender samples).

Hands-on experience helps to illustrate abstract methodological issues more vividly. Hence, research methods courses should include data collection involving measures obtained from actual human and animal subjects. Meaningful data gathering does not require a sophisticated laboratory or elaborate equipment. As part of the hands-on research component, students should learn to write their reports in APA style.

Some 2-year schools may have the faculty and material resources to support such research methods courses during a student's second year. More often, students who transfer from these schools should be urged to take these courses in their first term at a 4-year institution.

Psychometrics. Preparation in psychometrics is basic to the major. Many important questions and phenomena in psychology are not amenable to causal analysis and rely instead on the psychometric science of psychology (Cronbach, 1957). Knowledge of the concepts of standardization, validity, and reliability is essential; alternative measures of these constructs should be discussed. An understanding of the distinction between differences within groups and differences between groups is crucial. Major tests of intelligence and personality should be covered. Appropriate uses of traditionally administered and computer-based psychometric tests should be discussed, and their strengths, weaknesses, biases, and potential misuses should be emphasized. Psychometrics may be the most important aspect of scientific psychology for many students because tests are so much a part of modern life.

Instruction in statistics, research methods, and psychometrics should include a breadth of examples from all areas of psychology to help students understand the applications of methodology in various areas within the field. Also, examples should include appropriate studies of both genders and of various ethnic and racial groups.

Content Courses

A third group of courses covers the main content areas that typically define the discipline. Statistics and methodology courses should be prerequisites for some content courses. Selection from among these courses is necessary because it is neither appropriate nor reasonable, given the constraints of a liberal arts major, to expect students to take separate courses corresponding to every chapter in an introductory psychology textbook (e.g., perception, cognition, personality, etc.). The content courses should represent an intermediate level of generality, rather than cover topics that are too narrowly specialized (e.g., seminar topics on dreams, learning disabilities, or drugs). The curriculum should be structured to ensure that students are exposed to both the natural science and social science sides of psychology, including basic principles and applied areas.

One possible structure might provide two groups of courses from which students select a certain number. For example, students could choose three from each group:

Group A: Learning, Cognition, Biological Bases of Behavior, Perception, Animal Behavior

Group B: Developmental, Personality, Social, Abnormal

Other structures might divide the content courses into more groups, allowing a different pattern of choices but ensuring coverage of the core areas. For example, students could choose two each from Groups A and B and one each from Groups C and D:

Group A: Developmental, Personality, Social, Abnormal

Group B: Motivation, Learning, Cognition, Perception, Biological Bases of Behavior

Group C: Industrial–Organizational, Counseling, Drugs and Behavior, Tests and Measurements

Group D: African-American Studies, Developmental Disabilities, Psychology of Women, Human Sexuality

These two examples are neither prescriptive nor proscriptive; they simply illustrate organizational structures intended to ensure broad coverage. A department should design an appropriate structure for its own specific courses.

This approach to planning the psychology major will allow flexibility for programs that offer different career-interest tracks. For example, a student who wishes to pursue graduate work in biofeedback might be advised to take courses in learning, biological bases of behavior, and abnormal psychology.

Although much of the major consists of structured choices, some free electives should be preserved. Students can explore their special interests by these selections.

Integrative Experiences

The fourth and final level of the curriculum should include an integrative experience for seniors. This experience may take several forms, including internships, research projects supervised by a faculty member, or capstone courses.

Internships. One type of integrative experience is an internship, which is ideally embedded in an advanced seminar that requires regular meetings and a senior paper. The seminar and paper provide opportunities for students to appreciate their internship in a larger context that includes reflection on their own development as well as contextual analysis based on relevant psychological literature. In designing an internship, the student and faculty member should discuss the student's career interests and select a site that will adequately challenge the student working under appropriate supervision. Internships can involve a variety of settings, activities, and responsibilities. Some examples are: work with a college admissions counselor, testing in an urban police department, group counseling in a drug rehabilitation center, recreation counseling with emotionally disturbed adolescents, job placement and counseling with retarded adults, work with a foster parent agency, personnel work in a human resources development department of a corporation, marketing research in a local agency, and recreational work in a geriatric center.

Research Projects. Another type of practical experience is a research project that a student initiates and a faculty member supervises or that the faculty member initiates and offers the student a significant role in planning, data collection and analysis, and writing. Ideally, the student presents this project at a local or regional student research conference or at a professional convention.

Capstone Courses. A third type of integrative experience is a capstone course. When students take a variety of courses to ensure breadth of coverage, they sometimes fail to discern commonalities among different topics. They may have fragments of information and little or no organized framework. Despite their differences, several psychological specialties have the same or overlapping histories. For this reason, many departments offer History of Psychology as a capstone course. Another reason for offering capstone courses derives from the assumption that the content of the introductory course will be more meaningful for students after they have taken several other courses. This idea has led to capstone courses such as Advanced General Psychology and Great Ideas in Psychology. These approaches are sometimes combined in a course that reviews the histories of major topics in the discipline. Another alternative is a special topics course that examines two or three broad issues (e.g., gender, self-deception, or intelligence) from several perspectives. Some integrative courses can be combined with an internship or research project in a senior seminar.

Community College Curriculum

Our discussion thus far has emphasized the psychology major in 4-year colleges and universities. In contrast, most 2-year colleges (72%) do not offer a psychology major (Scheirer & Rogers, 1985). In the institutions that do have a major, requirements vary widely because some programs are designed for terminal degrees and others are planned as transfer programs.

In 2-year institutions that do not offer a psychology major, students who plan to transfer to 4-year colleges as psychology majors usually take several psychology courses but receive degrees in general studies or liberal arts. The statistics on majors at 2-year colleges in a report by Scheirer and Rogers (1985) are confusing. Most 2-year institutions indicated that they do not offer a psychology major, but they listed courses that psychology majors take. Many of these "psychology majors" were probably students who planned to transfer as psychology majors after completing a general degree program. The choice of "major" courses selected at the community college is often at the discretion of the student, who is usually advised to consult with the admissions office at potential transfer institutions. Most 2-year colleges have limited laboratory facilities and do not offer courses in experimental psychology. However, many 2-year colleges offer upper-level courses. In California, 93% of the community colleges surveyed by Farrell, Woodward, and Pollock (1990) reported offering upper-level courses at least once a year.

A key problem at community colleges is transfer credit for psychology courses. Some 4-year colleges will accept entire programs from community colleges; others insist that all courses in the major be taken at their institutions. Thus, the community college curriculum is often determined by decisions of faculty and administrators at neighboring transfer institutions. When articulation occurs between the psychology faculty at 2-year colleges and their counterparts at the 4-year institutions that they serve, students benefit from a more coherent curriculum and lose fewer credits when they transfer. Models of such articulation occur in the Dallas and Houston areas and in Arizona, where faculty from 2-year and 4-year colleges participate in consortia and discuss curricular issues as well as other issues. More 2-year and 4-year institutions should develop articulation agreements about transfer credits, and these agreements should be reasonably long-term.

In addition to students who plan to transfer as psychology majors, community colleges serve two other important constituencies: (a) students enrolled in 1-year certificate or 2-year associate degree programs and (b) members of the community who wish to enroll in one or more psychology courses. Although only 14% of 4-year colleges offer psychology courses specifically designed for students in other programs, more than 30% of 2-year colleges offer such support courses (Scheirer & Rogers, 1985). At 2-year colleges, these courses are most likely to be designed for students in technical or vocational degree programs and are selected from catalog listings by the program heads and their faculty, who usually have little or no background in psychology. Articulation between psychology faculty and the technical degree faculty is critical because students should recognize psychology as a scientific enterprise with applications that go beyond the focus of their specific technical or vocational programs.

The psychology program at community colleges should reflect the needs and interests of the entire community being served. Students choosing psychology courses may range in age from 15 to 96 and include people who have not completed high school as well as those who have earned advanced degrees. Introductory courses with an applied focus are most useful for some members of the community; other students will benefit from the traditional survey course described earlier in this chapter. Community college programs are challenged to expand the knowledge and skills of traditional and non-traditional students, who vary widely in age and ability.

Interdisciplinary and Service Courses

Psychology is one of the most popular undergraduate majors ("Fact File," 1991). In addition to accommodating its own majors, psychology provides courses for (a) students who select psychology courses to fulfill general education requirements; (b) students in departments, such as education, business, or nursing, that require at least one course in psychology; (c) students in interdisciplinary courses; and (d) students who select the psychology minor.

The psychology course that most often fulfills general college requirements is the introductory course. Few colleges require that every student take introductory psychology to graduate. More typically, students take this course to satisfy a social science requirement that offers other alternatives, such as anthropology and sociology. However, courses other than introductory psychology may also fulfill collegewide requirements; these courses may include developmental psychology, applied psychology, or human relations. Some schools have recently introduced general college requirements that are interdisciplinary in nature but that are commonly taught by psychology faculty members; these requirements include courses in multicultural issues, critical thinking, and biological bases of behavior.

Students majoring in other disciplines are sometimes required to take at least one psychology course. For example, many programs in business, education, nursing, and speech pathology require introductory psychology. Some of these disciplines specify additional requirements or electives, such as consumer psychology, industrial psychology, developmental psychology, or educational psychology. (In some programs, introductory psychology is not a prerequisite for more specialized courses.) Enrollments in these courses generate credits that support psychology faculty positions.

Psychology courses with an interdisciplinary focus provide options for still other students who are not psychology majors. For example, a course in psychobiology may enroll biology students as well as students in other disciplines (e.g., a premedical student with an English major). Interdisciplinary courses can be important mechanisms for faculty development because they encourage team teaching and may inspire collaborative research. These courses can be especially useful in 2-year colleges, where faculty members may welcome the opportunity to learn from their colleagues. In some cases, interests coalesce and new interdisciplinary departments or programs may develop (e.g., cognitive science, neuroscience, social ecology, and women's studies). Even when no formal interdisciplinary programs exist on a campus, some psychology faculty members teach interdisciplinary courses (e.g., American Studies, The African-American Experience, and Issues in Feminism).

Students who minor in psychology frequently major in another social science, but some major in humanities; natural sciences; fine arts; or professional areas, such as social work or criminal justice. Data are not available on students with psychology minors. We need information about the number of psychology programs that offer a minor, the number of students enrolled in these minors, and the requirements for them. A minor in psychology should require an introductory course and at least one methodology course, in addition to electives.

Teachers of psychology are both blessed and cursed with an inherently fascinating discipline that has practical applications in numerous other areas. High enrollments in psychology courses often mean that psychology majors are shortchanged. Many faculty members might teach the introductory course, or the department might offer one section with extremely large enrollments. Intermediate- and upper-level courses may then have large enrollments, resulting in fewer opportunities for seminar-type discussions and fewer writing assignments that encourage critical analysis and synthesis of ideas.

Psychology instructors welcome the opportunity to teach students from other disciplines, but there is a limit to the resources that can be allocated to nonmajors without eroding the quality of both the psychology major and the college's overall program. Because many institutions cannot add new faculty positions in psychology, these institutions need to develop creative ways to encourage more personalized teaching without overextending their resources.

RECOMMENDATIONS

As indicated earlier, this study led us to conclude that no one curriculum is ideal for all schools and students. Nevertheless, we believe that all programs should reflect certain common characteristics and emphases. Hence, to highlight important points covered in previous sections of this report, we recommend that planners of all undergraduate psychology programs strive to:

1. Ensure that psychology courses more accurately reflect the diversity of humankind, including ethnic, social, cultural, and gender diversity.

2. Help students understand psychology as a science, a profession, and a means of promoting human welfare.
3. Maintain the symbiotic relation between psychology and other aspects of education in the liberal arts.
4. Promote scientific thinking about facts, concepts, principles, and theories.
5. Design the major to begin with a required introductory survey course to be followed by required work in statistics and research methodology, which will be prerequisites for some later specialized content courses, and to conclude with an integrative experience for seniors. The structured curriculum should allow some electives.
6. Acquaint students with a broad range of methodologies, including statistics, research design, and psychometrics. For the psychology major, this goal implies taking required courses in which students collect and analyze data and write up their results using the citation and reference style of the *Publication Manual of the American Psychological Association*. At least one methodology course should be required for the psychology minor.
7. Ensure breadth of coverage by requiring courses that focus on both the natural science and the social science aspects of the discipline and ensure depth of coverage by providing courses that sequentially move students from elementary to advanced topics.
8. Provide students with the experience and understanding they will need to make the world a better place in which to lead productive and fulfilling lives.
9. Help students prepare for a variety of career goals. Such preparation will acquaint students with different specialties and careers in psychology and provide opportunities for practical experience (e.g., internships and research projects).
10. Emphasize communication skills in writing and speaking and provide appropriate opportunities for students to hone these skills, working toward clarity, conciseness, and felicity of expression.
11. Increase students' sensitivity to relevant ethical issues and familiarize them with ethical standards concerning research, teaching, and practice.

SUGGESTIONS

In addition to the foregoing recommendations, our discussion produced some suggestions that are not directly related to the curriculum per se. These are that:

1. Authors and publishers should be encouraged to include more information about human diversity and ethics in their psychology textbooks.

2. The *Publication Manual of the American Psychological Association* should be revised and updated to be more compatible with word processing technology and to be more helpful for students.[1]

3. The APA should gather and publish information on psychology minors and on interdisciplinary programs or courses related to psychology.

4. Colleges in a particular locale should work out formal agreements concerning transfer of psychology course credits from 2-year to 4-year colleges.

5. Psychology faculty should collaborate with members of other departments offering psychology courses (e.g., sports psychology and psychology of religion) to ensure the integrity of the discipline.

6. Psychology faculty should collaborate with members of other departments that require psychology courses to ensure the appropriate selection of courses for students majoring in other programs.

REFERENCES

American Psychological Association. (1982). *Ethical principles in the conduct of research with human participants.* Washington, DC: Author.

American Psychological Association. (1984). *Behavioral research with animals.* Washington, DC: Author.

American Psychological Association. (1990). Ethical principles of psychologists. *American Psychologist, 45,* 390–395.

Bok, D. (1986). *Higher learning.* Cambridge, MA: Harvard University Press.

Boyer, E. L. (1987). *College: The undergraduate experience in America.* New York: Harper & Row.

Buxton, C. E., Cofer, C. N., Gustad, J. W., MacLeod, R. B., McKeachie, W. J., & Wolfle, D. (1952). *Improving undergraduate instruction in psychology.* New York: Macmillan.

---

[1] Publisher's note: The Fourth Edition of the *Publication Manual* will be available in 1994.

Cronbach, L. J. (1957). The two disciplines of scientific psychology. *American Psychologist, 12,* 671–684.

Fact file: Earned degrees, by field of study, 1988–89. (1991, February 20). *The Chronicle of Higher Education,* p. A42.

Farrell, J., Woodward, C., & Pollock, S. (1990, April). *Psychology curriculum issues in California community colleges.* Paper presented at the meeting of the Western Psychological Association, Los Angeles.

Kimble, G. A. (1984). Psychology's two cultures. *American Psychologist, 39,* 833–839.

Kulik, J. A. (1973). *Undergraduate education in psychology.* Washington, DC: American Psychological Association.

Lewis, L. L., & Farris, E. (1989). *Undergraduate general education and humanities requirements* (Higher Education Surveys No. 7). Rockville, MD: Westat.

McGovern, T. V., Furumoto, L., Halpern, D. F., Kimble, G. A., & McKeachie, W. J. (1991). Liberal education, study in depth, and the arts and sciences major—Psychology. *American Psychologist, 46,* 598–605.

McKeachie, W. J., & Milholland, J. E. (1961). *Undergraduate curricula in psychology.* Chicago: Scott, Foresman.

Mill, J. S. (1979). *Utilitarianism.* Indianapolis, IN: Hackett. (Original work published 1861)

Perlman, B., & McCann, L. I. (1991). *A national survey of general education and proficiency requirements in undergraduate and psychology curricula.* Unpublished manuscript.

Scheirer, C. J., & Rogers, A. M. (1985). *The undergraduate psychology curriculum: 1984.* Washington, DC: American Psychological Association.

Wagner, D. L. (Ed.). (1983). *The seven liberal arts in the Middle Ages.* Bloomington: Indiana University Press.

Wegener, C. (1978). *Liberal education and the modern university.* Chicago: University of Chicago Press.

Winter, D. G., McClelland, D. C., & Stewart, A. J. (1981). *A new case for the liberal arts.* San Francisco: Jossey-Bass.

7

PROMOTING ACTIVE LEARNING IN PSYCHOLOGY COURSES

VIRGINIA ANDREOLI MATHIE, in collaboration with BARNEY BEINS, LUDY T. BENJAMIN, JR., MARTHA M. EWING, CHRISTINE C. IIJIMA HALL, BRUCE HENDERSON, DALE W. McADAM, and RANDOLPH A. SMITH

What takes place in the classroom is determined by many variables. The nature of the discipline; characteristics and goals of the instructor, students, and the institution; and the contemporary needs and expectations of society interact to influence what is taught, how it is taught, and how it is received. Increasingly, the quality of undergraduate education is evaluated in terms of how the classroom environment is responsive to the characteristics and needs of students. In the classroom of the next century, instructors will continue to deal with a diverse student population in terms of age, ethnicity, educational goals, background, learning styles, and socioeconomic status. In response to these diverse student populations, changes in the structure of the learning environment and the teaching strategies used in the classroom are needed (American Association of Community and Junior Colleges [AACJC], 1988; Cheney, 1989; Chickering & Associates, 1981; Kolb, 1984).

Instructors must also help students in all disciplines in higher education to develop skills to adapt to a rapidly changing, interdependent world.

Individuals are required to think critically and to synthesize large quantities of new information, to be sensitive to diversity, and to develop attitudes and skills that promote lifelong learning (National Institute of Education [NIE], 1984). However, reports on the quality of education in the United States (Association of American Colleges [AAC], 1985; Baker, Roueche, & Gillett-Karam, 1990; McKeachie, Pintrich, Lin, Smith, & Sharma, 1990; NIE, 1984, 1988) point out that there is too much information being offered to students and too little attention being paid to the strategies for learning, inquiry, and problem solving. To enhance the quality of education, instructors must broaden their repertoire of pedagogical techniques to include strategies that foster critical thinking and problem-solving skills and that instill a willingness and motivation to continue learning beyond the classroom (AAC, 1985). As McKeachie et al. (1990) stated, "When one takes life-long learning and thinking as a major goal of education, knowledge becomes a means rather than an end. . . . A course that dulls the student's curiosity and interest must be a failure no matter how solid the content" (p. 1).

To meet these challenges for enhancing the quality of education, advocates for educational reform have included among their recommendations the need for teaching that stimulates active learning. The NIE's 1984 report, *Involvement in Learning: Realizing the Potential of American Higher Education*, promoted active learning as the number one priority in American higher education, noting that it is crucial for the development of higher cognitive abilities. It is possible to integrate active pedagogical methods for teaching, learning, and assessment into all courses. This integration promotes achievement of objectives important to a discipline and at the same time addresses larger developmental purposes and societal challenges (Baker et al., 1990; Chickering & Associates, 1981; Sechzer & Pfafflin, 1987). Yet despite these important outcomes and a host of other benefits for students and faculty, active learning accounts for only a small part of the pedagogy in the typical college course (NIE, 1984). There is no indication that psychology teachers make any greater use of active learning than other instructors, although pedagogical resources exist for the psychology teacher and current psychological theories of learning and cognition support its use.

We hope that this chapter will be an impetus to teachers who have, as yet, made little use of active learning in their courses. After identifying the principles of active learning and discussing the rationale behind it, we describe how to incorporate active learning in psychology courses and how to respond to concerns and problems that discourage its use. We describe the principal teaching practices that increase active learning and suggest additional resources detailing such methods. We conclude with recommendations to enhance active learning in psychology classes; to spread its use across the entire curriculum; and to encourage its use by precollege, undergraduate, and graduate students while in school and beyond.

DESIGN PRINCIPLES OF ACTIVE LEARNING

Active learning connotes an array of learning situations in and out of the classroom in which students enjoy hands-on and "minds-on" experiences (e.g., Benjamin, 1991; Brothen, 1986; Frederick, 1987). Students learn through active participation in simulations, demonstrations, discussions, debates, games, problem solving, experiments, writing exercises, and interactive lectures (Schomberg, 1986).

This chapter identifies several design principles of active learning activities. Active participation by students is a key component of active learning, but other features must be present as well. Active learning should involve the entire class. Demonstrations, for example, that involve a few students may be active learning for those students doing the activity but not for the class as a whole. Active learning requires that all students have the opportunity for the complete experience.

Active learning is most effective when students understand the relevance of the exercise to the subject matter at hand, to other psychological course content, or to the events of the students' everyday life. Such activities should be flexible enough to encourage student-initiated learning.

Active learning stimulates learning at higher cognitive levels (Wittrock, 1984). Active learning methods require students not only to know and comprehend, but prompt them to apply, to analyze, to synthesize, and to evaluate (Bloom, 1956).

Active learning methods vary in the time they require in class and out of class. An instructor can design short activities that occupy a few minutes of class time or design an entire course with active learning as the sole learning practice.

Active learning exercises involve feedback (but not necessarily graded feedback) to the students. Such feedback may come from the instructor or from other students in the class, but it should be planned into the activity, ideally at the time of or soon after the learning experience. Out-of-class activities should involve feedback in a subsequent class.

WHY SHOULD WE PROMOTE ACTIVE LEARNING?

Too often students play a passive role in college courses. Studies using in-class observers report that the lecture occupies as much as 80%–95% of class time, regardless of class size (Eble, 1988; Lewis, 1982; Lewis & Woodward, 1984). We do not want to denigrate the lecture method. It has dominated the educational scene for centuries, and its survival is not due solely to tradition or inertia. The lecture has many advantages, perhaps the greatest of which is its ability to communicate a large amount of information in a short amount of time. Therefore, we are not proposing that faculty stop giving lectures. However, an overreliance on the lecture method tends to foster passivity on the part of students. Using a variety of teaching styles can increase student involvement (NIE, 1984) and can accommodate the diverse learning styles students bring to the classroom (Kolb, 1984). We are encouraging faculty to broaden their pedagogical techniques by replacing some lecture time with active learning techniques.

Active learning shifts the students' role from passive to one that requires participation and involves students in the process of learning. Student-generated learning activities have been shown to enhance student interest in courses, to foster intrinsic motivation for learning, and to create an interest in lifelong learning (Weimer, 1987). The authors of the NIE (1984) report concluded:

> There is now a good deal of research evidence to suggest that the more time and effort students invest in the learning process and the more intensely they engage in their own education, the greater will be their growth and achievement, their satisfaction with their educational experiences, and their persistence in college, and the more likely they are to continue their learning. (p. 17)

Active learning exercises increase the cognitive demands on students. They produce intellectual discrepancies that motivate the development of improved cognitive abilities such as critical thinking (Gorman, Law, & Lindegren, 1981; Halonen, 1986). Active learning involves the elaboration of meaning, the enhancement of context, and the processing of information at different levels. These are cognitive practices that facilitate learning and retention (Birch, 1986; DiVesta & Peverly, 1984; Hamil & Janssen, 1987; Hutchings & Wutzdorff, 1988; Slate & Charlesworth, 1989).

Students benefit from active learning in other ways as well. Active learning has been shown to improve interpersonal communication and human relations skills (Neer, 1987) and self-esteem (Johnson & Johnson, 1987). Because active learning exercises encourage students to talk with and learn from one another, students are exposed to different ideas and perspectives that offer social and cultural breadth (Bouton & Garth, 1983; Slavin, 1983). By encouraging student responses, active learning exercises engage student interests, thereby accommodating different learning styles and cultural backgrounds (Kolb, 1984; Lee, 1986).

Faculty members also benefit from the use of active learning activities in their courses (Jernstedt, 1982). They can monitor more closely the process and progress of learning. Faculty members' satisfaction with their courses often increases, and, not surprisingly, student evaluations of their courses also improve.

In short, strong evidence supports the value of active learning for students and faculty. That evidence comes from studies investigating active learning methods such as writing to learn, critical thinking, and cooperative or collaborative learning (Glover, Ronning, & Bruning, 1990; Pascarella & Terenzini, 1991). In the next section we discuss some of the issues instructors should consider before incorporating active learning strategies into their courses.

USE OF ACTIVE LEARNING

Like any pedagogical technique, active learning requires planning. Instructors must consider their students' reactions to this style of teaching and set the stage for its use. Instructors must determine the types of activities to use and when and how to integrate these activities with the course content. The next section of this chapter examines some of these issues.

Strategies for Increased Effectiveness

Because active learning is simply one teaching mode among others, the use of sound basic teaching principles should guide the instructor in setting the stage for its use. In this section we elaborate on some practices that increase the effectiveness of active learning activities.

Providing an Overview

At the beginning of the course, instructors should give students a detailed description of the active learning processes that will be used and a description of how active learning fits into the goals of the course. Instructors should tell students what is expected of them (participation, written work, discussion, etc.) during the semester and what can be expected of the instructor. Because students will be concerned about the grading process, the instructor should provide information about evaluation criteria for these activities.

Motivating Students

The importance of motivation to the success of active learning is an overriding consideration (Lowman, 1990). Students must be motivated to participate in discussions, exercises, and written assignments that are intellectually challenging and that require commitment and personal investment on the part of the students. Because people involve themselves more fully in those activities they choose to pursue as opposed to those activities they are made to do, giving students a choice of the types of activities in which they engage and the degree to which they do so should increase students' willingness and motivation to participate (Deci & Ryan, 1985). However, students do not always come to college with an orientation that allows them to see the classroom as an arena for choice. They may believe that school-related choices are not truly their own, and they may prefer to avoid making such choices. Many high school and first- and second-year college students are threatened by ambiguity and lack of structure and are uncomfortable making their own preferences or viewpoints known (Perry, 1970). They look to the instructor to provide structure (e.g., "Just tell me what I need to know") and the right answer. Instructors can provide an atmosphere of challenge and support that fosters cognitive development by helping students learn to evaluate alternative viewpoints and choices and to select their own course of action. When students have the opportunity to experience more autonomy in the learning process and change their motivational orientation, they will gain more from active learning activities.

Establishing Rapport and Climate

The importance of establishing rapport cannot be overemphasized (Lawry, 1990). Many faculty, particularly in large research universities, are oriented primarily toward their disciplines and secondarily toward their students. Coupled with large class sizes, infrequent class meetings, and scarce informal opportunities to engage faculty, the research and content bias of instructors gives students the impression—true or not—that faculty are cold, distant, and uncaring. It is not an unreasonable conclusion in many cases.

A learning environment must be carefully built; it does not automatically exist. Instructors should create a climate of trust for asking questions and participating in discussions. Faculty can build a rapport with students by interacting informally with students, working with them on common concerns, and communicating a passion for learning. These activities allow students and faculty to disclose to each other what they find important. Active caring enables students to engage in active learning more easily and more fruitfully.

Setting Limits

It is important for instructors to be sensitive to issues of privacy (Matthews, 1991). In some cases, instructors must establish guidelines on the type and amount of disclosure that is appropriate. One potential problem is that for some activities, some students could disclose issues that may be inappropriate in a classroom setting (e.g., unusual sexual activities, major family dysfunctions, psychological disorders). In addition, as students gain more autonomy in the classroom and become more willing to delve into controversial issues and try new experiences, there are more opportunities for them to become uncomfortable. If instructors are aware of these risks, they can develop strategies to deal with them. For example, students who wish to discuss personal issues or problems in more depth could be encouraged to see the instructor for guidance and referrals. Students who feel uncomfortable participating in an activity could be given an alternative activity.

Students should be given guidelines for nonjudgmental evaluation and feedback for particular exercises. Students should be encouraged to analyze, inquire, and synthesize information but in a nonjudgmental, constructive, and appropriate manner.

Sensitivity to individual differences in learning and participation must be taken into account when considering limits to be placed on students. Some active learning procedures may be discomforting to those students who are shy or who are not attuned to active discourse with teachers and fear to take such a risk (Neer, 1987). Individual differences arise from culture, gender, ethnicity, physical makeup, personal history, and personality. These differences affect the type and amount of interaction in class. This is not to say that students should be excused from participation, but rather that instructors must be sensitive to the boundaries these students may bring to class (Bronstein & Quina, 1988).

Structure and Content

Active learning is best introduced into courses gradually. The student who is not developmentally ready for an active learning exercise will not profit from it. Indeed, students may develop unfavorable attitudes toward active learning through an inappropriate introduction to it. Instructors must plan active learning activities so that the content and degree of structure are appropriate for students.

Preparation

Active learning is not do-it-yourself learning; it must be planned thoroughly by an instructor. There is a salient and important active teaching component to active learning that calls for preparation of materials suited to both the students and the course objectives. Instructors must review activities before selecting the ones most appropriate for the particular objectives and for the level of students. Instructors must design active learning activities or modify existing ones to fit specific course situations. Instructors must plan when to use an activity and must consider how it will be integrated with the other activities and content of the class. Instructors must think about the degree of structure to provide in the instructions, in the activity itself, and in the evaluation criteria. The type and amount of feedback to students and the criteria for evaluation should be determined in advance.

Nature of Material

Active learning is not a collection of exercises that entertain students; exercises must be relevant to the material being discussed. Exercises can introduce new concepts that are then discussed in class, or they can reiterate and demonstrate issues already discussed in lectures or presentations.

What sort of content is appropriate for active learning? On one hand, it is possible to teach almost anything with active learning. On the other hand, it has been our experience that active learning works particularly well with complex material that calls for the development, evaluation, and tempered acceptance of several alternative explanations. In terms of Bloom's (1956) taxonomy of cognitive activities, students can be challenged to analyze their alternatives, to apply them to concrete situations, to merge them through synthesis, and to weigh those contributions against specific evaluation criteria. The active learning process helps students become critical, informed, and autonomous builders and judges of different sophisticated worldviews.

Stepwise Progression

It is important to take a stepwise progression approach to active learning exercises. As with any course content, there should be a hierarchical sequence to the methods used and the information covered. For first- and second-year college students who are likely to be uncomfortable without structure (at the dualistic stage of intellectual development in Perry's, 1970, model), instructors can start with highly structured active learning activities that require a few simple pieces of information and that involve students in concrete activities (Parker, 1978; Widick, Knefelkamp, & Parker, 1975; Widick & Simpson, 1978). As students become accustomed to the active learning style or for students at later stages of development, the structure can be reduced and the complexity of the activities increased. A stepwise approach would be particularly important for activities that involve self-disclosure. Beginning exercises should require less personal and less threatening disclosure (e.g., sharing educational background and preferences for food or music). After trust is established, exercises involving issues that require more intimate self-disclosure (e.g., family, fears, attitudes) can be used.

Types of Activities

Experimentation with technology and pedagogy is certainly not new in psychology. Sanford (1910) recommended "the fullest use of demonstrations and class experiments, given always in such a way that the student shall not fail to grasp the psychological meaning" (p. 68). Walton (1930) provided descriptions, illustrations, and directions for the maintenance of demonstration devices for the classroom. In his directions for creating slides, Andrews (1946) reported that demonstrations would aid "retention by associating facts and principles with more vivid experiences" (p. 312). Although such early demonstrations and exercises may not have met our criteria for active learning, they show that psychology instructors wanted to engage students more actively in the learning process.

Interest in active learning has generated a plethora of activities to be used in all levels of psychology courses. Although instructors may find many of these activities suitable for classes of 25 (or fewer) to 50 students, there are a growing number of activities that have been field-tested in large classes of 200 to 300 students (e.g., Benjamin, 1991). The purpose of this section is to identify general categories of activities.

Active Learning in Note Taking

Active learning can be applied in situations frequently regarded as passive. For example, students can be taught systems of note taking (see Pauk, 1984) that will engage them with the material in lectures and that will facilitate a dialogue between students and the instructor in the form of overt questions or comments for the instructor or even in comments that go no further than the students' notes. Students should seek feedback about their note taking to make it an active learning process.

Demonstrations and Exercises

A primary method for active learning in the classroom involves demonstrations and exercises. Publications like *Activities Handbook for the Teaching of Psychology* (Benjamin & Lowman, 1981; Makosky, Sileo, Whittemore, Landry, & Skutley, 1990; Makosky, Whittemore, & Rogers, 1987), *Handbook for Teaching Introductory Psychology* (Benjamin, Daniel, & Brewer, 1985), *Teaching of Psychology* (the journal of the APA's Division 2), *The Psychology Teacher Network* (the APA's newsletter for psychology teachers from high school through college level), and the instructor's manuals in most textbook packages contain many suggestions. There is also a growing number of books describing exercises designed specifically to develop critical thinking skills (Bell, 1991; Chaffee, 1991) and describing laboratory exercises to accompany advanced courses (Abramson, 1990; Bennett, Hausfeld, Reeve, & Smith, 1981; Ewing, 1992; Power, Hausfeld, & Gorta, 1981). Although these activities must be critically evaluated by the instructor to ensure they meet the course objectives, the instructor's criteria for active learning, and the developmental level of the students, many activities meet the criteria for active learning outlined in this chapter, take only a few minutes of class time, have modest equipment requirements, and have minimal chances for failure.

Writing

Writing assignments are a traditional technique for active learning. Writing involves analysis of ideas and their presentation, deliberate shaping and elaboration of one's thoughts, and feedback from the reader (Fulwiler & Young, 1990; Nodine, 1990). Writing assignments can range from modest in-class paragraphs to extensive research papers (Tchudi, 1986). Although some exercises may be graded, Maimon, Nodine, Hearn, and Haney-Peritz (1990) provided examples of several ungraded writing exercises. However, even if not graded, all writing assignments should receive some feedback from either the instructor or other students.

Group Activities

Group projects, exercises, or discussion groups are excellent opportunities for active learning. Dividing the class into small groups can be particularly helpful for fostering active learning in large classes. For example, Benjamin (1991) described several small-group and dyadic activities used in large classes. Groups are opportunities for collaborative learning and the active enrichment of both the cognitive and social lives of students (Billson, 1986; Feichtner & Michaelsen, 1984; Johnson & Johnson, 1987).

Computer Usage

Growing universal access to computers presents new possibilities for active learning. Stoloff and Couch (1992) compiled a directory of software for psychology courses and Kahn and Brookshire (1991) described how to use computer bulletin boards and electronic mail as fast, interactive ways to engage students in a course. Unfortunately, many software packages present only the appearance of active learning. Be wary of packages that are merely on-screen study guides. The watchwords are *interactive* and *elaborative*. The program should seek to establish an interdependent relationship between the student and the computer. In their search for software that promotes active learning, instructors can profit from reading critical reviews (see *Teaching of Psychology* as well as reviews such as Anderson & Hornby, 1988, 1990; Beins, 1990; Hornby & Anderson, 1990) and testing the packages themselves to determine whether they meet specific active learning criteria.

Research

Student research is an important tradition in psychology training. It can involve varying levels of skill, commitment, independence, accountability, and active learning. Active learning in research can range from serving as a subject in an experiment and critically analyzing the experience to engaging in research activities incorporated into classes and laboratory courses or from working in a lab to learn laboratory techniques to conducting independent research to be presented as an honor's thesis, reported at a research conference, or prepared for publication. These activities help students become independent learners, formulating their own questions and seeking the answers to them (Beins, 1988; Ewing, 1991a, 1991b; Hovancik, 1984; Kierniesky, 1984; Palladino, Carsud, Hulicka, & Benjamin, 1982).

Field Experiences

Active learning occurs when students work in an applied community setting. Field placement and internship courses and volunteer service projects within other courses provide opportunities for students to observe real problems and to use personal and academic knowledge and skills to solve them (Fernald et al., 1982; Hutchings & Wutzdorff, 1988; Lestina, 1990; Sherman, 1982; VandeCreek & Fleischer, 1984; Ware & Millard, 1987). The internship or community service experience helps students evaluate their own skills and knowledge base and to identify deficiencies (Ryan, 1988). Internships and field placements also promote the personal growth of students in ways that foster an openness to lifelong learning. In evaluations of the Washington Center Internship Program (Ryan, 1988), students reported that internships helped them clarify their career goals, increase their awareness of world issues and social problems, increase their tolerance of diverse viewpoints, and improve their self-confidence.

Interns should have on-site supervisors who supervise students' daily activities and discuss how the agency serves its clients or does its business. Interns should also have on-campus faculty advisors with whom they meet periodically to discuss the academic aspects of their work, including papers they are expected to write and readings that supplement their applied work.

Undergraduate Teaching Assistantships

Another model of active learning uses advanced undergraduates as teaching assistants (TAs) in large introductory courses (McAdam, 1987, 1990; Mendenhall & Burr, 1983). University instructors may recruit TAs from within their own institution; community college instructors could recruit TAs from local universities. McAdam (1987, 1990) found that with ratios of 15 students per TA and 20 TAs per instructor, both TAs and students can engage in active learning throughout their contacts with each other and with the instructor. After extensive training and instructor feedback, TAs encourage active learning by applying principles of psychology to "data" consisting of student observations and experiences from daily life or from community service projects. TAs also encourage active learning by leading group discussions that require students to develop alternative explanations and to invoke alternative psychological principles. In McAdam's model, TAs also review students' journals, suggest appropriate readings and possible areas of observation, and design and supervise small-group projects for their students.

Non–Course-Related Activities

A non–course-related, yet departmentally sanctioned, active learning opportunity occurs when undergraduates take initiative through their own organizations. Psychology clubs or honorary organizations such as Psi Beta and Psi Chi offer social, informational, and academic programs for psychology majors and others interested in psychology. Students can generate program ideas, recruit speakers from the faculty or the community, arrange field trips, evaluate the quality of their events, and so forth. These activities let students learn firsthand about organizational and group dynamics. Interaction with peers and faculty in student clubs promotes social and affective development through the sharing of different views and cultural perspectives in an informal, less evaluative context.

Evaluation of Activities

After adding active learning activities to their courses, instructors must evaluate these activities. The easiest and most obvious evaluation is to determine whether the activity was successful in producing the results the instructor wanted. Was the demonstration carried out effectively? Did the discussion or writing assignments elicit the concepts, viewpoints, or principles the instructor had hoped would emerge? Was sufficient time allocated for the activity? With careful planning, procedural problems, if they occur, can be remedied without too much difficulty.

Outcome evaluation determines whether students learned what the instructor intended. This type of evaluation is more problematic. What processes ultimately occur in the student's "black box" are difficult to assess. However, assessment of students' understanding of a concept taught by an active learning exercise must be done. Assessment can include written or oral responses about what the students learned, analysis of reasons for unexpected results, and tests of long-term retention and understanding of the exercises at the end of the course. Instructors might also include questions on the course evaluation instrument that assess students' perceptions of the extent to which the active learning activities engaged them in the learning process, facilitated learning of various concepts, and stimulated further thought or reading. On the basis of the outcome evaluations instructors can revise active learning activities or delete them when other pedagogical techniques would be more useful.

PROBLEMS ENCOUNTERED IN USING ACTIVE LEARNING

Although the benefits of active learning are supported by research (Glover et al., 1990; Jernstedt, 1982; Johnson & Johnson, 1987; NIE, 1984; Pascarella & Terenzini, 1991), teachers still do not engage their students actively. Instructors give numerous reasons for their reluctance to include active learning strategies. Some of these reasons are concerns or misunderstandings about the activities themselves, personal styles or needs of individual instructors, and professional concerns such as how to document what is learned and how to evaluate it. These concerns are real and need to be addressed. In the next section, we identify some of the common barriers and offer arguments to counter them.

Concerns or Misunderstandings About Active Learning Activities

1. *Instructors believe they are already using active learning in their classes.*

Many faculty members have a basic misunderstanding of what active learning is, claiming that they are using such approaches just because they do not lecture constantly. Films, videotapes, outside speakers, and classroom demonstrations do not constitute active learning simply because they are substituted for lectures. A rat that presses a lever in front of the students is a valuable demonstration, but it is active learning only for the rat. Similarly, having a student wear visual-displacement goggles to show how visual adaptation takes place is active learning only for the student wearing the goggles.

Active learning is not busy work (e.g., study guides or workbooks) meant to occupy students when teachers have extra time to fill. We believe active learning activities should involve the entire class, stimulate students to think critically about issues, and provide feedback about or evaluation of the activities.

2. *Instructors are uncertain how to "do" active learning.*

Some faculty members have never heard of active learning approaches; others may not have used such strategies before. When reading about various active learning strategies, these instructors may not understand the activity from the description given or may need to see the activity demonstrated to them before they feel comfortable using it themselves. These concerns are probably related to the fear that an activity will not work.

If a description of an active learning device is unclear, contact the author. Teachers who are concerned about using demonstrations they have not observed firsthand can attend teaching-related sessions at APA meetings, regional association meetings, or various teaching conferences around the country (Hill, Palladino, & Smith, 1992) or observe colleagues' classes when such activities are used.

3. *Instructors believe that things are likely to go wrong.*

Fear of failure and evaluation apprehension are powerful motivators for using lectures. Teachers fear that a failed demonstration will not make the point they wished or, worse, it may leave a mistaken notion in students' minds. More important than failing to make a certain point is the possibility of personal embarrassment if a new strategy fails. This possibility threatens teachers' self-esteem and authority figure role.

Instructors may make an implicit assumption that things do not go wrong in a lecture. They believe they have more control over what is presented in lectures. The evidence of failed active learning activities is typically visible because such activities require evaluation or feedback. Although lectures may also go badly, the evidence of failure is less dramatic or immediate. Feedback during or after lectures is rarely requested; teachers simply assume that students understood and learned everything presented.

To decrease the chances of something going wrong, instructors can use active learning activities that have been published (e.g., see *Teaching of Psychology*) or ones they have seen demonstrated. Even if an activity turns out differently than expected, instructors can describe what should have taken place and use the opportunity to examine why it did not. Letting students know at the outset that these activities are learning experiences for teachers as well might mitigate evaluation apprehension.

4. *Instructors feel that active learning strategies are merely gimmicks or attention-getters without substance.*

This statement is often made by faculty members who resent recasting classroom presentations into short, entertaining, attention-getting, audiovisual episodes that fit the mold of sophisticated television productions. They believe that active learning strategies placate students who have limited attention spans. These faculty often view active learning activities as devoid of content and believe that active learning approaches generate superficial and short-lived learning.

The 1984 report sponsored by the NIE addressed this concern:

> By no means do these active approaches avoid the content or raw material of the disciplines. By no means do we intend to abandon standards of content in favor of exotic teaching techniques. Quite the contrary, our contention is that students are more apt to learn that content if they are engaged with it. (p. 28)

Successful active learning strategies should use psychological terminology and methodologies and be content oriented. When students complete such activities, they know more about psychology and about approaches to psychological knowledge. Active learning activities give teachers a double-edged sword. They are efficient learning strategies, and they increase students' interest in and motivation and liking for the material.

5. *Active learning strategies are too time consuming in preparation time, during the class period, and for evaluation.*

It takes considerable time, energy, and commitment to organize activities, integrate them into the course, create stimuli, provide students with appropriate background, and plan the evaluation. Any preparation for classes, when well done, is quite time consuming. Developing good lectures can be as time consuming as creating active learning activities. One can argue that once a lecture is written, it can be given repeatedly. Unfortunately, that is one of the possible drawbacks of lectures—they can lose their spontaneity and currency. Active learning strategies may also be used more than once, but because they are new for the students who are doing them, spontaneity will always be present. This is not to say that active learning activities cannot become dated. They do require systematic review and revision, but this is true of all course material.

Some instructors are concerned about the time needed during class to conduct active learning exercises. They fear that limited learning will emerge from a single demonstration that could take half a class period. Another fear is that details of an activity will obscure the point being made in an exercise or that the activity may destroy the flow of information during the lecture so that the relevance of connected, consecutive ideas may be lost to students. There is also the concern that the class will not have enough time throughout the semester to cover all essential material.

Such concerns have a logical basis, but the assumption that underlies them may be questionable. Teachers assume that students leave lectures knowing the main points that were covered; however, students' answers on tests often surprise even the most optimistic and supportive teachers (Barnette, 1947). Ericksen (1983) found that meaningful material was retained longer than a myriad of facts learned by rote. The goal of active learning strategies is to put the focal points in a meaningful context so that students understand them and know how they relate to other information and to their own experience. The personalized learning that can result from active learning exercises may help students remember better what they learn. "[W]e learn more, and more deeply, when learning touches on things that we care about" (Hutchings & Wutzdorff, 1988, p. 12).

Instructors who are concerned about time constraints should keep in mind that it is not necessary to cover in class all of the material in a textbook. As Benjamin (1991) pointed out, class time can be used to clarify material that is not explained well in the textbook and to present material that is not in the textbook. Furthermore, activities that take as little as 5 minutes or projects that students complete outside the classroom can be effective teaching tools that expend little class time.

With respect to evaluation, every exercise does not need to be graded, but feedback is absolutely crucial to point out to students their strengths and weaknesses and to document that what was intended to be learned indeed has been learned. To reduce evaluation time without sacrificing feedback, students can provide self-evaluation. This type of group work helps students focus on more effective approaches to a particular problem and lets them learn from the pitfalls that other students encountered. Instructors should keep in mind, however, that peer evaluations make some students uncomfortable. If students view the instructor as the authority, they may be reluctant to accept or value feedback from peers (Perry, 1970). Also, because they take evaluation personally, they may fear that peer evaluation, if it is critical in any way, will be viewed unfavorably and result in uncomfortable relationships with others in the class. To address these concerns instructors should provide structure to the peer evaluation process; make the evaluation criteria as concrete and clear as possible; reinforce the value of peer evaluation; and, if appropriate, make the evaluations anonymous.

6. *Instructors believe that active learning demonstrations are too expensive.*

Some faculty labor under the misconception that active learning strategies require large investments in equipment or laboratory space. Although instructors who have well-equipped laboratories and a sufficient budget for supplies can offer more sophisticated active learning activities and are sometimes motivated to do so, the lack of such facilities does not rule out the use of active learning approaches. There are many simple active learning exercises that can be used at institutions that have not yet acquired extensive laboratories. These exercises are suitable for either in-class or out-of-class use and may involve only the duplication of forms for students to use.

Personal Concerns

1. *Active learning activities reduce the instructor's control of the class and of the process and outcomes of learning.*

Lecturing gives instructors a sense of control of students' deportment and their learning. The individualized nature of active learning activities that allows for students' unique perception of and reaction to these activities may threaten instructors' sense of control and create anxiety and discomfort. At a time when the establishment and assessment of goals, objectives, and learning outcomes are receiving much attention (see chapter 1), instructors may believe that compared with lectures, active learning techniques limit their ability to ensure that course objectives are met and to document learning outcomes.

However, the control that teachers believe they have in a lecture format is really an illusion. Regardless of what information is presented in a lecture, there is no guarantee that it will be processed by all students who are physically present. Cameron (cited in Adler & Towne, 1987), using a time sampling procedure, found that at any given time, only 20% of a typical class was paying attention to the lecture and only 12% was actively listening to it. Even for the small percentage of students who are paying attention, many may forget what they are told or may take notes that are disorganized, fail to capture the essence of the lecture, or omit important information. The individualized experience and self-reflection that accompany active learning activities may elicit more focused attention.

A final point in examining the issue of control in the learning process is that giving control to students may actually be a favorable outcome of active learning. In addition to helping students learn complex skills and related information, active learning reinforces independent learning. In a passive learning environment, students rely on the interpretive and analytic skills of the instructor; in active learning, they generate their own hypotheses and evaluate them. As a result, with active learning they are exposed not only to knowledge about psychology, but also to the processes that lead to generating that knowledge. By learning how to take responsibility for their own learning, students are more likely to engage in lifelong learning.

2. *Instructors feel that an active learning approach does not fit their teaching style.*

Although some instructors believe active learning techniques are important and viable teaching techniques, they resist using them because this approach does not fit their own teaching and learning styles. Their own experiences may lead instructors to believe that the only way to learn material is to hear it directly from an instructor's mouth (Svinicki & Dixon, 1987). The faculty member's job is to present knowledge; the students' job is to acquire knowledge.

Kolb (1984) used the term *assimilators* to refer to individuals who prefer this style of learning. Assimilators tend to learn best when information is presented by an authoritative figure in an impersonal manner that emphasizes theory and systematic analysis and that permits impartial reflection. They tend to prefer lecture formats over more unstructured self-discovery exercises. In an informal survey of faculty using the Kolb Learning Inventory (Kolb, 1976), J. S. Halonen (personal communication, July 6, 1991) found that about 85% of the respondents were classified as assimilators. Given their own learning experience and a possible preference for the assimilator learning style, it is not surprising that instructors rely heavily on lectures and feel uncomfortable with more active modes of teaching.

However, not all students learn best by the lecture method. Kolb (1984) identified three other learning styles. *Convergers* favor structure, theoretical analysis, and hypothetical-deductive reasoning as well as the opportunity to experiment with and apply the information in projects and assignments. *Divergers* learn best when they are involved in real situations and can examine concrete experiences from many perspectives. Finally, *accommodators* have a strong "doing" orientation and prefer learning situations in which they are actively involved with the material and with new experiences. They are risk-takers who tend to solve problems by trial and error. Accommodators, in particular, benefit from an active learning orientation in the classroom, although elements of the converger and diverger learning styles suggest that they, too, would have much to gain from this teaching approach.

We are not recommending indiscriminate change in educational philosophy and practice. We are encouraging faculty to gradually move away from solely lectures to a style that incorporates active learning strategies along with lectures. Pedagogical diversity should broaden the appeal of courses and improve our capacity to reach students with different learning styles.

Professional Concerns

1. *Active learning and teaching are insufficiently rewarded.*

There are few rewards for teaching. Not only do teachers think that they do not have enough time, but they believe that time spent on teaching is not highly regarded by their colleagues. A collateral problem is that scholarly activity often does not include teaching, as reflected in the reward structure of most universities. Scholarly activity tends to be narrowly defined as publications related to research. There are few rewards for deviating from the traditional forms of inquiry (NIE, 1984). This system discourages faculty from spending the extra time required to incorporate active learning into their courses.

These comments are not trivial, given the higher status accorded to research activities compared with teaching and given the pressure to produce scholarly activity (i.e., published works). When institutions are interested in research alone, teaching activities will not be rewarded very highly. However, recent trends (e.g., Boyer, 1990) suggest an integration of teaching and research as partners in the definition of scholarship. Scholarship can include aspects of teaching, and publication in teaching journals (e.g., *Teaching of Psychology*) or in teaching issues of journals (e.g., *Contemporary Social Psychology*) can be viewed as scholarly productivity. There are possibilities for teaching-related presentations at regional and national teaching conferences and at regional psychological association meetings. Depending on one's institution, the development of new courses or the significant modification of existing courses to include active learning strategies may be viewed as scholarly activity. Recognition of these activities in promotion, tenure, and merit decisions motivates instructors to try teaching strategies that require more time for preparation and evaluation than lectures require.

There are rewards for using active learning within the classroom itself. Students' attitudes are often more positive; they tend to be more receptive to and willing to work at exercises that actively engage them in the learning process (Hutchings & Wutzdorff, 1988; Kolb, 1984; NIE, 1984). Instructors gain satisfaction from knowing that students are better prepared to succeed in courses that follow, not only because of their increased mastery of content but also because of their improved critical thinking skills and the acquisition of more sophisticated techniques in psychological investigation. Finally, students' evaluations may be enhanced. In departments in which good teaching is associated with the number of positive comments on the course evaluation, active learning strategies can benefit faculty as well.

Active learning strategies bring intrinsic rewards to instructors. Examining the content of a course from a new perspective, learning more about the intellectual and social development of students, and developing and honing new teaching skills offer instructors exciting challenges.

2. Peer pressure increases conformity to teaching practices that do not support active learning.

Young faculty may be reluctant to use active learning strategies because more experienced colleagues do not. Active learning strategies in their classes may be viewed not as good teaching but rather as an attempt to entertain students to get good student evaluations. This view can operate against the use of active learning in two ways. First, other faculty may feel threatened, believing that students will become critical of classes involving more passive modes of learning because those classes are perceived to be less interesting and less challenging and thus result in less learning. To keep their own evaluations favorable, they may pressure colleagues to use traditional methods. Second, in an open class that encourages analysis and constructive criticism, students may not only give more positive feedback, but they may also be more critical of some aspects of the course. Thus, instructors who use active learning approaches may increase their risks by getting student evaluations that may be construed by some colleagues to be unfavorable.

However, whole departments benefit from increased acceptance of and commitment to active learning. Colleagues may find themselves pleasantly surprised by students who participate more actively in classrooms beyond those in which active learning is used. Successful teachers may prefer students who are responsive versus those who are essentially passive. Students who develop active learning skills may generalize their active strategies in other contexts and enhance the classrooms of others.

RECOMMENDATIONS

To summarize, active learning is a valuable pedagogical tool. Students benefit from well-planned active learning activities that are integrated into the course in a meaningful way, that allow analysis and discussion of what students have experienced, and that provide feedback about what students have learned. Although there may be obstacles to overcome before active learning can be incorporated successfully into courses or the entire curriculum, these obstacles need not be insurmountable. This section of the chapter offers some recommendations to promote the use of active learning strategies in high school, community college, and college classes.

The Climate for Active Learning

A well-established perception is that undergraduate education generally is not held in high esteem in academe. A related perception is that many institutions have abandoned their traditional missions as centers of teaching. They have emulated or drifted toward the research university model and developed concomitant reward systems. The NIE (1984) stated that "While research and teaching can and should be mutually supportive and complementary, many of our colleges and universities overemphasize research and minimize quality teaching in personnel decisions, and this tradition has potentially damaging effects on student learning and development" (p. 59). Because the preparation, implementation, and evaluation of active learning exercises require large amounts of faculty time and effort, faculty members who use them may have less time for pursuits that maintain higher status, such as research and publication activities. Unless active learning activities are valued, a faculty member who uses them is at risk within the existing or developing reward systems.

The prevailing system of status and rewards is not likely to change without concerted action by organizations and individuals in leadership positions to make clear commitments to alternative models. Therefore we make the following recommendations for alternative models.

1. *Psychology faculty members and their colleagues should be encouraged to work with administrators to develop alternative reward systems, including mechanisms for reappointment, tenure, promotion, and merit pay.*

Model systems recognize that good scholarship should be the basis for teaching, research, and service (including practice) in psychology. Furthermore, these models recognize that there will be differences in the degree to which individual psychologist-scholars emphasize teaching, research, and service and that the same psychologist may place different degrees of emphasis on each component at different times. (See chapter 4 for a discussion of the developmental stages of a faculty career and of the needs and contributions of faculty.) The implementation of diverse models of the "ideal" professor will allow the development of reward systems that will explicitly reinforce the faculty member's investment of time and energy in developing and using active learning exercises.

2. *As an aid in creating a more positive climate for the adoption of active learning techniques, psychology departments, individual faculty members, and textbook publishers should seriously consider the wisdom of the concept that "less is more."*

When faculty members or textbook authors feel compelled to "cover it all" at the curriculum, course, class, or textbook levels, they are unlikely to leave time or space for active learning activities (McGovern, Furumoto, Halpern, Kimble, & McKeachie, 1991). A psychology curriculum designed to introduce students to all aspects of the discipline may not leave room for more time-consuming active learning experiences such as internships and research projects. Careful outcome assessments (see chapter 1 on assessment) are likely to show that students remember only a few ideas when these ideas are presented in the context of overwhelming numbers of new ideas and terms that have been presented briefly or superficially. The kinds of in-depth, elaborated, contextualized experiences provided in active learning experiences are much more likely to make a lasting impression (Ericksen, 1983; McGovern et al., 1991).

Isolation and Communication

There are many active learning exercises. The nonexhaustive references in this chapter suggest the breadth and depth of the available resources. We suspect that unpublished sources of ideas about using active learning exercises in psychology courses are at least as numerous as the published ones. However, many teachers of psychology do not have easy access to these materials. Teachers at small colleges and high schools are most likely to feel isolated. We make several recommendations to reduce isolation and increase communication between psychology teachers at various levels. There is a need for ongoing peer support to encourage and aid those who are willing to try innovative active learning techniques. (Readers should also refer to chapter 5 on networking across different levels of institutions.) The recommendations offered here are specific to disseminating information about active learning.

1. *Institutions should add or include training in the benefits and use of active learning techniques in faculty development workshops and in orientation sessions for new instructors.*

The lack of use of active learning activities may be due to misconceptions about what active learning is or to not knowing how to incorporate active learning activities into courses. When institutions provide workshops on active learning techniques, instructors who already use active learning activities can share ideas, experiences, and information about their effectiveness. For instructors who do not use them, the workshops can provide training in the use of these techniques. These workshops would most likely be coordinated by an institution's faculty development office, although instructors could organize workshops within their own department. Outside presenters or faculty at the institution who are using active learning techniques could serve as workshop leaders. Presenters should use and model active learning techniques in the workshop and allow participants to discuss their own ideas about and experiences with active learning. The format of the sessions could range from a 1-hour weekday session during lunch to weekend sessions or week-long summer workshops.

2. Instructors need to make an effort to disseminate information about active learning at a variety of conferences, including local conferences, independent of APA or its regional affiliates.

Many teachers of high school, community college, and undergraduate psychology courses are not affiliated with APA or do not attend APA conventions because of time or affordability. Instructors who are using active learning techniques must broaden the active learning network by presenting and attending workshops, papers, and posters at other conventions (e.g., American Psychological Society, Psychonomics, American Association of Higher Education, regional teaching conferences, and state association meetings); by encouraging convention coordinators to include these programs in the conference; and by organizing informal local conferences. Conferences that target high school and community college teachers should also be considered for this dissemination network. In addition to searching for new activities, many high school and community college teachers have good active learning activities to share with university faculty.

3. Instructors need to connect with other disciplines as well as with their colleagues in psychology to share ideas, activities, and resources.

Although instructors may be most likely to reach out to other psychology teachers for information and for sharing ideas about active learning, a wealth of information and experience can be gained from members of other disciplines. Although the content and perspective of activities will be different, some active learning techniques can be generalized across disciplines. This is particularly true in fields such as biology, sociology, education, and management in which there is much overlap with psychology. Psychology instructors can initiate these contacts through one-on-one discussions with colleagues. They can also review the teaching journals and newsletters of other disciplines (e.g., *Teaching of Sociology, Biology Teacher, Teaching Political Science, Teaching Professor*). Institutions can also facilitate this networking by providing opportunities for cross-disciplinary interaction in professional development workshops.

Curriculum Development and Restructuring

Active learning activities must be incorporated into courses in a meaningful and organized manner. This means that (a) thought and time must be given to develop the activities so that they reflect concepts, phenomena, ideas, and perspectives of the discipline; (b) adequate time must be allocated to provide for the integration of the activity and discussion of it in the classroom; and (c) the activities must be suitable for the skill level and developmental stage of the students. The committee therefore makes the following recommendations.

1. Institutional administrators must be educated to understand that psychology is a science, and students must be provided with space, supplies, and laboratory equipment that allow for active learning in laboratory experiences that are commensurate with those supported in the natural sciences.

It is more difficult to conduct active learning activities that reflect the scientific nature of psychology without appropriate space, supplies, and laboratory equipment. The equipment need not be expensive but it must foster hands-on experiences. Computers in particular are a minimal requirement for a psychology laboratory. The availability of software that provides challenging, active, learning-oriented experiences with psychology is increasing. Undoubtedly, as the demand continues to increase, more software will be made available through publishers and computer bulletin boards. Faculty must continue to request funds, and deans and academic vice-presidents must provide funds for the purchase of basic laboratory equipment and expendable supplies that are needed for active learning activities. Each institution must take responsibility for providing the basic resources required for the education of its psychology students.

2. Consideration should be given to expanding the time frame and increasing the credit hours for psychology courses that have a significant active learning component so that the laboratory experiences are commensurate with those in the natural sciences.

Active learning in psychology requires manipulation of variables, self-discovery exercises, natural observations, and so forth. Although this can be done in a typical 3–credit hour format, the number of activities and the time available for them would be limited. To allow sufficient time to conduct the activities and discuss the concepts underlying them, a laboratory component similar to that in the natural sciences could be added to courses. Of course this is not the only place where active learning activities are used, but the laboratory sessions could be devoted to activities that require more time or small-group interaction. The extra credit hour for such sessions would more accurately reflect the time spent by students on both in-class and out-of-class active learning activities and by instructors on preparation and evaluation of activities.

Laboratory or small discussion groups would be particularly beneficial in the case of large classes. Although it is not impossible to design active learning activities for large classes, it is certainly more difficult to do so than for small classes. Students are more likely to feel comfortable engaging in these activities and sharing diverse personal perspectives in small groups. To facilitate this exchange, large lecture classes can be divided into small laboratory or discussion groups once a week (Benjamin, 1991). Although this small group session could be one of the three meetings per week, it might be more effective and useful if it were added to the course as an additional credit hour.

Instructors need to identify activities to be included in the laboratory and discussion session, consider how to integrate these activities into the course as a whole, and initiate the appropriate course proposals. Department heads, deans, and academic vice-presidents need to provide support in the form of time and resources to accomplish these changes.

3. *Instructors and department heads should consider a stepwise orientation to incorporate active learning activities into courses and the curriculum as a whole and to foster the development of active learning skills in students.*

The development of active learning skills such as critical thinking, problem solving, writing, and oral communication require readiness and practice. High school and first- and second-year college students typically are threatened by ambiguity and lack of structure, unprepared to accept or be open to diverse or conflicting perspectives, and wary of divulging personal information or viewpoints (Perry, 1970). Active learning activities need to be highly structured when first introduced to these students. As students become more involved in the active learning process, structure can be reduced and demands for more self-examination and critical analysis can be increased. As students are asked to "stretch" themselves in these activities, they can be drawn into higher levels of cognitive development. As they become more open to diverse views and more willing to analyze and evaluate these perspectives and as they seek out feedback as an opportunity for personal growth, courses can require less structure, more choices by students, and more active learning experiences in general. Halonen (1986) described one model that could be used to design activities to produce this stepwise growth. From a curricular perspective, instructors and department heads could consider a coherent, hierarchically sequenced set of courses with clearly delineated skill levels to allow students to become increasingly skilled, active, and independent learners (Walker, Newcomb, & Hopkins, 1987).

4. *Instructors, department heads, deans, and academic vice presidents need to recognize the time it takes to restructure courses and the curriculum to include active learning experiences.*

It requires time to design good active learning activities that can be incorporated into a course in a meaningful way. Also, curricular changes in the sequencing of courses require time to ensure that the courses and course sequences are structured in such a way that they follow a logical pattern that builds on skills from previous courses. Consequently, instructors must be prepared to spend time reviewing courses and requirements for the major, developing the appropriate sequence of courses, and initiating the necessary curriculum changes. Administrators must allow for flexibility in teaching schedules and research and service activities to allow for such preparation time.

Resources

Faculty need to have resource materials that facilitate the use of active learning techniques. To this end, we offer these recommendations.

1. *Institutions, through their offices of sponsored research or similar administrative offices, should work with faculty to assist them in seeking external grants to fund laboratories and faculty development workshops that encourage the use of active learning.*

Funds to purchase equipment for active learning activities, to establish psychology laboratories, or to support faculty development workshops are not always available through the regular institutional appropriations. Instructors must often seek external funds. Although it is typically the responsibility of faculty members to write these grants, institutions can assist faculty members in the process. Institutional offices of sponsored research can provide names of agencies and programs, along with contact persons, that fund equipment and training projects. They can provide faculty the resources and time to visit these agencies and gather information about successful proposals. They can also provide basic outlines with sample text for grant proposals along with references and resource materials that deal with how to write successful grants and how to support requests. Institutions must recognize that the process may require several attempts before the grants are funded.

2. *Departments are encouraged to stretch potential resources within their own and nearby campuses.*

To aid instructors who seek assistance with active learning at 4-year institutions, advanced undergraduate students can be enlisted to act as laboratory and teaching assistants in lower level courses. Community college and high school teachers may be able to recruit students from local colleges and universities to serve in a similar capacity in their courses. To facilitate recruitment of assistants and provide an active learning experience for them as well, departments could include these positions in field placement or internship programs. Departments can institute laboratory fees to fund equipment and supplies. Departments could also consider locally producing print materials for active learning exercises and using any revenues from their sale to purchase additional equipment and material for active learning activities.

Evaluation of Active Learning Activities

To maintain the vitality and effectiveness of active learning, instructors must conduct regular evaluations of the activities they use. (Chapter 1 is a comprehensive discussion of the need for, benefits of, and methods available for assessment in psychology.) The recommendations below focus specifically on the assessment of active learning.

1. *Instructors should review existing resources documenting active learning activities to seek out evaluations of the activities they plan to use.*

Faculty should make every effort to evaluate activities before they use them to determine if the activities meet the criteria for active learning described in this chapter, are appropriately structured for the students' developmental level, and can be integrated into the course in a logical and meaningful way.

2. Instructors should conduct systematic evaluations of the active learning activities used in their courses and use the feedback from these evaluations to revise, add to, or delete activities as needed.

The effectiveness of active learning activities should be evaluated from three perspectives. Did the activity work without any technical or procedural problems? This is probably the easiest evaluation and can be done by instructors immediately following the activity. Did students experience and learn what the instructor intended them to learn? This assessment requires input from students as well as instructors. Discussions immediately following the activity, analysis of responses to test items, and comments from course evaluations completed by students at the end of the semester can provide data for this component of the evaluation. Was the activity integrated into the course content in a logical and meaningful fashion? Data for this component should also be gathered from students' discussions following activities and their comments on course evaluations.

3. Departments should include active learning as one of their objectives for the major and build into their regular assessment program an evaluation of the extent to which this objective has been achieved.

As noted in chapter 1, departments should identify specific learning objectives for psychology majors and conduct regular assessments to determine whether these objectives have been met. If active learning is to be integrated into the curriculum in a coherent, stepwise fashion, it must be explicitly identified in the department-wide objectives. By including active learning as an objective for the major, departments acknowledge its importance and emphasize their commitment to it. Departments and institutions are more likely to provide funds to promote and support active learning and the faculty who use this approach if it is an explicit objective that is assessed each year.

CONCLUSION

Incorporating active learning into psychology courses has many benefits for students and faculty. Resources are available to assist faculty who want to broaden their teaching style to include active learning. With careful planning, instructors can find or develop a variety of active learning activities and integrate them into their courses in a way that challenges students and enhances their learning without overwhelming them. The recommendations we offer in this chapter, if carried out, will facilitate this process.

REFERENCES

Abramson, C. (1990). *Invertebrate learning: A laboratory manual and source book.* Washington, DC: American Psychological Association.

Adler, R. B., & Towne, N. (1987). *Looking out/looking in: Interpersonal communication* (5th ed.). New York: Holt, Rinehart & Winston.

American Association of Community and Junior Colleges. (1988). *Building communities: A vision for a new century.* Washington, DC: Author.

Anderson, M., & Hornby, P. (1988). COMPsych: A computerized software information system. *Behavior Research Methods, Instruments and Computers, 20,* 243–245.

Anderson, M., & Hornby, P. (1990). Computer use in psychology instruction. *Behavior Research Methods, Instruments and Computers, 22,* 194–199.

Andrews, T. G. (1946). Demonstrations for the introductory psychology course. *American Psychologist, 1,* 312–323.

Association of American Colleges. (1985). *Integrity in the college curriculum: A report to the academic community.* Washington, DC: Author.

Baker, G. A., Roueche, J. E., & Gillett-Karam, R. (1990). *Teaching as leading.* Washington, DC: American Association of Community and Junior Colleges.

Barnette, W. L. (1947). Psychological boners. *American Psychologist, 2,* 369–371.

Beins, B. C. (1988). Teaching the relevance of statistics through consumer-oriented research. *Teaching of Psychology, 12,* 168–169.

Beins, B. C. (1990). Computer software for introductory psychology courses [Review of seven software packages from major publishers]. *Contemporary Psychology, 35,* 421–427.

Bell, J. (1991). *Evaluating psychological information: Sharpening your critical thinking skills.* Boston: Allyn & Bacon.

Benjamin, L. T., Jr. (1991). Personalization and active learning in the large introductory class. *Teaching of Psychology, 18,* 68–74.

Benjamin, L. T., Jr., Daniel, R. S., & Brewer, C. L. (Eds.). (1985). *Handbook for teaching introductory psychology.* Hillsdale, NJ: Erlbaum.

Benjamin, L. T., Jr., & Lowman, K. D. (Eds.). (1981). *Activities handbook for the teaching of psychology* (Vol. 1). Washington, DC: American Psychological Association.

Bennett, A., Hausfeld, S., Reeve, R. A., & Smith, J. (1981). *Workshops in cognitive processes.* Boston: Routledge & Kegan Paul.

Billson, J. M. (1986). The college classroom as a small group: Some implications for teaching and learning. *Teaching Sociology, 14,* 143–151.

Birch, W. (1986). Towards a model for problem-based learning. *Studies in Higher Education, 11,* 73–82.

Bloom, B. S. (Ed.). (1956). *Taxonomy of educational objectives: The classification of educational goals. Handbook 1: Cognitive domain.* New York: Longman.

Bouton, C., & Garth, R. (Eds.). (1983). *Learning in groups*. San Francisco: Jossey-Bass.

Boyer, E. L. (1990). *Scholarship reconsidered: Priorities of the professoriate*. Princeton, NJ: Carnegie Foundation for the Advancement of Teaching.

Bronstein, P., & Quina, K. (Eds.). (1988). *Teaching a psychology of people: Resources for gender and sociocultural awareness*. Washington, DC: American Psychological Association.

Brothen, T. F. (1986). Using active learning in large classes. In S. F. Schomberg (Ed.), *Strategies for active teaching and learning in university classrooms* (pp. 40–46). Minneapolis: University of Minnesota Teaching Center.

Chaffee, J. (1991). *Thinking critically* (3rd ed.). Boston: Houghton Mifflin.

Cheney, L. V. (1989). *50 hours: A core curriculum for college students*. Washington, DC: National Endowment for the Humanities.

Chickering, A. W., & Associates. (1981). *The modern American college*. San Francisco: Jossey-Bass.

Deci, E. L., & Ryan, R. M. (1985). *Intrinsic motivation and self-determination in human behavior*. New York: Plenum Press.

DiVesta, F. J., & Peverly, S. T. (1984). The effects of encoding variability, processing actively, and rule examples sequence on the transfer of conceptual rules. *Journal of Educational Psychology, 76*, 108–119.

Eble, K. E. (1988). *The craft of teaching: A guide to mastering the professor's art* (2nd ed.). San Francisco: Jossey-Bass.

Ericksen, S. C. (1983). Private measures of good teaching. *Teaching of Psychology, 10*, 133–136.

Ewing, M. M. (1991a). Involvement in psychology. *Community/Junior College Quarterly of Research and Practice, 15*, 327–338.

Ewing, M. M. (1991b). Learning is not a spectator sport. *Network: The Newsletter for Psychology Teachers at Two-Year Colleges, 9*(2), 6–10.

Ewing, M. M. (1992). *Life-span development: A laboratory manual*. New York: McGraw-Hill.

Feichtner, S. B., & Michaelsen, L. K. (1984). Giving students a part in the process: An innovative approach to team learning. *College Student Journal, 18*, 335–344.

Fernald, C. D., Tedeschi, R. G., Siegfried, W. D., Gilmore, D. C., Grimsley, D. L., & Chipley, B. (1982). Designing and managing an undergraduate practicum course in psychology. *Teaching of Psychology, 9*, 155–160.

Frederick, P. J. (1987). Student involvement: Active learning in large classes. In M. G. Weimer (Ed.), *Teaching large classes well* (pp. 45–56). San Francisco: Jossey-Bass.

Fulwiler, T., & Young, A. (Eds.). (1990). *Models and methods for writing across the curriculum*. Portsmouth, NH: Boynton/Cook.

Glover, J. A., Ronning, R. R., & Bruning, R. H. (1990). *Cognitive psychology for teachers*. New York: Macmillan.

Gorman, M. E., Law, A., & Lindegren, T. (1981). Making students take a stand: Active learning in introductory psychology. *Teaching of Psychology, 8,* 164–166.

Halonen, J. S. (Ed.). (1986). *Teaching critical thinking in psychology.* Milwaukee, WI: Alverno Productions.

Hamil, J., & Janssen, S. (1987). Active learning in large introductory sociology courses. *Teaching Sociology, 15,* 45–54.

Hill, G. W., IV, Palladino, J. J., & Smith, R. A. (1992). Live from across the country: A session of in-class demonstrations for teachers of psychology. *Teaching of Psychology, 19,* 54–55.

Hornby, P., & Anderson, M. (1990). A review of software for introductory psychology instruction. *Behavior Research Methods, Instruments and Computers, 22,* 184–193.

Hovancik, J. R. (1984). Individualized assignments in an experimental psychology course. *Teaching of Psychology, 11,* 52–54.

Hutchings, P., & Wutzdorff, A. (Eds.). (1988). *Knowing and doing: Learning through experience.* San Francisco: Jossey-Bass.

Jernstedt, G. C. (1982, May). Active learning increases educational effectiveness and efficiency. *Technological Horizons in Education Journal,* 97–100, 105.

Johnson, D. W., & Johnson, R. T. (1987). *Learning together and alone: Cooperative, competitive, and individualistic learning* (2nd ed.). Englewood Cliffs, NJ: Prentice-Hall.

Kahn, A. S., & Brookshire, R. G. (1991). Using a computer bulletin board in a social psychology course. *Teaching of Psychology, 18,* 245–249.

Kierniesky, N. C. (1984). Undergraduate research in small psychology departments. *Teaching of Psychology, 11,* 15–18.

Kolb, D. A. (1976). *The learning style inventory: Self-scoring test and interpretation booklet.* Boston: McBer.

Kolb, D. A. (1984). *Experiential learning: Experience as the source of learning and development.* Englewood Cliffs, NJ: Prentice-Hall.

Lawry, J. D. (1990). Caritas in the classroom. *College Teaching, 38,* 83–87.

Lee, M. W. (1986). The match: Learning styles of black children and microcomputer programming. *Journal of Negro Education, 55,* 78–90.

Lestina, T. (1990). Using student community service as part of a high school psychology course. In V. P. Makosky, C. C. Sileo, L. G. Whittemore, C. P. Landry, & M. L. Skutley (Eds.), *Activities handbook for the teaching of psychology* (Vol. 3, pp. 235–236). Washington, DC: American Psychological Association.

Lewis, K. G. (1982). *The large class analysis project* (Final Report). Austin: University of Texas, Center for Teaching Effectiveness.

Lewis, K. G., & Woodward, P. J. (1984, April). *What really happens in large university classes?* Paper presented at the meeting of the American Educational Research Association. (ERIC Document Reproduction Service No. ED 245 590)

Lowman, J. (1990). Promoting motivation and learning. *College Teaching, 38,* 136–139.

Maimon, E. P., Nodine, B. F., Hearn, G. W., & Haney-Peritz, J. (1990). Beaver College. In T. Fulwiler & A. Young (Eds.), *Programs that work: Models and methods for writing across the curriculum* (pp. 1–26). Portsmouth, NH: Boynton/ Cook.

Makosky, V. P., Sileo, C. C., Whittemore, L. G., Landry, C. P., & Skutley, M. L. (Eds.). (1990). *Activities handbook for the teaching of psychology* (Vol. 3). Washington, DC: American Psychological Association.

Makosky, V. P., Whittemore, L. G., & Rogers, A. M. (Eds.). (1987). *Activities handbook for the teaching of psychology* (Vol. 2). Washington, DC: American Psychological Association.

Matthews, J. (1991). The teaching of ethics and the ethics of teaching. *Teaching of Psychology, 18,* 80–85.

McAdam, D. W. (1987). Bringing psychology to life. *Teaching of Psychology, 14,* 29–31.

McAdam, D. W. (1990, January). *Undergraduate TA's bring life to psychology 101.* Poster presented at the 12th Annual National Institute on the Teaching of Psychology, St. Petersburg Beach, FL.

McGovern, T. V., Furumoto, L., Halpern, D. F., Kimble, G. A., & McKeachie, W. J. (1991). Liberal education, study in depth, and the arts and sciences major—Psychology. *American Psychologist, 46,* 598–605.

McKeachie, W. J., Pintrich, P. R., Lin, Y., Smith, D. A. F., & Sharma, R. (1990). *Teaching and learning in the college classroom: A review of the research literature.* Ann Arbor, MI: National Center for Research to Improve Post-Secondary Teaching and Learning.

Mendenhall, M., & Burr, W. R. (1983). Enlarging the role of the undergraduate teaching assistant. *Teaching of Psychology, 10,* 184–185.

National Institute of Education. (1984). *Involvement in learning: Realizing the potential of American higher education* (Report of the Study Group on the Condition of Excellence in American Higher Education). Washington, DC: U.S. Department of Education.

National Institute of Education. (1988). *A new vitality in the college curriculum.* Washington, DC: U.S. Department of Education.

Neer, M. R. (1987). The development of an instrument to measure classroom apprehension. *Communication Education, 36,* 154–166.

Nodine, B. F. (Ed.). (1990). Special issue: Psychologists teach writing [Special issue]. *Teaching of Psychology, 17.*

Palladino, J. J., Carsud, A. L., Hulicka, I. M., & Benjamin, L. T., Jr. (1982). Undergraduate research in psychology: Assessment and direction. *Teaching of Psychology, 9,* 71–74.

Parker, C. A. (Ed.). (1978). *Encouraging development in college students.* Minneapolis: University of Minnesota Press.

Pascarella, E., & Terenzini, P. T. (1991). *How college affects students*. San Francisco: Jossey-Bass.

Pauk, W. (1984). *How to study in college* (3rd ed.). Boston: Houghton Mifflin.

Perry, W. G., Jr. (1970). *Forms of intellectual and ethical development in the college years*. New York: Holt, Rinehart & Winston.

Power, R. P., Hausfeld, S., & Gorta, A. (1981). *Workshops in perception*. Boston: Routledge & Kegan Paul.

Ryan, M. (1988). The teachable moment: The Washington Center Internship Program. In P. Hutchings & A. Wutzdorff (Eds.), *Knowing and doing: Learning through experience* (pp. 39–47). San Francisco: Jossey-Bass.

Sanford, E. C. (1910). The teaching of elementary psychology in colleges and universities with laboratories. *Psychological Monographs, 12* (4, Whole No. 51), 54–71.

Schomberg, S. F. (Ed.). (1986). *Strategies for active teaching and learning in university classrooms*. Minneapolis: University of Minnesota Teaching Center.

Sechzer, J. A., & Pfafflin, S. M. (Eds.). (1987). *Psychology and educational policy*. New York: New York Academy of Science.

Sherman, A. R. (1982). Psychology fieldwork: A catalyst for advancing knowledge and academic skills. *Teaching of Psychology, 9,* 82–85.

Slate, J. R., & Charlesworth, J. R. (1989). Information processing theory: Classroom application. *Reading Improvement, 26,* 2–6.

Slavin, R. E. (1983). When does cooperative learning increase student achievement? *Psychological Bulletin, 94,* 429–445.

Stoloff, M. L., & Couch, J. V. (1992). *Computer use in psychology: A directory of software* (3rd ed.). Washington, DC: American Psychological Association.

Svinicki, M. D., & Dixon, N. M. (1987). The Kolb model modified for classroom activities. *College Teaching, 35,* 141–146.

Tchudi, S. N. (1986). *Teaching writing in the content areas: College level*. Washington, DC: National Education Association.

VandeCreek, L., & Fleischer, M. (1984). The role of practicum in the undergraduate psychology curriculum. *Teaching of Psychology, 11,* 9–14.

Walker, W. E., Newcomb, A. F., & Hopkins, W. P. (1987). A model for curriculum evaluation and revision in undergraduate psychology programs. *Teaching of Psychology, 14,* 198–202.

Walton, A. (1930). Demonstrational and experimental devices. *American Journal of Psychology, 42,* 109–114.

Ware, M. E., & Millard, R. J. (Eds.). (1987). *Handbook on student development: Advising, career development, and field placement*. Hillsdale, NJ: Erlbaum.

Weimer, M. G. (Ed.). (1987). *Teaching large classes well*. San Francisco: Jossey-Bass.

Widick, C., Knefelkamp, L. L., & Parker, C. A. (1975). The counselor as a developmental instructor. *Counselor Education and Supervision, 14,* 286–296.

Widick, C., & Simpson, D. (1978). Developmental concepts in college instruction. In C. A. Parker (Ed.), *Encouraging development in college students* (pp. 27–59). Minneapolis: University of Minnesota Press.

Wittrock, M. C. (1984). Learning as a generative process. *Educational Psychologist, 11,* 87–95.

III

CONCLUSION

TRANSFORMING UNDERGRADUATE PSYCHOLOGY FOR THE NEXT CENTURY

THOMAS V. McGOVERN

This book went to press as the American Psychological Association finished its centennial year celebrations. Metaphors abounded about the "second" century of the discipline. The *APA Monitor* spotlighted monthly our self-assertions of psychology's identity and growing stature in scientific, educational, and professional practice circles. Comments from psychologists about the contemporary state of public welfare were more guarded. Psychologists responded to the harsh, contemporary manifestations of cultural, social, and economic conflict in their work with homeless people, AIDS patients, and the daily victims of urban violence.

On university and college campuses, faculty continued to motivate their students to learn what Mann (1982) suggested for the discipline—psychology is about science, about healing, and about wisdom. The message was well received. In 1990, psychology awarded 53,586 baccalaureates, making it the most popular single discipline in the arts and sciences and the sixth most popular major field behind composite categories of business and management, social sciences, education, engineering, and health sciences ("Earned Degrees," 1992).

These numbers are a cause for optimism about undergraduate psychology. The overall population of undergraduate students is projected to increase in the coming decade as the children of the post–World War II "baby boomers" reach college age. Psychology will reap its share of this harvest.

This book is about our responsibility to renew continually our strategies to educate students. This final chapter has two purposes. First, I will place the St. Mary's conference in its historical context by comparing the ideas of this book's authors with those of the Buxton et al. (1952) text generated by the Cornell conference 40 years ago and with other subsequent reports. Second, I will discuss issues shaping higher education at the national level that will affect psychology programs into the next century. A theme for this chapter is that differences among the past, present, and future forms of undergraduate psychology reflect changes in the discipline and changes in the culture of higher education.

THE PAST AS PROLOGUE

Kiesler (1966) wrote a seminal article on psychotherapy effectiveness. He challenged what he labeled as the "uniformity assumption" prevalent at that time in the clinical field. Regardless of the type of client, the problem diagnosis, or the type of treatment applied, researchers and practitioners did not conceptualize effectiveness as a complex interaction of multiple variables. Kiesler's (1966) article changed the clinical field.

Kiesler was my senior colleague at Virginia Commonwealth University. As a faculty member affiliated primarily with the Counseling Psychology Program, I studied his work and routinely applied it to therapy research that I conducted with our graduate students. In 1981, when our department launched its first evaluation of the undergraduate program, I used Kiesler's interaction model to conceptualize the project (McGovern & Hawks, 1984). A similar interaction model was implicit in framing the seven critical questions for the St. Mary's conference.

Parallel to variables for psychotherapy research (outcome, patient, therapist, problem, treatment), an interaction hypothesis for undergraduate education in psychology could be stated as:

What kind of *outcomes* can be achieved with
What kind of *students* taught by
What kind of *faculty* using
What kind of *teaching methods* as part of
What kind of *curriculum?*

Different institutions are the contexts in which these variables interact in different ways to affect faculty and student learning.

The St. Mary's conference participants focused on all of these variables. In contrast, the Cornell conference participants were concerned only with outcomes and curriculum. A more thorough analysis of the similarities and differences between the Cornell and St. Mary's topics will highlight changes in higher education and in psychology over the past 40 years. Understanding these changes is the prologue to my discussion of the future and the continuing transformation of the discipline in the coming years.

Outcomes

Two issues are evident when comparing the Cornell objectives with those from St. Mary's. First, the Cornell group eschewed personal growth as an objective of their curriculum for reasons of privacy, lack of expertise of most psychologists in the "student personnel point of view" (Buxton et al., 1952, p. 39), and lack of empirical evidence for student change. Empirical research since then (Alexander & Stark, 1986; Astin, 1985; Feldman & Newcomb, 1976; Korn, 1986; Pace, 1979; Pascarella & Terenzini, 1991) on how students' cognitive, affective, and behavioral characteristics change during college supports chapter 1's expanded list of outcomes. Second, as chapter 1 aptly describes, broader forces in higher education and in society have had a direct influence on psychology programs in the past 40 years. In the following paragraphs, I want to analyze the differences apparent in the two conferences' perspectives on outcomes. I will return also to the higher education research on student outcomes in the final section of this chapter.

The preface to the 1952 Cornell conference report opens with this statement: "To improve our teaching requires an occasional review of what we have been teaching—an audit to determine the objectives, examine the content, and appraise the results of the instruction we have been giving" (Buxton et al., 1952, p. v). This report identified four potential objectives for undergraduate education, stressing three of the four, and recommended a curriculum.

The three objectives were knowledge or content (problems of psychology, facts and principles of psychology, psychology as science, structure and functioning of science); rigorous habits of thought (observation, quantitative thinking, multiple causation); and values, attitudes, or sets (knowledge as a value, attitudes of caution and responsibility). An objective described as "personal growth and an increased ability to meet personal and social adjustment problems adequately" (Buxton et al., 1952, p. 3) was deemed inappropriate. Although the authors recommended that the three objectives could be emphasized in planning a course or the curriculum,

> in actual teaching, emphasis will be upon the knowledge or content
> objective. . . . Application, transfer, and personal use of psychological

material remain the responsibility of the student rather than of an instructor who should not be expected to act as therapist, consultant in practical affairs, or reformer of character. (Buxton et al., 1952, p. 10)

In chapter 1 of this book, Halpern and her colleagues propose an array of objectives similar to those from the Cornell group. A knowledge base (content areas, methods, theory, and history), intellectual skills (thinking; communication; information gathering and synthesis; quantitative, scientific, and technological skills), and personal characteristics (thinking, interpersonal and intrapersonal skills, motivation, ethics, and sensitivity to people and cultures) are all identified as desirable outcomes for the psychology major (see Exhibit 1, pp. 28–29).

The Cornell group judged that "there are at present no means of determining whether or not a student has attained all of these objectives" (Buxton et al., 1952, p. 9). In contrast, Halpern and her colleagues offer an impressive set of assessment strategies, including conventional techniques (archival forms, class assessment activities, standardized testing, and capstone courses) and nontraditional qualitative measures (portfolio analysis, interviews, external examiners, performance-based assessment, conflict of ideas approach, and assessment of critical thinking). On the basis of mandates by state legislatures and regional accreditation associations, the faculty who worked on this chapter provide practical guidelines for designing, implementing, and evaluating a departmental assessment program. They conclude by observing that "student outcomes assessment is not only a tool for improving the teaching and learning process, it is the only way of determining what works in higher education" (p. 44). Determining "what works" has prompted a renewed emphasis on the students' essential role in their own learning.

Students

The faculty who met at Cornell to audit the undergraduate curriculum did not talk about students directly. The St. Mary's participants did, as reflected in separate chapters in this book on advising (chapter 2) and on ethnic minority recruitment and retention (chapter 3). Peripheral comments gleaned from Buxton et al. (1952) shed light on some similarities and differences in how the authors of the two reports saw students. There is similarity in the respect that faculty should have for their students and for the expected quality of instruction. The major differences are (a) perceptions in 1952 of the homogeneity versus in 1992 of the heterogeneity of the student population and (b) whether it is the job of faculty to address cognitive and affective goals.

The Cornell group described their reasons why psychology should not include these areas as curricular goals in chapters 3 ("Personal Adjustment

Courses") and 4 ("Technical Training in Psychology") of Buxton et al. (1952): "While we are not dealing with detached intellects and much of importance in college is not learned in class, we are charged with responsibility for educating a minority of the population which is able to achieve relatively high levels of intellectual attainment" (p. 40). In 1952, higher education was assimilating more and more World War II veterans into college classrooms. However, the full wave of "new students," of universal access, about which McKeachie and Milholland (1961) and Kulik (1973) commented, had not yet arrived.

The Cornell authors saw students' affective development as the province for professionals in college student personnel offices, not for academic course work or faculty. In a particularly disparaging statement, the authors commented on existing personal adjustment courses: "It is no more justified to consider such a course as a course in psychology than it would be to substitute a course on hygiene for introductory physiology or a course on household repairs for introductory physics" (Buxton et al., 1952, p. 41).

Ware (chapter 2), Puente (chapter 3), and their respective colleagues indicate how much has changed in student demographics, in faculty philosophy, and in departmental programs. Ware's group cite data on the national shifts in the age, gender, and ethnic minority status of undergraduates in general as well as of psychology majors in particular. Puente's group echo this message, commenting on the increased ethnic minority presence of students and faculty. For example, at the Berkeley and Los Angeles campuses of the University of California, White students now make up 49.4% and 50.9% of the students in attendance, respectively ("College Enrollment," 1992). Access and excellence have become defining characteristics of American higher education in the past 40 years.

Since the creation of higher education land grant institutions by the federal legislation of the Morrill Land-Grant Act of 1862, new students have been attracted to institutions by new programs. One consequence of increasing numbers and diversity of students has been an increasing expectation that higher education provides more specialized and vocationally relevant course work. However, the period of expansion after World War II was a time when institutions strengthened traditional arts and sciences programs as well; the numbers of baccalaureates awarded in arts and sciences and their proportion of total degrees rose between 1954 and 1968 (Turner & Bowen, 1990). The Cornell group affirmed unequivocally the value of liberal arts education, criticizing the trend toward applied courses reported in the Sanford and Fleishman (1950) national study of the psychology curriculum. The Cornell group concluded that "the high proportion of avowedly vocational bachelor's degrees in psychology seems unfortunate, because training in applied psychology without a supporting knowledge of general psychological facts and principles is probably not the best preparation for psychological jobs" (Buxton et al., 1952, p. 44).

Ware and his colleagues advocated broader faculty roles in fostering student development. For advising, they suggested the following dimensions for an effective program: (a) personal relationships between students and faculty; (b) achievement of academic, career, and personal goals; (c) use of institutional and community resources; and (d) responsiveness to student diversity. They reiterated the Cornell group's notion that such programs should be submitted to empirical scrutiny to evaluate their effectiveness. Ware's model for advising is consistent with the goals of active learning examined by Mathie and her colleagues (chapter 7) as well as with the empirical literature generated by college student personnel researchers and practitioners (e.g., Chickering & Associates, 1981). Good relationships between faculty and students are necessary but not sufficient; the partnership must yield enhanced decision-making skills. Understanding developmental issues and teaching problem-solving strategies to students who differ in gender, age, ethnicity, patterns of enrollment, and prior academic and life experiences are significant challenges.

In chapter 3, Puente and his colleagues amplify Ware's recognition of increased diversity among students. After describing a context for multiculturalism in contemporary higher education, they offer thought-provoking questions for a departmental self-study. These questions will stimulate faculty and student development and can enhance psychology's role in achieving institutional goals. What is especially insightful about Puente's recommendations is that they are construed as scientifically and intellectually important, not just politically correct. "Toward a psychology of variance" is a powerful stimulus intended "to go beyond . . . redressing the wrongs of the past . . .[to] serve as the foundation for the examination of why cultural competency and diversity are critical to understanding human behavior" (p. 89).

The chapters on advising and ethnic minority recruitment and retention focus primarily on students. The chapters on faculty issues written by the St. Mary's participants reflect another important variable that did not receive direct attention in 1952.

Faculty

Comments about faculty in the Cornell report were limited to the chapter on "Problems in Implementation of the Curriculum." However, a theme pervading the St. Mary's report is identical to one raised by the Cornell report and by the Michigan report in 1961:

The recommended program requires scholarship and attention to teaching techniques and other matters which can be hard work. Unfortunately, undergraduate instruction in some institutions carries little prestige and is regarded as a chore to be completed as effortlessly as possible, so that more important matters, usually graduate instruction and research, may be attended to. (Buxton et al., 1952, p. 50)

The Michigan group was even more forceful:

Teaching is not a prestigeful occupation in psychology these days. The research man is the status figure. . . . The situation worried us . . . because all our deliberations returned ultimately to the man, the teacher, without whose energy and motivation the curricular system ultimately falters and collapses. Again and again we found the dividing line between sterile and vital course content, between devitalizing and enriching experiences, between stagnation and growth, to lie in the teacher and his skill and not in the material itself. (McKeachie & Milholland, 1961, p. 6)

In chapters 4 and 5, Fretz and Weiten and their respective colleagues identify the same problem, and stress that it has not been ameliorated. Three common themes emerge from these two chapters. First, faculty development is a lifelong process. Second, there is no single, best approach to enhancing either faculty development or the building of academic community. Third, faculty learn best from one another. Fretz stresses this learning inside one's institution, whereas Weiten extends it to learning from kindred spirits, locally, regionally, and nationally.

Weiten and his colleagues extend Fretz's strategies beyond the boundaries of one's department. Their chapter is based on the premise that "problems, issues, tasks, and challenges facing psychology teachers at different levels of instruction, from high school to graduate school, are more similar than is widely believed" (p. 125). They suggest that different approaches to building community among psychology teachers and scholars should be based on the specific departmental or institutional situations. Their explicit theme is that "teaching and learning are communal activities" (p. 157).

There are obvious differences between such a strong emphasis on faculty development in these two chapters and the peripheral comments in the 1952 text. The 1992 emphasis should be understood in the broader context of the higher education community. Like assessment or response to changing student demographics, faculty development is part of a larger questioning of faculty roles and rewards that is gathering force in contemporary higher education. I will return to this issue in the last section of the chapter.

Curriculum

The St. Mary's authors establish the rationale for their recommendations using historical review of prior conference and task force reports. In chapter 6, Brewer and his colleagues capture the Cornell text succinctly.

After reviewing other curriculum reports (Kulik, 1973; McGovern, Furu-moto, Halpern, Kimble, & McKeachie, 1991; McKeachie & Milholland, 1961; Scheirer & Rogers, 1985), Brewer and his colleagues return to the Cornell theme of "the liberal arts tradition and the psychology major" (pp. 166–168). They reaffirm that "the fundamental goal of education in psychology, from which all the others follow, is to teach students to think as scientists about behavior" (p. 169).

Seven goals are stated for the curriculum: scientific thinking about behavior, attention to human diversity, a broad and deep knowledge base, methodological competence, practical experience and application, effective communication skills, and sensitivity to ethical issues. Four groups of courses should accomplish these goals: introductory psychology, methodology courses, content courses, and integrative experiences. The authors of chapter 6 do not define a single structure for the curriculum, recognizing as Kulik (1973) did that institutional and faculty differences preclude uniformity. They advocate that courses should be sequentially related and that major field requirements, however structured, should ensure student exposure to both the natural and social sciences sides of the discipline. Forty years ago, the Cornell group also asserted that all core courses should draw on social and biological materials for examples and research findings.

There are significant differences between the St. Mary's perspective on curriculum and on prior reports. First, there is a continual reference to the inclusion of topics and methodologies that incorporate new scholarship on gender and on ethnic minority groups. Second, there is a section on the community college curriculum, attending to this increasingly important constituency of faculty and students. Third, interdisciplinary and service courses are examined as opportunities and as liabilities for psychology in contemporary higher education. The authors of chapter 6 conclude with a set of recommendations and suggestions for future curriculum planning.

Active Learning

In chapter 7 of this handbook, Mathie and her colleagues pay special attention to pedagogy. This topic was implicit in 1952; it was given much more attention in McKeachie and Milholland (1961), and innovative pedagogy was a central theme in the Kulik (1973) volume. Active learning strategies have become more explicit, stated as specific approaches in course syllabi, and, like assessment and student development, are based now on solid, empirical grounds:

> Psychology is a young science, so close to its frontiers of research that even the beginning student can readily come to grips with unsolved problems, partly because its subject matter leads directly into such neighboring scientific fields as physics, biology, sociology, and anthro-

pology, and partly because its content, human experience and behavior, is so readily accessible. (Buxton et al., 1952, p. 6)

This zest for teaching students about scientific inquiry pervades the Cornell conference report. Ten years later, the psychologists who met at Michigan were more specific about alternative means to achieve this end. In their chapter on "The Beginning Course," McKeachie and Milholland (1961) described 16 objectives that are strikingly contemporary (e.g., critical thinking, understanding and acceptance of research findings on racial and cultural differences, etc.). In their discussion of "The Experimental-Statistical Area," the Michigan authors were specific about behavioral objectives and how to accomplish them.

Drawing on a wealth of literature on teaching and learning analyzed by McKeachie, Pintrich, Lin, Smith, and Sharma (1990), Mathie and her colleagues offer today's faculty empirically based means to transform their pedagogy. Active participation by the entire class, student-initiated activities, learning at higher cognitive levels, in-class and out-of-class tasks, and feedback to and from students can be woven into the fabric of all our courses. Ultimately, Mathie and her colleagues' conclusions and recommendations in chapter 7 intersect with every other chapter in this handbook. Those conclusions include respect for students' differences and for the quality of their learning, faculty development within a department and increased communication with colleagues at other institutions and at other levels of instruction, and the potential effectiveness of active learning across the curriculum.

FUTURE ISSUES AND INSTITUTIONAL DIFFERENCES

In this concluding section, I will examine several issues in higher education that will affect psychology departments in the future. My examination begins with some orienting comments about a set of interacting variables that are present in almost every undergraduate program in psychology. With a better understanding of these variables, faculty can focus more effectively on specific departmental issues for students, faculty development, and curriculum.

Conceptualizing the Common Variables in Undergraduate Psychology Programs

One predictable reaction when faculty or administrators read the analyses of problems and recommended solutions in this handbook could be, "That approach sounds good but doesn't apply to me or my institution." Expecting this reaction, the chapter authors deliberately avoided a prescriptive tone. They analyzed critical problems, described an array of potential responses, and evaluated the strengths of alternative solutions. In this section, I will examine effects that can be linked to specific institutional environments and those that transcend institutional differences.

We built a recognition of different institutional cultures into the St. Mary's conference by selecting diverse participants. Faculty from high schools, community colleges, liberal arts colleges, comprehensive universities, and research universities brought unique perspectives on every topic to every discussion at this conference. Yet, Weiten and his colleagues (chapter 5) observed that there are more similarities than differences among psychology faculty at different levels of education and in different types of institutions. It is important to identify some of the similarities and differences in faculty, student, and curricular issues that relate to institutional cultures.

Research on how the college experience affects students uses developmental theories to understand the stages, critical incidents, and predictable patterns of change on cognitive, attitudinal, and psychosocial dimensions. Psychologists have been key contributors to this research. Recent theories are less focused on intrapersonal development of students and more focused on sociological or environmental factors that contribute to the effects of the college experience. Pascarella and Terenzini (1991) reviewed the theoretical, methodological, and statistical roots of increasingly sophisticated findings of student change during the college years. Of particular interest is the general causal model used to explain the differential effects of college environments. The model identifies five sets of variables and was summarized by Pascarella and Terenzini (1991) as follows:

> Two of those sets, students' background and precollege characteristics and the structural and organizational features of the institution (for example, size, selectivity, residential character), together shape the third variable set: a college's or university's environment. These three clusters of variables, in turn, influence a fourth cluster that involves both the frequency and content of students' interactions with the major socializing agents on campus (the faculty and other students). Quality of effort, the fifth constellation of variables, is shaped by students' background traits, by the general institutional environment, and by the normative influences of peers and faculty members. Student change is seen as a function of students' background characteristics, interactions with major socializing agents, and the quality of students' efforts in learning and developing. (pp. 53, 55)

The conceptual model underpinning the St. Mary's conference topics was an extrapolation from attribute-by-treatment interactions in clinical intervention research. However, my comments about future issues for psychology students, faculty development, and curriculum derive from a model based on empirical studies directly related to the college student experience.

What do we know about how students learn in college? Three comprehensive studies (Bowen, 1977; Feldman & Newcomb, 1976; Pascarella & Terenzini, 1991) synthesized the extensive research findings on how a college education affects students. Although the findings are generally consistent across almost 30 years of research, the most recent synthesis had the advantage of examining increasingly sophisticated research in both design and data analysis methods. Pascarella and Terenzini's (1991) synthesis of findings on the results of college, in general, should guide psychology departments' agendas in the future. These investigators concluded that, by going to college, students (a) think more critically, complexly, and reflectively; (b) increase their cultural and artistic interests; (c) develop personal identities and healthy self-concepts; and (d) extend their intellectual interests, personal autonomy, interpersonal horizons, and overall psychological maturity. Going to college, not simply maturing with age, positively affects students' intellectual, moral, and career and economic development. There are enduring effects on these dimensions, as well as on values, attitudes, and quality-of-life indexes. However, a major limitation of the research on college impact is its lack of attention to individual differences. The research findings are about overall effects; effects attributable to "non-traditional" student status on campus—age, ethnic minority status, part-time or reentry enrollment patterns—need to be investigated and analyzed.

Pascarella and Terenzini (1991) further concluded that "similarities in between-college effects would appear to vastly outweigh the differences" (p. 590). Within any institution, the impact of college is directly related to how intensely involved students choose to become with their faculty, programs, peers, and opportunities that arise on campus. Within a major field, students' cognitive development is most demonstrable on subject matter tests directly related to their major or disciplinary emphasis of their field of study (e.g., humanities, sciences, social sciences).

In a conclusion that is directly applicable to this handbook's emphasis on psychology students, Pascarella and Terenzini (1991) stated,

> There is some evidence to suggest that departmental environment, whatever the department, may be more important than the characteristics of the discipline in shaping psychosocial and attitudinal changes among students. The interpersonal climate and value homogeneity and consensus within a department appear to be particularly important. (p. 614)

How can psychology programs accomplish student learning more effectively? First, the research on college effects and the recommendations from several higher education task forces indicate that the quality of student learning is directly related to the quality of students' involvement in their education. Astin's (1985) talent development model was an early catalyst for this perspective. Departmental environments in which (a) clear and high expectations are stated, (b) concerted faculty effort fosters active learning in every course or out-of-class activity, and (c) systematic assessment and feedback are provided are departments in which students and faculty thrive. The capacity to build these environments is not necessarily related to institutional resources or prestige; instead, the capacity is related to shared values in which administrators, faculty, and students recognize and reward quality effort on behalf of undergraduate learning.

A second way by which psychology programs can accomplish student learning more effectively is through the heterogeneity of the student population. This heterogeneity, recognized by McKeachie and Milholland (1961) and Kulik (1973) and examined so thoughtfully by Ware and by Puente and their respective colleagues in chapters 2 and 3 of this volume, will become a defining characteristic of psychology programs into the next century. To seek a common excellence in learning among all the different students who take psychology courses and who choose psychology as their major will require sensitivity by psychologists as teachers and as providers of university and community service. To achieve a common excellence in learning will require particular attention by psychologists as scholars to measure the differential effects of the psychology major and its faculty for a variety of undergraduate student characteristics. This research and evaluation effort can merge effectively with the assessment mandates already expected for departments and can be enhanced by the ideas set forth by Halpern and her colleagues in chapter 1.

Promoting an ethic of teaching a psychology of people will challenge faculty to extend themselves beyond their departments. In college student enrollment demographics reported for 1990, 50.9% of Native Americans, 42.9% of Asian Americans, 38.1% of African Americans, and 52.9% of Hispanics in higher education were enrolled in public, 2-year institutions ("College Enrollment," 1992). If psychology is to recruit more people of color into its ranks—as students and as future faculty members—partnerships must be initiated with the public community colleges as soon as possible.

In the latter half of the 1990s, overall college enrollments are projected to increase, but state expenditures for higher education and federally funded financial aid programs will not keep pace with student needs. Community colleges will maintain their role as a safe harbor for students with even minor academic or economic constraints. Weiten (chapter 5), Brewer (chapter 6), and Mathie (chapter 7) and their respective colleagues offer excellent suggestions on how to initiate these partnerships.

A third way to accomplish student learning more effectively is by a balanced emphasis on student access and curriculum excellence. Psychology's popularity will continue to increase, but faculty growth may not keep pace because of a lack of academically oriented and scientifically trained doctorates (see Howard et al., 1986), coupled with a sizable cohort of faculty who received their degrees between 1960 and 1970 and who are approaching retirement age in the year 2000. The potential response to too many students and not enough faculty will be pressures to decrease enrollments. More large universities will lower the number of majors by increasing admissions requirements into the major or by adding prerequisites (i.e., gatekeeping courses, often in statistics). Departmental conflict over undergraduate programs will focus more and more on achieving the difficult goals of access and excellence.

Advising programs will need to use more sophisticated strategies to respond to students' vocational needs. Departments can define liberal arts outcomes and career development as mutually possible (see Ware, 1992). As Ware and his colleagues' chapter in this volume (chapter 2) so effectively advocates, achieving a goal of career development in an undergraduate program requires cognitive elements and decision-making skills, not just a loose amalgamation of vocationally relevant practicum courses. The assessment of specific outcomes that derive from studying psychology is essential to both students and employers in promoting psychology as marketable. Halpern and her colleagues (chapter 1) offer a realistic list of outcomes and an excellent inventory of assessment strategies to measure the achievement of such outcomes.

What are the changes in the ethos of higher education that will stimulate faculty development in the coming decades? Weiten and his colleagues (chapter 5) made a persuasive argument that psychology faculty, regardless of institutional type, experience similar feelings of isolation and strive for similar images of academic community. Studies on the professoriate (e.g. Boyer, 1990; Schuster, 1990) attest to a national sense of malaise and hope among current faculty. Other authors confirm such faculty sentiments but suggest that differences are based on institutional settings and academic disciplines as well. A recent national study by Syracuse University's Center for Instructional Development describes some of the tensions in faculty values at research universities (Gray, Froh, & Diamond, 1992). These tensions result from perceived differences among faculty and administrators about how faculty spend their time and how they should be rewarded, especially in finding an appropriate balance between time spent on research and on undergraduate teaching. These authors concluded that narrowly defined reward systems on many campuses not only stress research over undergraduate teaching, but emphasize the quantity rather than the quality of research and scholarly work.

In their study, Gray et al. (1992) received more than 23,000 surveys (50% response rate) from faculty, unit heads, deans, and central administrators at 33 public and 14 private universities identified as Research I and II and Doctoral Granting I and II institutions. Respondents were asked to rate this statement: "In relation to each other, currently how important are research and undergraduate teaching." Respondents were asked to rate this statement in three different categories: "you personally," "the direction that you think our university is going," and "the direction that you think our university should go." The mean ratings by faculty, unit heads, and deans for how the university "should go" uniformly tended toward a perfect balance between teaching and research. (This question was not asked of central administrators.) For how the university "is going," the ratings indicated greater emphasis on research for three groups of respondents; central administrators saw more of an already established balance between teaching and research. It should be noted that 40% of the total faculty sample responding to this survey spent no time teaching undergraduates.

The authors' analyses revealed that (a) there was more variability within each of the three groups (faculty, unit heads, and deans) than among them; (b) each level perceived the group above them as more biased toward research over teaching than the higher level reported for themselves; and (c) faculty and unit heads advocated the teaching side of the continuum, personally and for how the university should go, the longer they had been at the institution.

These data, analyzed by academic areas and disciplines, are even more provocative than the aggregate responses because the respondents included 530 psychologists. When compared with 75 other academic areas or single disciplines, psychologists reported the fourth-highest personal preference for research over teaching, just lower than economics, microbiology and immunology, and physiology and anatomy faculty. Psychologists had the second-highest rating for how the university should emphasize research over undergraduate teaching, with economics faculty only slightly higher.

The authors of this study calculated a stress index, defined as the difference between respondents' perceptions of how their institution is going and how they believe it should go. Psychology was lowest in stress, along with computer science, chemistry, physics, and zoology. Psychology faculty's similarity in satisfaction with their science department colleagues in this study reaffirms earlier research by Kimble (1984) in his portrayal of "psychology's two cultures." However, psychologists' general satisfaction with perceived university priorities for emphasizing research over teaching is very different from the high levels of stress reported by their faculty colleagues in business and management, communication, education, engineering, fine and performing arts, and the humanities.

Rice's (1991) article on "the new American scholar" is another thought-provoking piece about contemporary faculty values. Rice's title comes from Ralph Waldo Emerson's address to the Phi Beta Kappa Society at Harvard in 1837 in which he articulated an American definition of academic scholarship, distinguishing us from our European ancestry. At the heart of Emerson's and Rice's argument is the almost 200-year-old struggle to define what is a distinctively American university. For the research university, as Kerr (1982) noted, the concept of a "university" must be replaced by the "multiversity," in which there are many communities with many, and often conflicting, values. Gray et al.'s (1992) findings of different levels of satisfaction reported by faculty in different academic specialties attest to that concept. Faculty in comprehensive universities, as noted by Boyer (1990) and Rice (1991), suffer the most from a lack of clear institutional priorities about balancing scholarship and teaching:

> It is the comprehensive universities that have struggled most with the established definition of scholarship and the hierarchy that reinforces it. Sixty percent of the public universities are in this category, and almost all were created or designated as universities during the postwar period. . . . The recent emergence of these institutions and—ironically—their success in terms of growth and prestige, have blurred their mandate and sent confusing signals to faculty; there is no clear indication of what is valued. (Rice, 1991, p. 9)

At the other end of the continuum from this lack of clarity prevalent in comprehensive universities is the sense of purpose and concomitant satisfaction expressed by faculty in liberal arts colleges and community colleges. Rice and Austin's (1988) study of small liberal arts colleges showed a correlation between faculty satisfaction and clarity of their institutional missions. In the same national study that revealed the predominant malaise about which so much is now being written, the Carnegie Foundation for the Advancement of Teaching (1989) found that community college faculty and liberal arts faculty reported having the highest levels of quality of life and sense of academic community in their institutions. However, along with the clarity of purpose derived from a strong teaching emphasis, there is the lack of support for research. Fewer than 25% of community college faculty reported receiving funds for research activities, but commitment to their academic discipline or department was not reduced by lack of support for research.

What do national studies indicate for psychology faculty development in the coming decade? First, faculty's intellectual development, often manifested in traditional forms of research activity but always required for effective teaching regardless of institutional setting, is paramount. New definitions of scholarly activity will be discussed at psychology faculty meetings in all settings.

Rice's (1991) synthesis of the different ways of knowing with Boyer's (1990) four forms of scholarship (scholarship of discovery, scholarship of integration, scholarship of practice, and scholarship of teaching) is a good starting point for the discussion:

> What is being proposed challenges a hierarchical arrangement of monumental proportions—a status system that is firmly fixed in the consciousness of the present faculty and the academy's organizational policies and practices. What is being called for is a broader, more open

field, where these different forms of scholarship can interact, inform, and enrich one another, and faculty can follow their interests, build on their strengths, and be rewarded for what they spend their scholarly energy doing. All faculty ought to be scholars in this broader sense, deepening their preferred approaches to knowing but constantly pressing, and being pressed by peers, to enlarge their scholarly capacities and encompass other—often contrary ways—of knowing. (Rice, 1991, pp. 15–16)

Second, Fretz and his colleagues' (chapter 4) incorporated the growing research on human development and specific work settings into the practice of faculty development. As the research cited earlier indicates, faculty in community colleges and liberal arts colleges seem to have personal and institutional clarity about their roles and rewards. Faculty in research universities may have to decide with which academic communities to identify. Scott (1991) predicted that administrative units labeled "department of psychology" will disappear and be replaced by specialized, organizing descriptors such as departments of "cognitive science" or "human and applied development." According to Scott, these units will reflect where the creation of new knowledge has led faculty and where the specialized training of graduate students is more likely to take place. The implications for undergraduate education of these administrative and intellectual transformations is an open question as well (McGovern, 1992).

In the coming decade, faculty in comprehensive universities will feel the most pressure and role confusion. As enrollments increase, there will be more administrative and external demands to shift institutional missions more toward teaching and community service. Without a concomitant redefinition of the relation between scholarship and teaching, or a redefinition of roles and rewards, faculty in these institutions will struggle without clear signals about priorities and without a sense of support for their own intellectual development that renders good teaching all but impossible.

To assist faculty in their efforts, in chapter 2, Ware and his colleagues offer an excellent analysis of the costs and benefits to the institution of more support for faculty advising efforts. In chapter 4, Fretz and his colleagues suggest ways for departments to build effective faculty development programs. And in chapter 5, Weiten and his colleagues offer helpful strategies for some faculty who will seek their sense of community and intellectual stimulation outside their own institutions.

Transforming the Curriculum for the Next Century

The first issue of *Current Directions in Psychological Science*, a journal of the American Psychological Society, appeared in February 1992. The editors (Scarr & Gallistel, 1992) described its purpose as follows:

Readers can track major research developments while keeping in view the broad scope of scientific psychology and its increasingly important role in shaping our conceptions of ourselves, our social organizations, and the impact of behavior on our personal lives, communities, and public policy. (p. 1)

Their plan was to cover the breadth of scientific psychology as ambitiously as authors of current, introductory psychology textbooks. I was struck by the primary authors' departmental affiliations for the 10 articles in this first issue. Three were from departments of psychology. The remaining seven used a variety of addresses: Center for the Study of Child and Adolescent Development; Institute for Social Research; Institute of Cognitive and Decision Sciences; Cognitive Development Unit; Centre for Visual Sciences, Research School of Biological Sciences; Institute for Research in Cognitive Science; and Center for Neural Science. Because most discussions of the curriculum begin with faculty arguing about the essential knowledge base of the discipline, the specialization portrayed by these authors and predicted by Scott (1991) will be an important issue in the coming decade. What is psychology? What curriculum covers it?

To understand that changing definitions of knowledge are reflected in the labels of administrative structures, Trapp's (1984) list of departmental addresses for psychologists at the University of Arkansas from 1884 to 1950 is instructive: Psychology, Ethics, Sociology, and Evidences of Christianity (1884); Psychology, Ethics, and Political Economy (1886); Psychology of Ethics (1889); Philosophy and Pedagogy (1898); Philosophy (1912); Education (1913); Philosophy and Psychology (1918); and finally, Psychology (1950). After reviewing catalogs of 20 institutions for the years 1890, 1900, 1910, and 1920, I was amazed at the similarity between curricular transformations that took place at the turn of the last century and those that are beginning to take place now.

For example, faculty discussion about curricular change will continue to be influenced by the breadth-versus-depth theme that has characterized the debate for the entire century. Faculty proponents of depth will advocate curricular requirements that are linear, sequential, and modeled on those of other sciences. For faculty in research universities, such a position is easy to advocate as the undergraduate equivalent of specialized graduate study. Faculty of like mind, but in institutions without the staff expertise to offer such a specialized course of study leading to a new baccalaureate, will advocate tracks or minors that mirror some of these new content areas. Assessment of student learning outcomes will be easiest in such programs because of the narrow content focus.

Faculty who advocate that psychology remain a liberal arts discipline, in which breadth and depth are parallel goals, will find an effective model in chapter 6 by Brewer and his colleagues. Their curriculum is adaptable for the comprehensive universities at which students often graft 2 years of general education courses and lower-level psychology courses at a community college to upper-division major field requirements at the senior institution. Assessment of student learning outcomes for such programs will be more difficult because the varied inputs (student demographics and courses presented for the degree) produce aggregate evaluations that are ambiguous.

In addition, a new focus on synthesis is reflected in recent reviews of undergraduate curricula. A three-volume work was sponsored by the Association of American Colleges in collaboration with faculty representatives from 10 arts and sciences disciplines, interdisciplinary studies, and women's studies (Project on Liberal Learning, Study-in-Depth, and the Arts and Sciences Major, 1991a, 1991b, 1992). Two important reviews encompassing arts and sciences outcomes and professional school curricula were completed by Stark and Lowther (1986, 1988). These recent groups focused on the academic major. The initiative to examine assumptions and requirements of major fields grew out of pervasive discontent with undergraduate education in general and with definitions of general education in particular (Bennett, 1984; Boyer, 1987; Project on Redefining the Meaning and Purpose of Baccalaureate Degrees, 1985; Study Group on the Conditions of Excellence in American Higher Education, 1984).

In coming decades, the renewed questioning of curricular objectives stimulated by these national groups, coupled with the transformation of disciplinary fields and their curricula by new knowledge, will prompt new university definitions of "general education" and the "major." There will be structural changes and content changes in the psychology curriculum.

Structurally, psychology will become a broad, general education, distribution category. This is similar to what took place at the end of the 19th century when scientific psychology differentiated itself from philosophy as the overarching disciplinary category. In the future, instead of introductory psychology serving as one option among several in social and behavioral sciences departments (e.g., sociology, anthropology, political science), students will choose among two to three courses (e.g., brain and behavior, social psychology, philosophy and psychology of moral dilemmas) to learn about individual and social behavior from the scientific or humanistic research conducted by psychologists.

The content objectives of individual psychology courses will also change in one of two ways. As the span of knowledge under traditional, disciplinary umbrellas widens, faculty may direct their teaching toward common outcomes such as literacy, critical thinking, and multicultural understanding. These outcomes will begin to look more and more like any other field's outcomes or for that matter, like general education goals. A second change in the content of psychology courses will be stimulated by current scholarship in the humanities and feminist theory that challenges our contemporary epistemologies. As I noted in the opening paragraphs of this chapter, future curricular objectives for psychology may strive to incorporate all of Mann's (1982) orientations—science, healing, and wisdom.

In short, transforming undergraduate programs for the next century will require an understanding of larger issues that shape our perspectives about students, faculty, and the curriculum. For psychology in particular, the transformation will be further stimulated by our own discipline's scholarship on individual differences and life-span development and by the continuing pursuit of new knowledge that has characterized our efforts for more than 100 years.

CONCLUSION

Derek Bok initiated the Harvard Assessment Seminars to enable faculty to discover how to help students learn more effectively. After 5 years of the project, 570 undergraduates had been interviewed by more than 100 faculty members. Light (1992) summarized the findings as follows:

> All the specific findings point to, and illustrate one main idea. It is that students who get the most out of college, who grow the most academically, and who are the happiest, *organize their time to include interpersonal activities with faculty members, or with fellow students, built around substantive, academic work.* (emphasis in original; p. 6)

Benjamin (1987) wrote about the legacy of Nebraska psychologist Harry Kirke Wolfe (1858–1918), titling his piece "A Teacher Is Forever." One of Wolfe's students remembered him this way:

> His scholarship had a foundation of courage. When he had worked out something and was satisfied of its truth, he was willing to abide by it even if the heavens were to fall. He had the utmost contempt in the matter of scholarship for faintheartedness or wavering, for padded pretensions. Let a man stand up for what he was, let him speak what he knew, let him prove what he alleged. But woe unto him if he were a parrot or purveyor of hot air. It was not sufficient in his classes to say "I know because Ladd says so." He was no rubber stamp himself and he wanted none of his pupils to be ditto-marks. An examination answer might be graded by him perfect, though it came to conclusions exactly the reverse of what he himself held, if only the answer showed that the writer had been thinking and really knew what he was trying to say. (Benjamin, 1987, p. 73)

The message from Nebraska students at the turn of the 20th century and from Harvard students entering the 21st century is clear. Benjamin summarized one faculty member's legacy, paraphrasing a quotation from Henry Adams, who said, "A teacher affects eternity. He never knows where his influence stops" (Benjamin, 1987, p. 74). Participants in the APA

National Conference to Enhance the Quality of Undergraduate Education in Psychology understood that message. It is our hope that this handbook will help others to communicate a similar zest for the teaching and learning of psychology.

REFERENCES

Alexander, J. M., & Stark, J. S. (1986). *Focusing on student academic outcomes.* Ann Arbor, MI: National Center for Research to Improve Postsecondary Teaching and Learning.

Astin, A. W. (1985). *Achieving educational excellence.* San Francisco: Jossey-Bass.

Benjamin, L. (1987). A teacher is forever: The legacy of Harry Kirke Wolfe (1858–1918). *Teaching of Psychology, 14,* 68–74.

Bennett, W. J. (1984). *To reclaim a legacy: A report on the humanities in higher education.* Washington, DC: National Endowment for the Humanities.

Bowen, H. R. (1977). *Investment in learning.* San Francisco: Jossey-Bass.

Boyer, E. L. (1987). *College: The undergraduate experience in America.* New York: Harper & Row.

Boyer, E. L. (1990). *Scholarship reconsidered. Priorities of the professorate.* Princeton, NJ: Carnegie Foundation for the Advancement of Teaching.

Buxton, C. E., Cofer, C. N., Gustad, J. W., MacLeod, R. B., McKeachie, W. J., & Wolfle, D. (1952). *Improving undergraduate instruction in psychology.* New York: Macmillan.

Carnegie Foundation for the Advancement of Teaching. (1990). *The condition of the professorate: Attitudes and trends, 1989.* Princeton, NJ: Author.

Chickering, A. W., & Associates. (1981). *The modern American college.* San Francisco: Jossey-Bass.

College enrollment by racial and ethnic group. (1992, March 18). *The Chronicle of Higher Education,* p. A35.

Earned degrees, 1989–90. (1992, May 13). *The Chronicle of Higher Education,* p. A37.

Feldman, K. A., & Newcomb, T. M. (1976). *The impact of college on students.* San Francisco: Jossey-Bass.

Gray, P. J., Froh, R. C., & Diamond, R. M. (1992). *A national study of research universities: On the balance between research and undergraduate teaching.* Syracuse, NY: Syracuse University Center for Instructional Development.

Howard, A., Pion, G. M., Gottfredson, G. D., Flattau, P. E., Oskamp, S., Pfafflin, S. M., Bray, D. W., & Burstein, A. G. (1986). The changing face of American psychology: A report from the Committee on Employment and Human Resources. *American Psychologist, 41,* 1311–1327.

Kerr, C. (1982). *The uses of the university* (3rd ed.). Cambridge, MA: Harvard University Press.

Kiesler, D. J. (1966). Some myths of psychotherapy research and the search for a paradigm. *Psychological Bulletin, 65,* 110–136.

Kimble, G. A. (1984). Psychology's two cultures. *American Psychologist, 39,* 833–839.

Korn, H. A. (1986). *Psychological models of the impact of college on students.* Ann Arbor, MI: National Center for Research to Improve Postsecondary Teaching and Learning.

Kulik J. A. (1973). *Undergraduate education in psychology.* Washington, DC: American Psychological Association.

Light, R. (1992). *The Harvard Assessment Seminars: Second report: Explorations with students and faculty about teaching, learning, and student life.* Cambridge, MA: Harvard University Graduate School of Education and Kennedy School of Government.

Mann, R. D. (1982). The curriculum and context of psychology. *Teaching of Psychology, 9,* 9–14.

McGovern, T. V. (1992). And whither the undergraduate major in psychology? *American Psychologist, 47,* 1149–1150.

McGovern, T. V., Furumoto, L., Halpern, D. F., Kimble, G. A., & McKeachie, W. J. (1991). Liberal education, study in depth, and the arts and sciences major—psychology. *American Psychologist, 46,* 598–605.

McGovern, T. V., & Hawks, B. K. (1984). Transitions and renewal of an undergraduate program in psychology. *Teaching of Psychology, 11,* 70–74.

McKeachie, W. J., & Milholland, J. E. (1961). *Undergraduate curricula in psychology.* Fair Lawn, NJ: Scott, Foresman.

McKeachie, W. J., Pintrich, P. R., Lin, Y-G., Smith, D. A. F., & Sharma, R. (1990). *Teaching and learning in the college classroom: A review of the research literature* (2nd ed.). Ann Arbor, MI: National Center for Research to Improve Postsecondary Teaching and Learning.

Pace, C. R. (1979). *Measuring outcomes of college: Fifty years of findings and recommendations for the future.* San Francisco: Jossey-Bass.

Pascarella, E. T., & Terenzini, P. T. (1991). *How college affects students.* San Francisco: Jossey-Bass.

Project on Liberal Learning, Study-in-Depth, and the Arts and Sciences Major. (1991a). *The challenge of connecting learning* (Vol. 1). Washington, DC: Association of American Colleges.

Project on Liberal Learning, Study-in-Depth, and the Arts and Sciences Major. (1991b). *Reports from the fields* (Vol. 2). Washington, DC: Association of American Colleges.

Project on Liberal Learning, Study-in-Depth, and the Arts and Sciences Major. (1992). *Program review and educational quality in the major: A faculty handbook* (Vol. 3). Washington, DC: Association of American Colleges.

Project on Redefining the Meaning and Purpose of Baccalaureate Degrees. (1985). *Integrity in the college curriculum: A report to the academic community.* Washington, DC: Association of American Colleges.

Rice, R. E. (1991). The new American scholar. Scholarship and the purposes of the university. *Metropolitan Universities, 1*(4), 7–18.

Rice, R. E., & Austin, A. E. (1988, March/April). High faculty morale. *Change, 20,* 50–58.

Sanford, F. H., & Fleishman, E. A. (1950). A survey of undergraduate psychology courses in American colleges and universities. *American Psychologist, 5,* 33–37.

Scarr, S., & Gallistel, C. R. (1992). Keeping up with psychological science. *Current Directions in Psychological Science, 1,* 1.

Scheirer, C. J., & Rogers, A. M. (1985). *The undergraduate psychology curriculum: 1984.* Washington, DC: American Psychological Association.

Schuster, J. H. (1990). The need for fresh approaches to faculty renewal. In J. H. Schuster, D. W. Wheeler, & Associates (Eds.), *Enhancing faculty careers: Strategies for development and renewal* (pp. 3–19). San Francisco: Jossey-Bass.

Scott, T. R. (1991). A personal view of the future of psychology departments. *American Psychologist, 46,* 975–976.

Stark, J. S., & Lowther, M. A. (1986). *Designing the learning plan: A review of research and theory related to college curricula.* Ann Arbor, MI: National Center for Research to Improve Postsecondary Teaching and Learning.

Stark, J. S., & Lowther, M. A. (1988). *Strengthening the ties that bind: Integrating undergraduate liberal and professional study* (Report of the Professional Preparation Network). Ann Arbor: University of Michigan.

Study Group on the Conditions of Excellence in American Higher Education. (1984). *Involvement in learning: Realizing the potential of American higher education.* Washington, DC: National Institute of Education.

Trapp, E. P. (1984). *A century of psychology at the University of Arkansas.* Paper presented at the 25th Anniversary of Doctoral Programs in Psychology, Fayetteville, AR.

Turner, S. E., & Bowen, W. G. (1990). The flight from the arts and sciences: Trends in degrees conferred. *Science, 250,* 517–521.

Ware, M. E. (1992). Collegiate career advising: Status, antecedents, and strategies. In A. E. Puente, J. R. Matthews, & C. L. Brewer (Eds.), *Teaching psychology in America: A history* (pp. 39–69). Washington, DC: American Psychological Association.

Appendix A

STEERING COMMITTEE MEMBERS

Original Members of the Committee on Undergraduate Education

Douglas Bernstein	University of Illinois
Jane Halonen	Alverno College
Thomas V. McGovern (Chair)	Arizona State University West
Carole Wade	College of Marin

Additional Members Recommended by the Board of Educational Affairs

Ludy T. Benjamin, Jr.	Texas A&M University
Andrew B. Crider	Williams College
Wilbert J. McKeachie	University of Michigan
Barbara Nodine	Beaver College
Pamela T. Reid	City University of New York Graduate Center
Richard Suinn	Colorado State University

APA Office of Educational Affairs Administrative Staff

Ira Cohen
Cynthia Baum
Martha Braswell

Appendix B

CONFERENCE PARTICIPANTS

A call for conference participants appeared in the June 1990 *APA Monitor*. Approximately 200 individuals submitted applications to be named one of the 50 participants. The Steering Committee used several selection criteria. Faculty were to be chosen from different types and sizes of institutions representing different geographical areas of the country. The Steering Committee identified faculty from universities, colleges, 2-year institutions, and high school programs. Although several excellent faculty members applied from the same schools, only one individual was chosen from any given institution. Every effort was made to recruit ethnic minority faculty as participants, to gender balance the group, and to include faculty who were less highly visible in prior APA service but who communicated innovative ideas in their applications.

The final roster, including the 10 Steering Committee members, was composed of 32 men and 28 women. Of these 60 participants, 11 were ethnic minority faculty members. There were 5 faculty members from 2-year colleges, 2 high school teachers, and 2 "international" members (Canada and Puerto Rico). Patricia Hutchings, director of the Teaching Initiative of the American Association for Higher Education (AAHE), was invited because of her particular expertise on several topics and because of AAHE's contributions to assessment, minority recruitment and retention, and innovative teaching and program development.

The Steering Committee chose seven task force chairs on the basis of their established reputation, expertise in one of the topic areas, and group leadership skills.

Conference Participants Listed by Group

Outcomes Assessment

Diane F. Halpern (Chair)	California State University at San Bernardino
Drew C. Appleby	Marian College
Susan E. Beers	Sweet Briar College
Catharine L. Cowan	Southwest State University

John J. Furedy	University of Toronto
Jane S. Halonen	Alverno College
Carrell P. Horton	Fisk University
Blaine F. Peden	University of Wisconsin–Eau Claire
David J. Pittenger	Marietta College
Patricia Hutchings	American Association of Higher Education

Advising

Mark E. Ware (Chair)	Creighton University
Nancy A. Busch-Rossnagel	Fordham University
Andrew B. Crider	Williams College
Lisa Gray-Shellberg	California State University at Dominguez Hills
Karyn Hale	Crater High School
Margaret A. Lloyd	Georgia Southern University
Eduardo Rivera-Medina	University of Puerto Rico–Rio Piedras
Joseph A. Sgro	Virginia Tech

Minority Recruitment and Retention

Antonio E. Puente (Chair)	University of North Carolina at Wilmington
Evelyn Blanch	Wilberforce University
Douglas K. Candland	Bucknell University
Florence L. Denmark	Pace University
Carol Laman	Houston Community College
Neil Lutsky	Carleton College
Pamela T. Reid	City University of New York Graduate School
R. Steven Schiavo	Wellesley College
Richard Suinn	Colorado State University

Faculty Development

Bruce R. Fretz (Chair)	University of Maryland
Antoine M. Garibaldi	Xavier University
Laraine M. Glidden	St. Mary's College
Wilbert J. McKeachie	University of Michigan
John N. Moritsugu	Pacific Lutheran University
Kathryn Quina	University of Rhode Island
Jill N. Reich	Loyola University Chicago
Barbara Sholley	University of Richmond

Faculty Networks

Wayne Weiten (Chair)	College of DuPage
Stephen F. Davis	Emporia State University

Jane A. Jegerski	Elmhurst College
Richard A. Kasschau	University of Houston
K. Bates Mandel	Carver High School of Engineering and Science
Carole Wade	College of Marin

Curriculum

Charles L. Brewer (Chair)	Furman University
J. Roy Hopkins	St. Mary's College
Gregory A. Kimble	Duke University
Margaret W. Matlin	State University of New York at Geneseo
Lee I. McCann	University of Wisconsin Oshkosh
Ogretta V. McNeil	College of the Holy Cross
Barbara F. Nodine	Beaver College
Virginia Nichols Quinn	Northern Virginia Community College
Saundra	Montclair State College

Active Learning

Virginia Andreoli Mathie (Chair)	James Madison University
Barney Beins	Ithaca College
Ludy T. Benjamin, Jr.	Texas A&M University
Martha M. Ewing	Collin County Community College
Christine C. Iijima Hall	Arizona State University West
Bruce Henderson	Western Carolina University
Dale W. McAdam	University of Rochester
Randolph A. Smith	Ouachita Baptist University

Steering Committee

Thomas V. McGovern (Chair)	Arizona State University West
Cynthia Baum	APA Educational Programs
Martha Braswell	APA Educational Programs

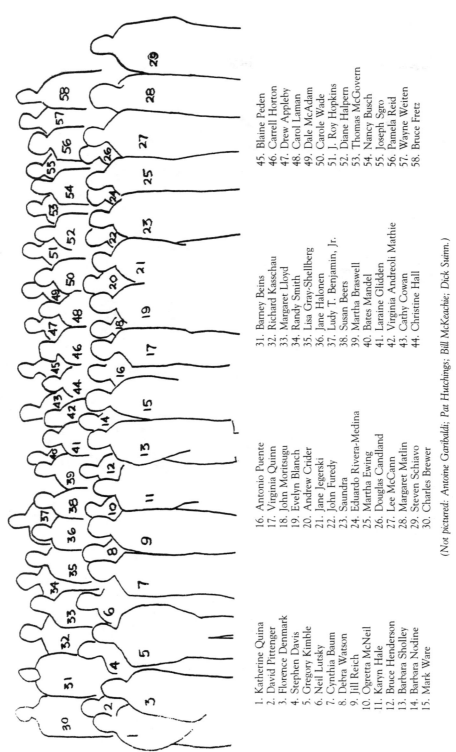

1. Katherine Quina
2. David Pittenger
3. Florence Denmark
4. Stephen Davis
5. Gregory Kimble
6. Neil Lutsky
7. Cynthia Baum
8. Debra Watson
9. Jill Reich
10. Ogretta McNeil
11. Karyn Hale
12. Bruce Henderson
13. Barbara Sholley
14. Barbara Nodine
15. Mark Ware

16. Antonio Puente
17. Virginia Quinn
18. John Moritsugu
19. Evelyn Blanch
20. Andrew Crider
21. Jane Jegerski
22. John Furedy
23. Saundra
24. Eduardo Rivera-Medina
25. Martha Ewing
26. Douglas Candland
27. Lee McCann
28. Margaret Matlin
29. Steven Schiavo
30. Charles Brewer

31. Barney Beins
32. Richard Kasschau
33. Margaret Lloyd
34. Randy Smith
35. Lisa Gray-Shellberg
36. Jane Halonen
37. Ludy T. Benjamin, Jr.
38. Susan Beers
39. Martha Braswell
40. Bates Mandel
41. Laraine Glidden
42. Virginia Andreoli Mathie
43. Cathy Cowan
44. Christine Hall

45. Blaine Peden
46. Carrell Horton
47. Drew Appleby
48. Carol Laman
49. Dale McAdam
50. Carole Wade
51. J. Roy Hopkins
52. Diane Halpern
53. Thomas McGovern
54. Nancy Busch
55. Joseph Sgro
56. Pamela Reid
57. Wayne Weiten
58. Bruce Fretz

(*Not pictured:* Antoine Garibaldi; Pat Hutchings; Bill McKeachie; Dick Suinn.)

Participants in the APA National Conference on Enhancing the Quality of Undergraduate Education in Psychology
St. Mary's College of Maryland, June 1991

Appendix C

CONFERENCE SITE

A call for conference site proposals appeared in the March 1990 *APA Monitor*. Seven proposals were submitted. Two institutions offered to underwrite all of the conference participants' expenses and to provide extensive library, computer, and staff support on their campuses. In August 1990 at the APA Annual Meeting in Boston, the Steering Committee unanimously approved the proposal submitted by St. Mary's College of Maryland. Roy Hopkins of St. Mary's was designated as the on-site host for the conference and joined the Steering Committee at all subsequent meetings.

St. Mary's College of Maryland is a public liberal arts college of 1,500 students located in historic St. Mary's City. Founded in 1840, St. Mary's was originally a female seminary, then a junior college, and since the late 1960s it has been a 4-year, state-supported liberal arts college. In recent years, the National Endowment for the Humanities recognized the college for its outstanding core curriculum. *U.S. News & World Report* named it the number one regional liberal arts college in the northeast.

During the conference, participants were lodged in townhouses overlooking the St. Mary's River. Seven townhouses were equipped with a computer workstation and printer, and each townhouse had an adjacent room that served as a small-group discussion area. An eighth townhouse staffed by St. Mary's undergraduate psychology majors became the social and problem-solving center for the conference.

Evening meals were a veritable liberal arts education in history with venues including a 17th-century inn and a southern plantation, as well as a traditional Maryland crabfeast on the banks of the river. The splendid environment and the gracious support of campus administrators, faculty, staff, and undergraduate psychology students were essential ingredients in the conference's successful outcomes.

Appendix D

RECOMMENDATIONS FROM THE APA NATIONAL CONFERENCE ON ENHANCING THE QUALITY OF UNDERGRADUATE EDUCATION IN PSYCHOLOGY

Specific recommendations for departments and their faculty are listed in the previous chapters. Those recommendations should stimulate discussion and suggest specific activities for internal renewal of an undergraduate program. The following pages synthesize those recommendations aimed at organizations and constituencies external to one's campus. They form an "action agenda" from the intellectual and organizational creativity generated by the conference. Conference participants saw the need to challenge a number of national organizations, such as the APA, National Science Foundation (NSF), Council of Graduate Departments of Psychology (COGDOP), and American Psychological Society (APS), to focus their efforts more effectively on behalf of undergraduate education. By including such different individual voices and institutional perspectives among the participants at the St. Mary's Conference, the Steering Committee is confident that the recommendations generated from this conference should be uniquely persuasive to a broad array of constituencies.

RECOMMENDATIONS FOR UNDERGRADUATE EDUCATION ACTIVITIES FROM THE STEERING COMMITTEE FOR THE APA NATIONAL CONFERENCE ON ENHANCING THE QUALITY OF UNDERGRADUATE EDUCATION IN PSYCHOLOGY

In January 1992, the Steering Committee for the conference prioritized the following recommendations to the APA.

Dissemination of Conference Outcomes

The major foci of the conference were to address critical concerns in undergraduate education, to stimulate discussions of these issues, and to prompt activities to improve undergraduate education in psychology.

Recommendations for Action

1. Publish this handbook for college and university faculty and administration on the enhancement of undergraduate psychology. Distribute announcements and brochures regarding this publication broadly to APA members and other academic psychologists through convention displays of Publications and Communications and the Education Directorates, through announcements in the *APA Monitor*, and through direct mailings.
2. Adopt as official APA policy the Principles for Quality Undergraduate Psychology Programs that have been abstracted from the recommendations of the conference (see section 1). The process of policy adoption (dissemination for feedback by Committees and Boards of the Association, external academic groups, and the broader APA membership) is designed to generate discussion and action related to undergraduate education. As APA policy, these Principles may aid academic faculty in resource acquisition for program improvement.
3. Sponsor workshops, presentations, and symposia regarding the conference and its outcomes at annual APA meetings. Facilitate dissemination at regional psychological association meetings, regional and national teaching conferences, and meetings of other academic organizations (e.g., Council of Graduate Departments of Psychology, Council of Teachers of Undergraduate Psychology, Council of Undergraduate Programs in Psychology).

Information must reach broader audiences, including non-APA members, and foster feedback from the field. Dissemination activities should enhance the perception of the APA's commitment to undergraduate education.

Central Communications Network

Recommendation for Action

Establish a central network for communication about teaching as a means of promoting linkages nationwide.

A central communication network would build on the work of the conference and would spur continued development of the themes discussed at St. Mary's. The network would address two critical needs: (1) to establish communication links between faculty members around the country; and (2) to serve as a clearinghouse of information on topics discussed at the conference, including assessment, advising, minority recruitment and retention, faculty development, curriculum, preparation of syllabi, and active learning. Sophisticated technology for electronic networks and bulletin boards is expanding rapidly and the APA should help undergraduate educators move toward the 21st century.

Requirements for the Central Communication Network. At a minimum, the Central Communications Network would require

- A strong indexing system, so that a potential user could quickly and easily access relevant information
- A quality assurance mechanism, for example, to protect the organization from copyright liability
- Strong technical support, especially during the development phase of the project
- Mechanisms for linking individuals and departments who have access to the system with those who do not.

Interim steps to achieve the goal. The APA should

- Investigate existing models
- Ask the Science Directorate to expand their grant network to include seeking grants relevant to undergraduate education
- Place E-mail addresses in the next edition of the *Directory of the APA*
- Prepare a directory of Division 2 members, including E-mail addresses
- Establish contact with Division 2 members who are collecting course syllabi and ideas for active learning.

Recruitment and Retention of Ethnic Minority Students

Recommendations for Action

Develop support materials to enhance recruitment and retention of ethnic minority students. Although the psychology major is faring well overall, demographics suggest that the major is not as attractive as other fields to ethnic minority students. This is particularly problematic in our efforts to increase diversity among psychologists.

1. Develop a series of brochures targeted toward ethnic minority high school and early major students to address the following topics:
   a. How an undergraduate psychology major contributes to success in a variety of career paths (This brochure would address employment at the baccalaureate level.)

b. Examples of successful minority men and women at work who have majored in psychology, emphasizing what worked and how they did it

　　c. Exploration of how psychological research addresses numerous social issues

　　d. Exploration of psychology majors as preparation for a variety of professional careers requiring postbaccalaureate education.

2. Develop videos targeted toward ethnic minority students to:

　　a. Highlight the achievement of minority psychologists

　　b. Identify the research and practice contributions to ethnic minority communities

　　c. Expand the emphasis on minority issues and baccalaureate level employment opportunities in the revision of the APA publication *Careers in Psychology*.

Psychology Teacher Preparation

Recommendations for Action

Promote efforts to improve the preparation of graduate students and new faculty as teachers of undergraduate psychology. The majority of psychology faculty have had little or no formal training for their role as teachers. Effective programs for preparing psychology faculty already exist and having access to them early in one's career can have beneficial effects not only on the growth of one's teaching skills, but on attitudes toward teaching and impact on students. The APA's endorsement of the importance of teaching preparation programs would indicate its concern for future generations of citizens informed about psychology as well as its concern for attracting future generations of psychologists.

1. Recommend to all graduate programs that

　　a. Graduate students in psychology have supervised teaching experience

　　b. Students be prepared for their role as teachers through course work or programs on teaching principles and methods

　　c. Preparation programs reflect the topics and methods found to be effective in existing programs.

2. Gather, compile, and disseminate information about the most effective teacher preparation programs in psychology.

3. Sponsor continuing education and preconvention workshops for teachers with various levels of experience.

4. Develop a Distinguished Teacher Lecture Series Program, parallel to the APA Science Directorate's Distinguished Sci-

ence Lecture Program, in which support would be provided to outstanding teachers for making presentations at meetings of regional association.

Data Needs

Recommendation for Action

Develop a national database on 2- and 4-year programs in psychology to support the ongoing national evaluation of undergraduate programs in psychology. The Steering Committee had to rely on dated and limited APA samples of undergraduate programs to prepare for the national conference.

1. Institutionalize the regular collection and updating of census data on undergraduate programs and practices (e.g., curriculum, assessment practices, advising practices, ethnic minority recruitment practices, faculty development).
2. Support the current planning by the Office of Demographic, Employment, and Educational Research (ODEER) to seek funding for a comprehensive database in support of the work of the Education Directorate. Planning for this project should include action item 1 (i.e., census of and descriptive information on undergraduate programs and practices).
3. Include representatives knowledgeable about and active in undergraduate education on the advisory group of any data collection activity.

ORIGINAL RECOMMENDATIONS FROM CONFERENCE PARTICIPANTS

Conference participants generated recommendations to multiple organizations external to an individual campus. In the following pages, these original (sometimes overlapping) recommendations are itemized. The ones addressed to the APA were synthesized by the Steering Committee to develop the aforementioned priorities.

Recommendations to the APA

The major audience for the conference participants' recommendations was the American Psychological Association, whose sponsorship of the St. Mary's conference was indicative of their concern for undergraduate education in the discipline. The coming decade will require systematic and aggressive advocacy for undergraduate issues if the science and the practice of psychology are to flourish in the 21st century. To this end, we urge review and approval of the following recommendations.

Students

- Collect annual statistics for a database on undergraduate majors and graduates, including ethnic minority breakdown, transfer students, salaries and employment placements for graduates, and attrition rates.
- Recognize successful undergraduate students, their mentors, and their programs.
- Develop a pamphlet for ethnic minority student recruitment and distribute to high school counselors, college minority affairs offices, and so forth.

Faculty

- Support E-mail networks for teaching and a clearinghouse for teaching materials.
- Coordinate networks for active learning exercises and related ideas and information.
- Develop a means of disseminating faculty development information through newsletters and E-mail/bulletin boards.
- Disseminate information about innovative assessment practices.
- Involve school psychologists in the recruitment and promotion of psychology to ethnic minority high school students and to high school counselors.
- APA Council of Representatives should endorse use of multiple reward systems that are commensurate with diverse missions of institutions that offer the undergraduate psychology degree.
- Disseminate the conference book as widely as possible, supplemented by workshops at regional and national meetings sponsored by the APA and other groups.
- Provide expertise, assistance, consultation, and a clearinghouse for the grant-writing process to obtain funds for faculty and curriculum development activities. The Education Directorate must play a stronger advocacy role with granting agencies, Congress, and other professional associations on behalf of undergraduate education.
- Develop a model grant proposal for teaching-related programs and cosponsor as appropriate.
- Aggressively pursue the development of academic alliances in psychology. Prepare information materials on steps to form

alliances and assist/consult in the development of local proposals for seed-money grants.

- Develop an Association of High School Psychology Teachers.
- Develop a national network of ethnic minority teachers who are concerned about recruitment and retention.
- Develop a master mailing list of psychology teachers at all levels of institutions, including those who are not members of the APA.
- Consolidate two specialized newsletters aimed at high school and community college teachers.
- Expand continuing education efforts for teachers at national meetings.
- Fund a pilot program for developing a Distinguished Teacher Lecture Series at regional meetings.
- Increase the representation of high school, community college, and small 4-year colleges in the APA governance activities.
- Prepare lobbying materials for national and state associations and for universities on the importance of funding faculty development initiatives, that is, direct beneficial outcomes for students and others of such initiatives.
- Build a resource library of materials and list of consultants on faculty development.
- Develop a model for a self-managed faculty development program for those in relatively isolated, small academic communities where opportunities for more formal interactions are limited.
- Implement a study of plateaued (dormant) faculty for the purpose of using the results to form effective faculty development programs.
- Develop collaborative relationships with the Professional and Organizational Network in Higher Education in behalf of faculty development efforts.

Curriculum

- Instruct undergraduate site visitors to attend to the needs of ethnic minority students and to specific elements of diversity in the curriculum.
- Psychologists who are college or university administrators (presidents, chief academic officers, or deans) should endorse the principles of active learning in particular and those of quality programs in general.

- Produce a videotape that demonstrates a wide variety of active learning exercises.
- Encourage publishers to support the use of active learning in psychology courses by publishing more books that focus on these techniques.
- Encourage authors and publishers to include more information about human diversity and ethics in their textbooks.
- Revise and update the *Publication Manual of the American Psychological Association* to be more compatible with word processing technology and to be more helpful to students.[1]
- Gather and publish information on psychology minors and interdisciplinary programs or courses related to psychology.
- Colleges in a particular locale should work out formal agreements concerning transfer of psychology course credits from 2-year to 4-year colleges.
- Prepare a "Guidelines for Publishers" regarding the materials that should be included in all instructor's handbooks, especially to assist new teachers. These materials should include but not be limited to classroom discussion topics, exercises to stimulate critical thinking, primary source readings, audiovisual materials, and software.
- APA's Education Affairs Office should become a clearinghouse for information on assessment practice and consultation resources and should develop a handbook on exemplary practice.
- Design a study to evaluate the use of the St. Mary's conference recommendations and materials as an effective means (or not) of enhancing the quality of undergraduate education.

Recommendations to Other Organizations

The above recommendations were intended primarily for the APA. However, a number of them apply as well to the regional organizations of psychology and to other national organizations. The need for systematic resource development that serves undergraduate education in psychology is paramount. Some audience-specific recommendations include the following.

Division 2 of APA

- Continue support for the targeting of previously underrepresented groups for membership; urge continued efforts to recruit more high school and community college faculty.

---

[1]Publisher's note: The Fourth Edition of the *Publication Manual* will be available in 1994.

- Develop and disseminate a pamphlet explaining the procedures for establishing regional teaching conferences and student research conferences.
- Work more closely with CTUP to increase teaching-related programs at regional conventions. Investigate the development of local representatives and local chapters.
- Division 2 should consider changing its name reflecting its more diverse membership and that members need not belong to the APA. Aggressive recruiting efforts would be enhanced if non-APA members would be joining a group that bills itself as more than a special interest group of the APA.
- Affiliate (non-APA) members should not be excluded from any membership privileges other than those that are absolutely essential to the maintenance of the division's alliance with APA.

American Psychological Society (APS)

- The APS should correct its minimal attention given to undergraduate education, especially given that its membership is primarily academic. Rather than duplicate all of the resources developed by the APA on behalf of undergraduate education, the APS should carefully examine its mission, interest, and commitments and define a clear role it wants to play for undergraduate education.
- Like the APA, the APS should heighten its advocacy role with grant-sponsoring agencies in behalf of undergraduate psychology teachers.
- The APS should earmark more of its annual convention time to distinguished addresses, papers, and symposia related to the teaching of psychology.

Council of Teachers of Undergraduate Psychology (CTUP)

- Continue and expand efforts to develop programs on teaching issues at regional meetings (alone or in concert with Division 2).
- Recruit high school teachers and graduate students as members who could participate with CTUP in regional meetings on teaching issues.

National Science Foundation (NSF)

- Psychologists need to submit more teacher enhancement proposals to NSF; reviewing by psychologists is considered unnecessary when so few proposals are forthcoming.

- NSF should more actively solicit and fund proposals related to the teaching of psychology.

Regional Psychological Associations

- Regional associations should formally commit to the teaching track of programs at their meetings. Ideally, the call for programs would specify such a track and invite submissions directly.
- Work with the APA to establish a Distinguished Teacher Lecture Series for regional meetings.
- Regional meetings should consider inclusion of content area update lectures, similar to the APA's G. Stanley Hall Lectures, at their meetings.
- Regional associations should become more aggressive in soliciting the attendance and participation of high school and community college teachers at their meetings.

INDEX